Rough Guide to Sustainability
A Design Primer

3rd edition

by Brian Edwards

RIBA ＃ **Publishing**

© Brian Edwards, 2010
First edition published in 2001
Second edition published in 2005

Published by RIBA Publishing, 15 Bonhill Street, London EC2P 2EA

ISBN 978 1 85946 332 1

Stock code 69040

The right of Brian Edwards to be identified as the Author of this Work has been asserted in accordance with the Copyright, Design and Patents Act 1988.

All images © Brian Edwards, unless otherwise stated.

British Library Cataloguing in Publications Data
A catalogue record for this book is available from the British Library.

Publisher: Steven Cross
Commissioning Editor: Lucy Harbor
Editor: Melanie Thompson
Designed by Phillip Handley
Typeset by Academic + Technical Typesetting, Bristol
Printed and bound by Pureprint, Ukfield

While every effort has been made to check the accuracy and quality of the information given in this publication, neither the Author nor the Publisher accept any responsibility for the subsequent use of this information, for any errors or omissions that it may contain, or for any misunderstandings arising from it.

RIBA Publishing is part of RIBA Enterprises Ltd.
www.ribaenterprises.com

The name **Rough Guide** is a registered trademark of the publishers Rough Guides Ltd, 80 Strand, London WC2R 0RL, and is used here with their consent. The publishers have no editorial connection with this publication. Rough Guide travel guides, music guides, phrasebooks and reference books are available at all good bookstores or at www.roughguides.com.

Contents

Contents

Preface to the Third Edition

The first edition of the Rough Guide to Sustainability was published in 2001. This was less than 10 years after the problem of climate change really captured the attention of the public (via the Rio Earth Summit), and before UK government legislation had begun to have a substantial impact on building design.

Almost a decade later, there have been significant changes to buildings-related regulations in the UK and in Europe, global political changes (notably in the USA), and – most recently – dramatic changes to the global economy caused by the 'credit crunch', which has had unforeseen consequences for the construction industry.

Yet the need to press on to improve the sustainability of the nation's building stock is ever more urgent. The most recent climate change predictions, for instance, suggest there could be a rise in the number of days with high temperatures everywhere, fewer frosty days, and an increase in the number of 10-day dry spells across the UK. This not only highlights the urgent need to cut emissions to stem the escalation of global warming, it suggests that new buildings (and refurbishments) must be designed to cater for the demands of a changing climate.

As the demands upon buildings increase, so too has the size of the Rough Guide. The second edition was substantially larger than the first, and included sections on vernacular buildings, offices, schools and housing. This third edition of the Rough Guide to Sustainability builds on those additions, in particular, incorporating new projects by Ken Yeang, BIG Architects and Eco-systema.

The content of the book has been comprehensively re-organised to take account of the growing body of historical information surrounding the sustainable development movement and its impact on buildings, and to reinforce the urgent need for architectural education to keep pace with contemporary practice. This has been achieved by the creation of four self-contained 'essays' on the history, economics, aesthetics and pedagogical aspects of sustainable development and the role of 'green' design.

The fundamental aim of the first edition was to provide an authoritative source of information, clearly and logically structured so that students and practitioners alike can dip in and out of the book during their daily work. This aim holds true today, and therefore this new edition has reorganised the content into clearly defined sections – for science and policy; assessment tools; resources; and design – to enhance the reader's experience.

What this book seeks to show through argument and example is the way architecture, nature and culture are combining to provide a quiet revolution. Over the past decade we have seen growing governmental intervention in the environment, increasingly sympathetic clients and consumers to the green cause, and real worries over the cost and availability of future energy supplies. These have fuelled a movement which the first edition sought to describe but which today has grown to occupy centre stage for designers and contractors alike.

Sustainable design now forms the central focus for many projects and as new regulations are enacted and new science on issues such as climate change emerges, there are corresponding innovations in the way we design, construct and engineer buildings.

Brian Edwards
Copenhagen, 2010

Acknowledgements

The author wishes to thank Spon Press, Architectural Press, Earthscan and John Wiley & Sons Ltd for permission to adapt parts of earlier books and journal articles by the author for use in this edition. This includes the section on school design from *Green Buildings Pay* (Spon Press: Edwards, 2003), sections on waste, materials and pollution from *Sustainable Architecture* (Architectural Press: Edwards, 1999), sections on sustainability and nature from *Green Architecture* (AD/ Academy: Edwards, 2001) and the essay by the author on professional education from *The Sustainability Curriculum* edited by John Blewitt and Cedric Cullingford (Earthscan, 2004). It also includes articles adapted from the journals *Sustainable Development* published by John Wiley & Sons Ltd and *Research in Education* published by Manchester University Press.

The author also wishes to thank the many architects or their clients who have provided illustrations used to support the arguments in this book.

Special appreciation is extended to the European Environment Agency and Danish Architecture Centre (especially the Sustainable Cities unit) and in particular to the author's employer, the Royal Danish Academy of Fine Arts, School of Architecture. Here the author wishes to single out Torben Dahl, Peter Henning Jørgensen, Winnie Friis Möller, Ola Wedebrunn and Søren Nielsen for special mention.

Finally, the author wishes to acknowledge the enthusiastic help of Royal Institute of British Architects' (RIBA) former President Paul Hyett and the work over the past decade of the RIBA Sustainable Futures Group.

Introduction

Around half of all non-renewable resources consumed across the planet are used in construction, making it one of the least sustainable industries in the world. However, our daily lives are carried out in and on constructions of one sort or another: we live in houses, we travel on roads, we work and socialise in buildings of all kinds. Contemporary human civilisation depends on buildings and what they contain for its continued shelter and existence, and yet our planet cannot support the current level of resource consumption associated with them.

Estimate of global resources used in buildings	
Resource	(%)
Energy	45–50
Water	50
Materials for buildings and roads (by bulk)	60
Agricultural land loss to buildings	80
Timber products for construction	60 (90% of hardwoods)
Coral reef destruction	50 (indirect)
Rainforest destruction	25 (indirect)

Estimate of global pollution that can be attributed to buildings	
Pollution	(%)
Air quality (cities)	23
Global warming gases	50
Drinking water pollution	40
Landfill waste	50
Ozone thinning	50

Buildings are long-lived, and cities have even longer lives: they stretch into the future realm – a future of unknown resources, pollution and unstable climate.

Typical life-expectancy of different aspects of construction	
Building finishes	10 years
Building services	20 years
Buildings	50+ years
Infrastructure (roads, railways)	100+ years
Cities	500+ years

Clearly, for the good of the environment, something has to change, and architects – as the leading building designers – have an important role to play in that change. But that is only part of the equation.

Architects design buildings, which in turn create wealth. Half of all fixed capital formation annually is vested in buildings, which, taken together with the inherited assets of buildings, represents about 75 per cent of all UK wealth.[1]

The long-term asset value of a building depends on its ability to satisfy user needs, changing environmental conditions and evolving expectations of design quality. Naturally lit and ventilated buildings, those that utilise alternative energy sources and those that are attractive to consumers are more likely to be sound wealth investments than those which are over-dependent on fossil fuels or which ignore the fundamental human need for a healthy and wholesome lifestyle. The typical ratio of economic costs of commercial building over a 50-year period is:

cost of design and construction : operating costs : staff costs
1 : 2 : 10

With this perspective in mind, it is therefore prudent to address environmental issues at the outset; otherwise our created wealth will be undermined.

For the architect, sustainability is a complex concept.

As we shall see in **Section A**, the definition of sustainability has grown out of a number of important world congresses, and encompasses not just energy but all the resources needed to support human activity. A large part of designing sustainably is concerned with addressing the global warming that is driving climate

The challenge of sustainability
☐ Mankind and nature are locked into a dynamic asymmetrical system
☐ Human society has rarely been sustainable
☐ The nature of unsustainability is always changing
☐ The complexity of sustainability is a barrier to progress
☐ Human society is living on the 'capital' of the planet, not its 'interest'
☐ Political decisions are short-term; natural systems long-term
☐ Short-term damage requires long recovery time

Green aesthetics
☐ Ecological accounting informs design
☐ Making nature visible
☐ Design with nature
☐ Learn from nature's structures
☐ Everybody is a designer
☐ Solutions grow from place

change; using energy conservation and techniques such as 'life-cycle assessment' to maintain a balance between capital cost and long-term asset value. However, designing sustainably is also about creating spaces that are healthy, economically viable and sensitive to social needs. Increasingly, 'green architecture' – a term used frequently in this book – is concerned with respecting natural systems and learning from ecological processes: creating a better balance between human need and the wider environment.

The history of environmentalism and architecture underlines the gradual understanding of the importance of resource use at a global level, and the inclusion of more philosophical or spiritual concerns along with measurable criteria.

Development of environmental priorities		
1970s	⇒	Energy scarcity
1980s	⇒	Global warming Concept of 'sustainable development' Ozone thinning
1990s	⇒	Water distribution and quality Rainforest protection Biodiversity
2000s	⇒	Health of cities Sustainable design and construction Sustainability and health World poverty and disease

The UN Earth Summit in Rio de Janeiro in 1992 formalised the need to jointly address the imperatives of energy, environment and ecology. Until then, energy had been the primary cause for concern, partly because of the threat of diminishing supplies, but increasingly as a consequence of global warming. The agreement at the Rio Earth Summit effectively widened the environmental debate to bring all resources into the frame, particularly the ecological well-being of the planet.

Thus energy as a single topic has lost its supremacy and is now an element, albeit a major one, in the bigger picture of 'sustainable development'. Other topics have begun to emerge as related aspects of environmental design – such as climate, health, stress and productivity and, although poorly defined, sustainability – has become the intellectual framework for reconciling many competing interests.

Humankind is now placed squarely within the ecological system rather than adopting the typical Western view of a separation between humans and nature.

Origins of sustainability			
Nature as support	Nature as inspiration	Ecological systems	Environmental protection
Food Shelter Water	John Ruskin William R. Lethaby Frank Lloyd Wright	Habitats Rainforests Biodiversity	Global warming Waste and pollution Resource depletion

The repositioning of environmental imperatives at the Rio Earth Summit forced a reassessment of key relationships, influencing not only the environmental sciences but also other areas such as business, farming and the world economic order itself. Although it takes time for the new order to become widely apparent or influential, the Rio Earth Summit planted the seeds of change.

What does this mean in practice?

The concept of sustainability embraces the notion of the environment as a holistic cross-disciplinary system.

Sustainability influences:

- how we design buildings
- how we construct buildings
- how we manage buildings.

Sustainability challenges the fragmentary view of:

- low-energy technologies that are not integrated within ecological design
- high art, high-consumption architecture
- profit at high social or environmental cost.

Sustainability supports:

- an ethical view of architect's role
- a multi-disciplinary approach

- community, social and cultural value
- a new aesthetic language for architecture
- ecological thinking.

There are three broad factors which lead to improvements in the sustainability of the built environment: technology push, policy pull and enlightened self-interest. All three are evident to a greater or lesser extent in sustainable design, but the balance of importance of each varies according to the priorities of clients, the enthusiasms of architects and engineers, and the prevailing political ethos.

Thus the main drivers for change are:

- **Legislation** – new laws demand new thinking.
- **Materials** – as new materials and technologies are developed these lead to new design approaches.
- **Scarcity** – as minerals and other global resources become scarce, the price rises and this influences design choices.
- **Consumerism** – as demands from users of buildings rise, so too do design expectations, so consumers are increasingly demanding green living and working environments.
- **Ethics** – professionalism has begun to embrace environmental ethics, changing the moral basis of architecture.

As Richard Weston notes[2] '… all architecture worth the name embodies a vision of how we might live …' and the challenge is to materialise that vision through construction in a sustainable way.

Normally, a green building will involve a combination of innovative technologies, connection in some way with UK or EU government policy (including any financial incentives which may be available), and a client who recognises the health or social benefits of low-energy design. Added to this, clients need to feel that there is a business case for sustainable design, which shows real benefits in the balance sheet.

The thorny question of whether a building is 'sustainable' or not, or to what degree it reaches the idea, is discussed in **Section B**.

Design is the practice of visualising, shaping and then making the human environment. It involves modifying nature, yet working within nature's rules; it is concerned with giving meaning to our lives, and generating – through space, light, shelter and artefacts – a certain pleasure in living. Design goes beyond creating habitats for mere existence. It involves generating happiness.

Architects help make sense of things; they give order to a disordered world. That order in the age of sustainability derives its basis from ecology. Design may be inspired by nature but there are no direct precedents in the natural world for the things made by man. That is why architectural design is so difficult and why green design presents such a challenge. Earlier generations of architects could solve problems using materials from any continent and from energy resources that were perceived to be infinite, with little regard for cultural or social impact. In the green age, designers are constrained by new laws, new scarcity, and new expectations. Green buildings have to face the challenge of creating beauty and delight using materials and resources, including energy, that are increasingly scarce and expensive. **Section C** presents an overview of the difficult and sometimes conflicting decisions that must be taken during the design of a sustainable green building.

Design is what architects do, and green design is what architects will do more of in the future. Many architects will argue that sustainable design is what they have always sought since the treatises of Vitruvius and Alberti influenced building practice. However, as the science of construction evolves, architects develop new skills and apply new technologies. What makes today different is not the underlying practice of architecture but the urgency of current problems – particularly global warming, which is driving climate change. The resource stresses society face, especially in the field of energy, modify established practices and design assumptions.

However, although we have new tools, new technologies, and face new problems, the design and building professions must not throw away well-honed skills. Design for a sustainable future will continue to involve four key processes[3]:

Defining the problem This will involve searching for appropriate precedents, identifying the knowledge needs, reviewing recent research and distinguishing critical from non-critical factors. Without a strong definition of the problem (and any associated key issues), there will be little chance of innovative green design.

Sharing the problem   Involving the client in the identifying the key issues and in the design process itself is often key to the successful delivery of green buildings. Participation by all stakeholders (users, community groups, consultants, planning officer, building standards officer) throughout the process leads to better design.

Innovation   Innovation comes normally in two forms – either existing technologies are applied in new ways or new technologies are developed and applied in the project for the first time. The latter is rare and full of potential hazard for the client, user and reputation of the design team. More commonly, old techniques and construction processes are modified to suit the particular brief and site in hand. As Darwin pointed out nearly two hundred years ago, new species evolve from old ones, not from scratch. To search for new solutions the whole time is not how nature works.

Ownership   Most of a building's environmental impact starts at occupation and ends a hundred years later – at demolition. The client who has collaborated in the design process becomes the owner and is responsible for the life-cycle costings that follow. By adopting a collaborative approach to the design process, the architect can cultivate real ownership and care of the building by the client.

As Darwin pointed out nearly two hundred years ago, new species evolve from old ones, not from scratch. To search for new solutions the whole time is not how nature works.

Green design is more than style. It is a fundamental reordering of basic design and technological principles, and hence refigures architecture in all of its essential elements.

One has only to look at how major international architects such as Renzo Piano, Lord Rogers, Sir Nicholas Grimshaw and Lord Foster have used good design to 'shop-window' certain ecological principles. In the process they have created an environment of patronage which has helped younger practices and encouraged students to push at the frontiers of sustainable design.

Section D reviews the fundamentals of green design, and highlights and discusses exemplars in several core building types (including schools, homes, offices) and at the macro level – cities.

The aesthetics of sustainability is a poorly understood concept, lacking in theoretical underpinning and rarely articulated through practice. This book seeks to develop a body of knowledge around green design practices and, hence, green aesthetics. The argument is based on the premise that society will more readily accept the discipline of ecological design if it is also beautiful. This discussion is expanded at key points in the book, in the form of a series of 'Essays' that delve deeper into the cultural and political impact of sustainable design.

Art and architecture inspired by nature have the power to challenge the supremacy of other socio-cultural orders. In this, 'sustainable design' can present an alternative vision allowing eco-aesthetics to gradually emerge as a new style or movement in architecture. As such, 'green' can become a powerful cultural force beyond its technological and social assumptions.

The challenge for the architect is to create more beauty with less intervention and more recycling: to do, in fact, what nature does in our own backyard. This is why this book refers frequently to green or 'ecological' design, as well as to low-energy design, and puts sustainability into a cultural context as well as a technological one.

NOTES

[1]   Richard Saxon, 'Sitting on our assets', *Building Design*, 7 November 2003, p. 9.
[2]   Richard Weston, *Materials, Form and Architecture*, Laurence King, 2003, p. 229.

[3]   This list is adapted from lecture by Rogier van der Heide of ARUP given at the Royal Danish Academy of Fine Arts, School of Architecture on 22 January 2009.

Section A
The science and politics of sustainability

1 The Theory and Science of Sustainability

The European heat wave of 2003 is thought to have killed between 22,000 and 35,000 people; and in the same year the World Health Organization (WHO) estimated that global warming was causing 150,000 deaths a year.

How could the WHO be sure that these deaths were caused by global warming, and not just by established weather cycles? This chapter summarises the scientific basis for global warming, surveys the evidence, and reflects on the global impacts that are already evident.

HOW DOES GLOBAL WARMING WORK?

The greenhouse effect is the result of a protective low-level envelope (known as the troposphere) which, positioned about 15 km above the Earth's surface, traps solar radiation. Without the protective shield of the troposphere, the planet would be over 30°C cooler. The troposphere is a delicate embrace that keeps us warm and sheltered from both the excesses of solar radiation and from the chilling effect of night-time cooling.

Only about half of all the energy of solar radiation is absorbed by the Earth; the rest is reflected as infrared radiation (heat). This heat is unable to escape into the outer atmosphere because of the presence of the certain gases in the troposphere, which readily absorb the radiation. This simple process is the reason that life on Earth is possible, and has been termed the 'greenhouse effect' because it works in essentially the same way as the familiar greenhouses where humans grow plants.

The gases that form this protective layer around the globe are thus known as 'greenhouse gases' (GHGs), and include carbon dioxide, methane, nitrous oxide and the man-made compounds chlorofluorocarbons (CFCs).

Carbon dioxide, being the most abundant of the GHGs, is the gas we most readily associate with the greenhouse effect and 'global warming'. The other gases, though present at much lower concentrations, are more potent, that is, due to their molecular make-up, they are capable of absorbing (and therefore holding on to) much more infrared radiation.

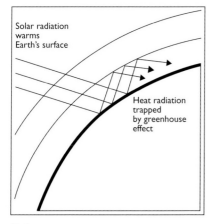

Solar radiation warms Earth's surface

Heat radiation trapped by greenhouse effect

Fig 1
How global warming works.
Source: Newman Levinson Architects

Carbon dioxide (CO_2)

Until the Industrial Revolution, most of the atmospheric CO_2 was derived from natural sources. During daylight, plants absorb CO_2 from the atmosphere and, through the chemical process of photosynthesis, store it as food or use it for growth.

Burning trees or plant material releases this stored CO_2 into the atmosphere. This phenomenon is the reason why locally grown biofuels can – in specific circumstances – be regarded as 'carbon neutral', because during their growth they stored as much CO_2 as they emit when they are burnt.

Fossil fuels such as coal, oil and gas are the end product of this natural CO_2 storage process that began millions of years ago. Ever since fossil fuels became the primary source of energy for humans, we have been releasing this vast reservoir of 'stored' CO_2 back into the atmosphere. With the Industrial Revolution came a massive increase in the burning of fossil fuels (mainly coal, to begin with); and likewise rapid population growth led to ever-increasing energy requirements.

Two hundred years ago there were 590 billion tonnes of CO_2 in the atmosphere; now there are 760 billion tonnes. All this additional CO_2 means that more heat is trapped in the troposphere. This has led to the prediction that the average global temperature could rise by as much as 4°C over the next 100 years – and by twice that amount over the next 500 years.

Methane

The second most significant greenhouse gas, by volume, is methane. Methane is particularly damaging because it depletes atmospheric chemicals which help to break down other greenhouse gases. Globally, there has been a 1 per cent increase per year in methane emissions, part of which is attributed to the growth in domestic waste. In the UK, the construction process generates around 40 per cent of all waste, with buildings in use (i.e. the activities of the people in them) being the principal source of the remainder – amounting to half a tonne of waste per person per year. The other main source of methane is farming and agriculture.

Nitrous oxide

Nitrous oxide (NO_2) is a potent greenhouse gas, about 300 times as powerful as CO_2. Although by volume it is considerably less prevalent than CO_2, it is responsible for nearly 4 per cent of global warming.

NO_2 (and other nitrous compounds – NO_x) comes mainly from animal-based agriculture such as dairy and sheep farming, where it is released mainly in the form of urine (compared with methane which is mainly a by-product of digestion and released from dung). The meat and dairy sectors are growing worldwide, consequently so too are nitrous oxide emissions.

Other factors

Chlorofluorocarbons (CFCs) are highly potent man-made chemicals introduced in the 20th century for use in aerosol spray cans and industrial and domestic refrigeration equipment. Evidence gathered in the 1980s demonstrated that these chemicals were accumulating in the upper atmosphere where they were absorbing ozone – a compound that was protecting the Earth from excessive solar radiation. The thinning these chemicals created in the ozone layer over the Antarctic allows excess solar radiation to hit the Earth's surface, and thus exacerbated the greenhouse effect. The use and manufacture of CFCs was banned by an international treaty (the Montreal Protocol) which came into force in 1989; but even though this has halted the growth of the ozone hole, CFCs (and their substitutes) persist.

FROM GLOBAL WARMING TO CLIMATE CHANGE

Climate change is, essentially, a chain reaction resulting from a rise in average global temperatures (global warming). A small rise in the overall temperature means that water stored in ice-caps and glaciers begins to melt, so sea levels rise a little. Warmer temperatures mean that more water vapour evaporates from the oceans, so more moisture is available for rain (precipitation); and the presence of excess moisture in the air (clouds) contributes to shifting wind and weather patterns.

Thus, although the term 'global warming' suggests an even heating of the Earth, the reality is climate change and a great deal of regional instability. For example, the intensity of storms increases, with higher rainfall, stronger winds and less seasonal predictability for countries near to major oceans. Conversely, drought makes farming unsustainable in formerly productive areas (e.g. Texas, Sudan) and, as a result, nations become dependent on food aid, threatening health and prosperity. Meanwhile melting polar ice and the thermal expansion of the oceans in turn, alters the patterns of ocean currents, which cause further changes in the weather patterns.

The scale of the problem

In spite of international agreements (such as those signed at the Rio Earth Summit and at Kyoto), CO_2 emissions continue to rise; and that in spite of improvements made to the energy efficiency of buildings. There are three main reasons for this:

- the rise in human population (over 6 billion at the turn of the 21st century and expected to reach 10 billion by 2050)
- the legacy of older, inefficient buildings (the existing building stock globally is replaced at a rate of less than 2 per cent per year)
- rising consumer standards, with the corresponding growth in air-conditioning, electrical gadgets of various kinds, and increasing comfort expectations.

There are wide regional variations in the use of fossil fuels and hence man-made greenhouse gas production. In the USA, GHGs are mainly the result of oil used in transportation and gas used for domestic heating. In much of Eastern Europe and China, coal is a major problem, in terms not just of GHGs but also of other pollutants such as sulphur compounds (SO_2 and SO_x), which are responsible for respiratory diseases and acid rain. Coal is the basis of 70 per cent of China's energy, making China the second biggest producer of GHGs after the USA (although compared with the USA, China produces only about one-fifth per head of population).

CO_2 production is increasing faster in newly industrialised countries (China, India and Brazil) than in rich Western countries. Although conservation measures and the switch to renewal energy technologies is a theme of the West, particularly Europe, the economic expansion of other parts of the world poses an ever-increasing challenge to emissions control.

Socio/political/economic threats of global warming
- ☐ Reduction in economic growth
- ☐ Increase in the migration of people
- ☐ Change in global agricultural and fisheries production
- ☐ Increased risk of political instability and wars
- ☐ Inundation of sea-level world cities

Stabilisation of climate change will take more than a century after the last barrel of oil has been burnt. The time–temperature lag means that the world climate may be 4–5°C higher at the end of the fossil fuel age than at the beginning.

Nearly 45 per cent of man-made GHG emissions are derived from the burning of fossil fuels in support of the use of buildings, and about half of the remainder is generated in transporting people and goods to and from buildings. Cities, therefore, are responsible for about 70 per cent of all anthropogenic (man-made) CO_2 emissions, and so it is cities that are the main source of global warming. Debate currently centres on the degree of warming; estimates vary from 1.5°C to 4°C over the next 100 years. Bearing in mind the life span of buildings (typically 50–150 years), it is clear that many buildings designed today will need to survive quite different climatic conditions in the future. With a combination of global warming and a reduction in global dimming (the masking of the sun by air pollution), if the temperature of the planet were to rise by 4°C, it would lead to sea-level rise of about a metre by the end of the century and perhaps seven metres over a millennium. Furthermore, it is thought that at anything more a 2-degree increase in global average temperature, the cycle of change would accelerate and become irreversible.

One of the main guardians of the climate change debate is the International Panel on Climate Change (IPCC). Its annual reports influence governments and IPCC research is highly regarded and forms one of the main sources of climate prediction employed by the European Environment Agency. It was also influential it shaping the EC report (2007) *Adapting to Climate Change in Europe – options for EU action*.[1] Along with the UK Meteorological Office, IPCC has warned recently that earlier predictions of climate change may have underestimated the problem.

The IPCC predictions[2] suggest that the main direct effects of global warming are:

- rise in sea level
- increase in storm activity
- differential regional temperature rise
- expansion of deserts
- increase in episodes of high temperature, especially in unlikely places

Fig 2
The effects of climate change.

Fig 3
The Roman town of Palmera in Syria, which collapsed when the water supply failed.
Source: Syrian Tourist Authority

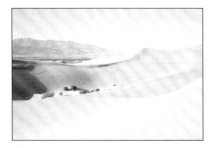

Fig 4
Global warming is leading to the expansion of deserts, stressing many poor nations. Sub-Saharan Morocco.

- increase in convective action (leading to soil drying)
- stress on world forests and uncontrolled fires.

And the main indirect effects of global warming are[3]:

- extra air pollution due to ozone thinning
- displacement or migration of species (plants, birds, insects)
- decline of summertime tourism in hot countries
- extra deaths due to extreme summer weather
- storm damaged cities
- flooded cities and lost agricultural land.

Indeed, the WHO attributes the main causes of the 150,000 deaths per year cited at the beginning of this chapter to sea-level changes affecting agricultural production, lack of rainfall and the evaporation of drinking water supplies.

CLIMATE CHANGE DRIVERS

The evidence that global warming exists is now overwhelming. Climate science has established the correlation between burning fossil fuels, planetary warming and weather instability. However, other human activities – such as the destruction of rainforests (often to supply the world's construction industry), the creation of landfill waste (and the associated release of methane), and the use of ozone-thinning chemicals – are also accelerating the rise in global temperatures.

Global warming is an uncomfortable fact for politicians (some of whom until recently remained in denial), building designers, the construction industry and the human race. It is also an uncomfortable reality for many other global species, whose habitats are threatened by sea-level rise and desertification. Global warming not only places our species under threat, but also stresses the whole ecosystem upon which farming and fishing depend.

The increase in CO_2 production is essentially an urban consequence, but the level of emissions depends on many factors: climate, land use patterns, density, lifestyle and population.

Fig 5
Half the human population now lives in cities of over one million. This example is Sydney.

Fig 6
Mixing land uses reduces the need for transport and hence lessens the consumption of fossil fuels.
Source: LDDC

Land-use patterns have a big impact on carbon emissions. The dispersed, single land use city generates a great deal more CO_2 than the traditional mixed-use neighbourhood. The extra consumption of fossil fuels, and the accompanying increased CO_2 emissions, is the result of private modes of transport and energy-inefficient detached buildings. Population density is a significant issue: public transport only becomes economically viable in compact cities. Dense urban patterns with a diversity of land uses achieve significantly lower CO_2 generation than typical modern suburban cities. This is why carbon dioxide production per head of population varies between countries. It is the pattern of living that is the key.

Lifestyle is clearly a related issue. As we become more prosperous, we desire and consume more. Consumption carries a corresponding burden of resource use, waste generation and, ultimately, CO_2 production. Buildings that are necessary to support life and consumption, could, through better environmental design, reduce adverse ecological impacts. The great irony is that the world's most advanced nations are also its greatest polluters, in spite of having the greatest knowledge of the environmental consequences. Industrialisation sows the seeds of its own destruction by generating high levels of carbon emissions, leading directly to global warming. Architecture alone cannot solve global environmental problems, but it can make a significant contribution to the creation of more sustainable human habitats.

Comparison of the impact of building construction and buildings in use		
Impact	Building construction	Building use
Energy resources	Medium	High
Water resources	Medium	High
Mineral resources	High	Low
Transport	Medium	High
Air pollution	Low	Medium
Water pollution	High	Low
Noise pollution	High	Medium
Visual impact	High	Medium
Wildlife impact/biodiversity	High	Low
Waste	High	High
Health	High	Medium

Fig 7
Low-density cities such as Milton Keynes depend on high levels of fossil fuels and require drastic remodelling to make them sustainable in the future.
Source: Milton Keynes Development Corporation

Fig 8
Rapid industrialisation in China and India is further stressing planet Earth.
Source: HKPD

Factor four

The environmental think tank The Rocky Mountain Institute predicts that society can achieve a fourfold improvement in productivity without consuming further resources. This 'factor four' concept is based on the assumption that leaner technologies, greater use of recycling, and better management and design will allow mankind to grow without further ecological damage.

Underpinning this idea is the notion of 'natural capital' – a kind of global accounting system for all ecological resources (see ESSAY: Natural capital). Ecological resources will come to resemble stocks and shares from the world's financial markets. Ecology will be traded: as ecological richness becomes scarce its value will increase, thereby ensuring its survival. It is an attractive idea but has, at its root, the concept of free market economies. The 'factor four' concept, however, contains many lessons for those who design, engineer and commission buildings. Like the 'cradle-to-cradle' movement, the Rocky Mountain Institute is against greater environmental regulation, believing that it is in the best interests of companies to conserve resources since they will acquire a competitive edge by so doing. It is a position which runs counter to that of the European Union, with its emphasis on environmental regulation, highlighting the political difference between Europe and the USA on this issue.

Improvements in living conditions, aided by the ever-increasing average rate of energy use per person globally (from 0.6 kW in 1900 to 2.6 kW in 2009), have led to an increase in human numbers and life expectancy. During the past 50 years, average life expectancy around the world has risen from 46 years to 63 years and the difference in longevity between people in the developed and developing worlds has shrunk from 26 to 13 years. As we live longer, we consume more, and in old age our dependency on heat, light and transportation increases. Food production has more than doubled over the past century from a diminishing area of productive agricultural land. Land has been lost to urban expansion, to desertification and to pollution, but thanks to new technologies (particularly irrigation, fertilisers and pesticides) and greater energy input, total agricultural productivity has increased. In achieving this, biodiversity has suffered, and Rachel Carson's prediction of a 'Silent Spring' has become a reality in large parts of agricultural Europe. Carson writes[4] about a landscape without birdsong – places which are productive but devoid of beauty or ecological richness.

The stresses imposed by population growth touch upon resources of various kinds (as well as the waste chain), and force society to better manage the conflicts between economic, environmental and social sustainability. The main question facing ecologists is whether human success as a species will be constrained by resource scarcity or by the scale of human-generated pollution. Will waste

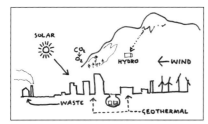

Fig 9
The post-petroleum city of the future, with its dependence on renewable energy and waste as a resource.

Fig 10
Urbanisation leads to increased consumption of scarce resources, as here in Yokohama, Japan. Urban design is the key to unlocking constraints to sustainable development.

succeed in limiting growth more effectively than the ability to secure an ever-increasing supply of resources? These tensions will be felt primarily in mega-cities and will lead to stressing of existing infrastructure to the same degree as they will demand a fresh approach to designing buildings. Architecture will need to address the resource and waste equation, exploiting waste as a potential source of energy or future construction material.

The trouble with cities

Environmental damage will be manifested first in our cities, in the form of rising temperatures, health problems caused by air pollution or contaminated water, disease, food shortages and energy scarcity. In the near future, individual buildings may still function adequately but the collective landscape of cities and their relationship to the global ecosystem may begin to fail. This is because cities are a cocktail of impacts – the waste chain is long, deep and pervasive. Cities are also increasing the scale of their ecological footprints and becoming more densely inhabited.

The drift of the human population to cities puts pressure on housing land, water and energy supplies, and sewage and waste capacity. The year 2000 marked the first time in human history that the urban population exceeded the rural one. Of a global population of 6.8 billion, a greater number of people now live in cities than in the countryside.

Over half of all humans now live in urban areas; about one-third of those live in cities with over a million inhabitants, and half of them live in 'mega-cities' of over eight million people. These mega-cities are where global environmental stress is already most in evidence – in the big conurbations of Tokyo, Mumbai, Mexico City and São Paulo. By the end of the current century it is estimated that over three-quarters of the human population will live in such cities. In the meantime, the task is one of developing new technologies and new design solutions to deal with the adverse impacts we have already identified while working out how to manage the unavoidable future consequences.

The move to cities not only entails an intensification of urban problems (pollution, space crowding and resource stress) but it also raises expectations of an enhanced lifestyle. The personal goals of air-conditioning, cars and energy-consuming gadgets of various kinds (including over a quarter of a billion

Fig. 11 *(right)*
The American model of urbanism is a threat to both the global environment and personal safety. San Francisco.

Fig 12 *(far right)*
The European model of urbanism favours streets for people and low-energy design. City of London.

mobile phones discarded each year) require resources whose supplies seem infinite but are, in reality, ever more limited.

As the human species becomes more urbanised we consume more, waste more and pollute more. This, as the architect Lord Rogers has pointed out, shifts the emphasis from single buildings to urban design; from simple design choices (such as energy efficiency) to complex ones (such as sustainability); and, ultimately, from a profit-driven agenda to an ethical one. If current trends continue it is likely that, by 2050, the human race will have four times the environmental impact it had in 2000 (based on a 2 per cent annual economic growth and a global population of 10 billion).

Global warming and building design
☐ Half of all fossil fuels are used in the construction and operational use of buildings
☐ A quarter of all fossil fuels are used in transportation of people and goods to buildings
☐ Air-conditioning use is increasing as global temperatures rise
☐ Energy policy and regulation is driving building design
☐ Energy price is increasingly effecting design choices for consumer
☐ Energy scarcity and security is leading to a shift from fossil fuels to renewable technologies

CHALLENGES FOR THE BUILT ENVIRONMENT

Over the past generation there has been a shift in emphasis about the nature and scale of environmental problems faced, and hence there emerged different perspectives on how these problems were to be solved. In the 1970s, following the OPEC oil embargo, there was concern over oil supplies; then the *Limits to Growth* report by a group of academics known as the Club of Rome[5] predicted growing resource scarcity and the end to unlimited consumption. By the 1980s there was international anxiety over acid rain and coal production was curtailed in Europe in favour of gas. In 1987 the term 'sustainable development' was coined by a UN Commission which in turn fuelled debate about global warming, its root causes and the action needed to slow down the process. Subsequent agreement has proved difficult politically although the European Union has pushed ahead with various environmental laws, regulations and agreements among its internal partners. These are increasingly seen as a model for other nations to follow. By the early 21st century the security of energy supplies and rising costs of oil and gas encouraged the impetus to address the broader picture of energy and environment.

Ecology began to emerge as a unifying discipline – a framework on which human impacts and the carrying capacity of planet earth could be measured and ultimately reconciled.

According to the World Wide Fund for Nature (WWF),[6] forests the size of Greece are lost each year to serve the construction industry, resulting in the extinction of hundreds of species a year (most before they have been discovered). In addition, it is estimated that each of us carries several hundred synthetic chemicals in our bodies that were not present in our grandparents. As the global construction industry is responsible for much of the forest clearing (to create timber products used in buildings) and for putting the new chemicals into people (by way of the materials they specify), architects and architecture schools share some of the responsibility.

The interaction between architecture and agriculture is highlighted by an increasing rate of severe flooding as witnessed in the UK, Italy, Germany, Cambodia, Vietnam and India in the period 2000–8. The combined effect of urban expansion and agricultural intensification has exceeded the capacity of the land to absorb exceptional levels of rainfall. At the same time, rainfall has become more intensive, concentrated and erratic due to global warming. The design of buildings and landscapes therefore has a role to play in absorbing the new rainfall peaks, and thereby reducing stress on drains and river systems. Hard surfaces

Fig 13
The ICI Visitor Centre, Runcorn, designed by
AMEC Design brings nature and architecture
together.
Source: Amec Design and Build

Fig 14
Nature influenced the design of the Wetlands
Centre at Slimbridge, from site planning down
to construction details.
Source: ECD Architects

Fig 15
Bath stone used in new office near Bath,
designed by Bennetts Associates.

should be replaced by those which act as a sponge to soak up moisture and release it gradually using sustainable urban drainage systems (SUDS).

The farming landscape too is less able to absorb water than in the past. Agricultural land that surrounds cities is over-farmed and over-grazed, with the result that the rainwater quickly runs off all surfaces. For example, the sheep population in the UK is around 30 million (one sheep for every three humans), and fields not grazed are ploughed for winter cereal production. In Denmark there are more pigs than people, with much of the landscape trampled and water courses polluted by the run-off from mega piggery units. Under this kind of intensive regime, rainwater cannot percolate through to ground aquifers and instead runs off to flood the valleys where buildings are concentrated. River speeds increase, eroding banks and flooding the houses, shops and industrial premises which make up the urban landscape. Every doubling of a river's velocity increases its destructive power fourfold.[7]

Historically, many world cities are located at sea level. Trade by boat and the need for international communication led to the growth of coastal cities, many at the mouths of large rivers such as London (on the Thames), Hamburg (on the Elbe) and Rotterdam (on the Rhine). These, and many other cities such as Mumbai, Sydney, New York and Hong Kong, are located at sea level, and their survival depends on the construction of ever more ambitious flood protection measures. These cities may in time become the new Venices of human civilisation. It is not just the flooding of roads which will make these great urban centres untenable, but also the loss of the underground services upon which they depend – water supply, sewers, fibre-optic cables, metro systems. Even those who do not live or work in the city are affected. Most food production comes from the rich agricultural lands of former flood plains, and as sea levels rise much of this land will be lost by inundation. For example, around a third of the European population lives within 50 km of the sea and about 3 per cent of these people are at risk of rising sea levels.

By the year 2050 it is likely that the world will double its demand for of energy. Much of the demand will be for the fossil fuels that are needed for conventional electricity generation (with consequent further pressure on price, energy security and consequences in terms of global warming) but a growing percentage will be energy produced from renewable sources. Meeting the challenge of

Fig 16
The long-term view of: (a) fossil fuels; and (b) climate change.

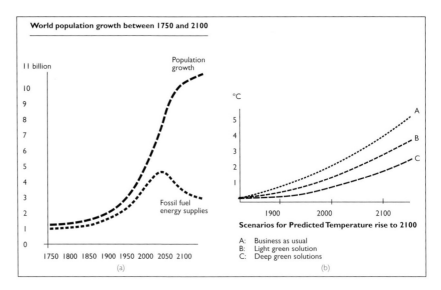

World population growth between 1750 and 2100

(a)

Population growth

11 billion

Fossil fuel energy supplies

1750 1800 1850 1900 1950 2000 2050 2100

°C

A

B

C

1900 2000 2100

Scenarios for Predicted Temperature rise to 2100

A: Business as usual
B: Light green solution
C: Deep green solutions

(b)

Fig 17
Buildings help to test the performance of new environmental approaches. BRE building, Watford.

satisfying rising energy expectations in areas of the world such as China, Africa and India, which are already substantially industrialised, requires action by architects to promote the exploitation of renewable energy in building projects in preference to oil and gas. The development of renewables offers an energy solution which does not damage human health (through air pollution), blight local environments (via petrochemical plants) or threaten natural systems (by global warming).

It is argued that as oil and gas supplies become exhausted, society will return to coal consumption for heating and electricity generation. Coal deposits, either in pure or shale deposits, have the potential to supply human need throughout the 21st century, but the side effects of coal burning limit its use. Not only is the carbon footprint of coal high, but there are also many unpleasant side effects, such as SO_2 pollution (which leads to acid rain) and other toxic pollutants. Although new technologies allow for the cleaner burning of coal, it remains a last resort.

At present one-third of humanity (or 2 billion people) is dependent on biomass energy sources – typically firewood and animal dung – for cooking and heating. The consequences are felt not just in the area of poverty but in environmental

Fig 18
Five approaches to electricity production.
Top: nuclear power; coal-fired power station;
Below: wind generators; photovoltaic cells;
waste/combined heat and power.

stress. As trees are felled for firewood, the landscape becomes more arid with a decline in agricultural capacity. The downward spiral increases as further firewood is extracted, often involving lengthy journeys into the bush. Children are the usual gatherers of fuel, so time spent on this activity eats into time for schooling. When there are lengthy journeys also for water, the basic needs of many in Africa and parts of Asia are determined by the demands of survival rather than developing an economy which creates time for skills training.

The World Summit on Sustainable Development held in Johannesburg in 2002 set a target of halving fuel poverty by 2015. Part of the solution proposed was in the development of rural solar power systems. Since fuel poverty is most marked in relatively sunny, underdeveloped countries the potential of solar energy is obvious. What is being promoted by the United Nations Development Programme (a by-product of the Summit) is a shift towards a low-carbon energy system based on solar power in developing countries, hydrogen fuel cells for already industrialised ones, and greater use of biofuels for world transport.

Fig 19
The design of schools can do much to promote an understanding of sustainable design. Swanlea School, Whitechapel, London, designed by Percy Thomas Architects.
Source: Percy Thomas Architects

The UN Millennium Development Goals[8] (MDGs) seek an environmental and social partnership which crosses political, regional and cultural frontiers. Ambitious and utopian in spirit, the ten main goals seek to improve the human condition through better education, healthcare and infrastructure provision

Fig 20
Water filtration plant in New York, designed by
Grimshaw. The design is based on the water lily.
Source: Grimshaw

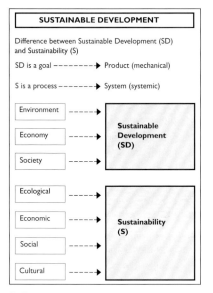

Fig 21
The difference between sustainable
development and sustainability.

including architectural projects. Like the UN Development Programme, there is a clear role for design professionals in the area of building-related infrastructure which is a recurring theme of the MDGs. Architects are increasingly involved in implementing aid-assisted developments on the ground, not always at the cutting edge of technological development, but in designing buildings able to accommodate fast-changing environmental priorities and new evolving social programmes.

THE FUTURE ROLE FOR ARCHITECTS

Architects have a key role to play in helping to manage climate change. Their professional involvement with the adaptation of existing buildings (currently making up about 60 per cent of total construction workload) should aim at reducing the consumption of energy and prepare structures for much altered future climates. Architects are also active players in shaping the future through the design choices they make. It is ethically unacceptable to ignore the challenge of global warming as a designer or as a teacher of architecture. Carbon neutral architecture will be the agenda of the next generation. Unfortunately a great deal of cost is attached to engineering these changes. The economic slow-down following the credit crunch of 2008 limits the freedom to choose expensive energy adaptation or innovative green technologies. However, the recession does provide nations with breathing space to take stock of alternative visions of the future.

Action to limit CO_2 production can be taken on many fronts. Microclimates can be modified to enhance human comfort levels, thereby using less energy. Cold northern cities can benefit by improving shelter and harvesting solar radiation, both relatively simple and cost-effective solutions. In hot climates, trees and climbers can be used to create shade and the cross-section of buildings can be altered to channel natural air currents, thereby reducing the need for air-conditioning.

There are three main strategies needed to address and manage climate change:

- reduce the burning of fossil fuels
- limit damage by mitigation and adaptation of existing conditions (cities, buildings, etc.)

Fig 22
The Park in Abu Dhabi designed by PRP is a mixed-use building containing: (a) a hotel; and (b) an office development that achieved high scores in LEED and Estidama environmental assessment.
Source: PRP

Fig 23
This office tower, designed by Hamzah & Yeang for Manesar, India, blends ecological and architectural principles to produce a form of future wealth that is less exposed to rising energy costs than most modern buildings.
Source: T.R. Mamzah & Yeang Sdn. Bhd.

- design for a fossil free future (zero carbon buildings).

Reduce reliance on fossil fuels

Buildings in both the developed and less developed worlds are required to facilitate and test knowledge transfer from the science laboratory into the field in areas such as micro-generation of electricity, alternative technologies and power grid independence. In this sense, enlightened clients such as the World Bank and NGOs expect buildings to be exercises in design innovation with all the subsequent monitoring and potential failure that this entails. As UN and government initiatives change, so too do building briefs and client expectations in the critical fields of energy or water conservation.

Addressing environmental stress can only be achieved by the use of more intelligent technologies, better design practices linked to greater economy in the use of natural resources, and a shift from fossil fuel resource exploitation to developing self-sustaining renewable supplies. City planning has a key role to play in the quest to establish a more symbiotic relationship between buildings, energy, land and nature. Here sustainable transport – involving architects rather than engineers in the decisions concerning design and social provision – is important.

Damage limitation and mitigation

The relationship between global warming, land use and architecture is one that society needs to understand quickly. The old idea of separate urban and rural ecologies is no longer valid, although it is the basis for much official thinking, implied, for example, in the term 'town and country planning'. Designers can play their part by rethinking the choice of surfaces around buildings, by introducing

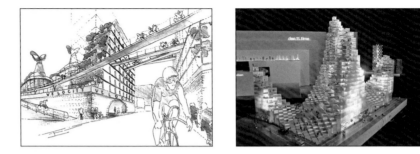

Fig 24 *(right)*
Bill Dunster's vision of cycle-based urbanism known as 'Velocity' – an interesting blend of ecology and carbon-free transport.
Source: Bill Dunster Architects

Fig 25 *(far right)*
Lego Towers model, designed and built by BIG (Bjarke Ingels Group), shows the potential of modularisation in creating new eco-city forms.
Source: BIG Architects

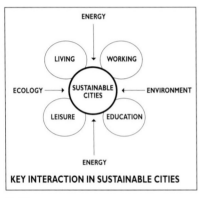

KEY INTERACTION IN SUSTAINABLE CITIES

Fig 26
Key interactions in sustainable cities.

more bio-engineering methods of flood control, by questioning the validity and use of green belts, and by avoiding development on flood plains. If building must be constructed on flood plains then the ground floor should be able to be evacuated speedily and provision made for mobility by boat as well as car.

In some ways the professional and subject discipline boundaries which have grown up act as barriers to environmental learning. Whereas landscape architecture students are aware of the benefits of natural drainage and food plain protection, such knowledge does not always extend to architecture, urban planning or civil engineering students. Ecological design methods may be understood at the building scale but too few architecture students know how to apply the principles at a regional level. Designing buildings and cities able to withstand seasonal floods and sea level rise is one of the biggest challenges for the future.

Equally, the habitats that architects create have their place in satisfying the needs of both humans and other species. Biodiversity is everybody's responsibility: designers, engineers, farmers, politicians and so on. Architects can play their part in three ways:

Fig 27
Traditional farming settlements: (right) on a flood plane of Elbe; and (far right) the author's sketch of flood risk housing design.

20

Fig 28
Designing in anticipation of rising sea levels will become increasingly important in the future.

- They can design natural habitats as part of the development process – these could include ponds or wetlands, tree planting, turf roofs, creeper-clad walls, natural grasslands (flower-rich and left uncut).
- They can source construction materials from an ecological point of view, helping to maintain local or regional biodiversity by the choice of products or materials employed.
- They can bring nature into closer contact with people's lives. This can entail interior as well as exterior planting and the exploitation of views to enhance the perception or visibility of the natural world. The objective is to ensure that the human species is not disconnected from the natural world. Just as television has done much to bring an appreciation of wildlife and an understanding of ecology into our lives, buildings can play their part in providing a window on biodiversity.

Poverty, rural areas and ethical responsibilities

Climate change will have a greater impact on everyday days for poor rather than wealthy nations. The G8 leaders acknowledged their global responsibilities at Gleneagles in 2005 but took little meaningful action to help poorer nations adapt to altered climates. The creation of an infrastructure of basic services and public buildings is essential if Africa is to pull itself out of the current cycle of environmental and social decline. Sustainable development can only be achieved if aid is directed to the engineering infrastructure needs of water supply, roads and sanitation and the equally important building infrastructure provision of schools and health facilities. In both areas climate change and regional conflict elevates construction to beyond that of basic human rights.

The particular problem of remote rural areas provides a challenge for designers of schools, houses and local health centres. Grid-based energy systems rarely exist in rural areas, where electrical energy is generated from oil and heat from burning wood. Solar power provides an obvious solution in the form of photovoltaic

(PV) generated electricity. Gridless electricity is necessary in remote areas, making local generation essential. Both wind- and solar-generated electricity suit people living in villages or remote homesteads and relieve pressure on local timber reserves. For governments and aid agencies, PV technology is the cheapest and quickest way to deliver electricity. With electricity come other benefits to rural communities – light for reading and study, connection to radio and television, and energy for cooking, boiling water and mobile phones. Off-grid solar power liberates the rural poor from dependency on imported and expensive non-renewable energy supplies. It costs about £800 to install a basic solar system to a house and £9000 to a school in developing countries. Although, by the standards of other construction costs, solar installation costs are quite high (perhaps 20 per cent of the total building budget), the long-term benefits socially, economically and environmentally are significant. Although off-grid power is normally solar-driven in developing countries, it can also be wind or water-driven.

Fig 29
The roof as habitat and extra layer of insulation.
Source: Erisco Bauder

Fig 30
Harmony between architecture and nature
at the Mountain in Copenhagen, designed by
BIG, and in the suburbs of Madrid, designed by
Foreign Office Architects.

Fig 31
The Bo01 Green City of Tomorrow project
in Malmo received generous backing from the
Swedish government.

Fig 32
Roof-mounted PV system at University of Gloucester, designed by Feilden Clegg Bradley.

Research for sustainable design
☐ Knowledge creation   Blue sky
☐ Knowledge testing   Laboratory
☐ Knowledge transfer   Design studio or
                        office
☐ Knowledge application Building
☐ Knowledge sharing   Teaching and
                        publication

Fig 33
Design for low-carbon sports village in Malmo, Sweden, by BIG Architects. The project uses geothermal energy and water harvesting.
Source: BIG Architects

Design for zero carbon

It is ironic that about 20 per cent of the world's solar panels are now manufactured by oil companies such as Shell and BP. If the world does double its energy consumption by 2050 it can do so only by diversifying the sources of energy production. In the first half of the 21st century it is expected that the newly industrialised or still developing countries will need five times more energy than at present, and most of this will have to come from renewable sources.[9] Without the infrastructure of refineries, pipelines and power grids, large areas of rural Africa, Asia and Latin America will be dependent on non-grid supplies. Such a demand may push down the price of PV panels to that of a few gallons of petrol.

With the globalisation of architectural services, professionals in the developed world will need to learn how to use renewable technologies if they hope to work in the rapidly expanding developing world. The architectural and engineering professions face distinct challenges in meeting the demands that lie ahead; so too does education of the new professionals who will provide the services. After all, 'zero carbon' means offsetting the inevitable carbon footprint that results from constructing the building by using energy generated at the building over its lifetime. With current PV efficiency levels, an active building (in an energy generating sense) may need 30–40 years to balance its carbon equation. Then of course, it is carbon negative and becomes a mini power plant for the community.

NOTES

[1]   EC report: *Adapting to Climate Change in Europe – options for EU action*, 2007.

[2]   IPCC, *Climate Change 2007 – The Physical Science Basis; Contribution of Working Group I to the Fourth Assessment Report of the IPCC*, Cambridge University Press, 2007. See www.ipcc.ch

[3]   Adapted from *Impacts of Europe's changing climate – 2008 Indicator-based Assessment* (joint EEA-JRC-WHO report no 4/2008).

[4]   Rachel Carsen, *Silent Spring*, Houghton Mifflin (Trade), 1962. See in particular chapter 2.

[5]   Donella H. Meadows et al., *The Limits to Growth, A Report to The Club of Rome*, 1972, available online at www.clubofrome. org/docs/limits.rtf

[6]   Source: www.worldwildlife.org/what/ wherewework/amazon/threats.html, and The Amazon's Vicious Cycles (PDF, 2.5MB) www.worldwildlife.org/what/ wherewework/amazon/publications.html

[7]   Jonathan Theobold, 'Overgrazing has Stripped the Soil', *The Guardian*, Society Supplement, 15 November 2000, p. 11.

[8]   See www.un.org/millenniumgoals/ development

[9]   Peter Davies, *Putting Energy in the Spotlight*, BP Report, London, 2005. See www.bp.com

Essay – A Short History of Sustainable Development

Through its various conferences the United Nations (UN) has been the environmental conscience of the world. Although much more needs to be done, the UN in partnership with other international agencies[1] such as the European Union, has obtained a remarkable level of agreement among often sceptical nations.

Major global environmental conferences or agreements	
1972	Stockholm Conference on the Human Environment (UN)
1980	World Conservation Strategy (IUCN)
1983	World Commission on Environment and Development (UN)
1987	Montreal Protocol on Ozone Layer (UN)
1987	*Our Common Future* (Brundtland Commission) (UN)
1990	Green Paper on the Urban Environment (EU)
1992	Rio de Janeiro Earth Summit (UN)
1996	Habitat Conference (UN)
1997	Kyoto Conference on Global Warming (UN)
2000	The Hague Conference on Climate Change (UN)
2002	Johannesburg Summit on Sustainable Development (UN)
2006	Helsinki Conference on Carbon Trading and Global Warming (UN)
2007	Bali Conference on Climate Change (UN)
2008	Poznan Conference on Climate Change and Carbon Trading (UN)
2009	Copenhagen Conference on Climate Change (UN)

DEFINING SUSTAINABLE DEVELOPMENT

In 1987 the UN Environment Commission, chaired by Gro Harlem Brundtland, defined sustainable development as:

> '… development that meets the needs of the present without compromising the ability of future generations to meet their own needs'.

Now known as 'the Brundtland definition' of sustainable development, this is a virtuous but imprecise concept, open to various and often conflicting interpretations. However, it remains the global standard. It addresses the needs of both the present and future generations in terms of environmental resources. The definition Brundtland coined may well be the single biggest imperative for global development in the 21st century. The consequences have been enormous.

The Brundtland definition has spawned a series of sub-definitions to meet particular sector needs. Typical of these is that used by the practice of Foster and Partners, which defines 'Sustainable design as creating buildings which are energy efficient, healthy, comfortable, flexible in use and designed for long life'. The Building Services Research and Information Association (BSRIA) defines 'Sustainable construction as the creation and management of healthy buildings based upon resource efficient and ecological principles'.

The UK government has gone further, stating ambitiously that 'Sustainable development means a better quality of life now and for generations to come ...' with the aim to '... avoid using resources faster than the planet can replenish them ...' and to join up '... economic, social and environmental goals'.[2] Furthermore, four key areas for activity all of which impact upon the professional life of those in the design and construction industries: sustainable consumption and production (changing the way products and services are designed, produced, etc.); climate change and energy (reducing greenhouse gas emissions and adapting to future climate change); natural resources (understanding the limits of resources); and sustainable communities (maintaining existing urban resources and building an energy-efficient future).

These various definitions show the value of coining terms of reference for specific topics – be they building types, services provided, or levels of development. In summary, the Brundtland definition outlines a philosophy that benefits from a degree of imprecision. There is a general understanding and set of principles which allow useful sub-definitions to be framed within its broad embrace.

Within these broad definitions and interpretations there are three recurring dimensions that provide the focus for action by different interested parties:

- environmental sustainability
- economic sustainability
- social sustainability.

The Brundtland Commission argued that economic and social systems could not be divorced from the 'carrying capacity' of the environment – the idea that growth and social welfare has to be balanced by the conservation of

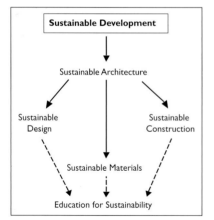

Fig 34
The concept of sustainable development spawns several sub-definitions relevant to building design.

Fig 35
The Johannesburg World Summit on Sustainable Development stimulated investment in clean energy technologies, such as photovoltaic cells (PVs).

environmental resources by the present generation for the benefit of future generations. Hence the term 'sustainable development' has wide ramifications for architects – the people who are carrying out the 'development'. But it also begs the question of whether environmental and economic sustainability are truly reconcilable. Are architects fooling themselves into thinking that 'development' can ever be sustainable?

A key word in the definition of sustainable development is that of 'future'. Architects are always designing for the future – that is what the blueprint is about. However, the time horizon was extended by Brundtland by the inclusion of another key phrase 'future generations'. Designers of the built environment are accustomed to thinking across decades, even centuries, as they make the difficult material and energy choices. But buildings survive for such a long time and the urban infrastructure even longer, so the obligation to think long-term has raised questions about the architects' professional role and the knowledge base that underpins professional practice.

Fig 36 *(right)*
Project ZED – a low-energy office, design by Future Systems, points to a new eco-aesthetic.
Source: Future Systems

Fig 37 *(far right)*
The skills of architectural design are a form of cultural capital. GLA Building, London.
Source: Foster and Partners

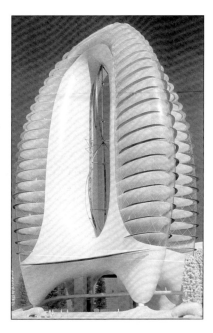

Further refinements to the definition

The UN Conference on Environment and Development held in Rio in 1992 elaborated on some of the key concepts encapsulated in the Brundtland definition. Among these was the adoption of the 'precautionary principle' which stipulates that:

- no environmental action should be taken which was not reversible
- designers should use the best scientific knowledge available
- scientists had a duty to develop environmental knowledge
- ignorance was no defence under international law for ecological damage.

There were far reaching implications for the development industry.

The 2002 Johannesburg World Summit on Sustainable Development then introduced the concept of 'sustainable consumption and production' leading to a number of international agreements. The key principle was to establish a link between productivity, resource use and levels of pollution. Specifically, the agreement was about:

- ensuring that economic growth does not cause environmental pollution at a global and regional level
- improving efficiency in resource use
- examining the whole life cycle of a product
- giving consumers more information on products and services
- exploiting taxation and regulation to stimulate innovation in clean technologies.

Although the Johannesburg World Summit had an economic bias, the ramifications have been felt by architects and the wider construction industry ever since. The agreements, for instance, stimulated investment in new energy technologies and in new ways of recycling or reusing waste. They also encouraged the development of concepts linked to sustainability such as 'added value' and 'cradle to cradle', and provide encouragement to the formulation of arguments around 'productivity' benefits of green buildings. Since more information was being made available to consumers following Johannesburg, designers benefited from both the environmental credentials then being displayed on products and the pressure for more green solutions which flowed from better informed clients.

Fig 38
The Swiss Re building consumes only half the fossil fuels of a typical modern office block in London.
Source: Foster and Partners

Key definitions

☐ **Sustainable development** is 'development that meets the needs of the present without compromising the ability of future generations to meet their own needs' (Brundtland, 1987).

☐ **Sustainable design** is the 'creation of buildings which are energy efficient, healthy, comfortable, flexible in use and designed for long life' (Foster and Partners, 1999).

☐ **Sustainable construction** is the 'creation and management of healthy buildings based upon resource efficient and ecological principles' (BSRIA, 1996).

☐ **Sustainable materials** are 'materials and construction products that are healthy, durable, resource efficient and manufactured with regard to minimising environmental impact and maximising recycling' (Edwards, 2004).

THE RIO EARTH SUMMIT: INTEGRATING THE THREE ES

The UN Earth Summit in Rio de Janeiro in 1992 formalised the need to jointly address the imperatives of the 'three Es' – energy, environment and ecology. Until then, energy had been the primary resource concern, partly because of the threat of diminishing supplies, but increasingly as a consequence of global warming. The Rio agreement effectively widened the environmental debate to bring all resources into the frame, particularly the ecological well-being of the planet.

The main environmental agreements at the Rio Earth Summit focussed on:

- energy – global warming (future supplies)
- ecology – biodiversity (rainforest protection)
- environment – water resources (land and farming).

The repositioning of environmental imperatives at the Rio Earth Summit forced a reassessment of key relationships, influencing not only the environmental sciences but also other areas such as business, farming and the world economic order itself. Although it takes time for the new order to become widely apparent or influential, the Rio Summit planted the seeds of change.

Fig 39
The widening influence of sustainability.

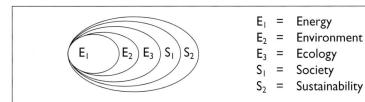

E_1 = Energy
E_2 = Environment
E_3 = Ecology
S_1 = Society
S_2 = Sustainability

Action to achieve the 'three Es': Energy, Environment and Ecology		
Energy	Move from fossil fuels to renewable energy sources	Employ low-energy design See building as generator of energy Consider all energy uses (heating, lighting, ventilation, transport) Use heat recovery and super-insulation Use orientation to reduce energy load Consider embodied energy and energy in use
Environment	Consider environmental impact on broad front	Consider resource conservation (land, water, materials) Restore land and buildings as part of development process Avoid pollution through design Design for durability, flexibility and recycling Design for health, comfort and safety
Ecology	Consider effect of choice of materials on biodiversity	Link design systems to ecological systems See development as closed loop with recycling of waste Maximise diversity from minimum resources Use development to extend or create natural habitats Use planting for shelter and energy efficiency

The Rio agreements formed a convenient three-point framework of global concerns, requiring human activities to be within it rather than outside it. Development, including building design, was to be informed by new concerns. Architects now had to consider not only energy but also other environmental resources (particularly water use) and how the building impacted on the wider ecology (timber sourcing). For some the new agenda was too broad; for others it provided an inspiring fresh basis for architectural design.

Fig 40
The trilogy of the three Es and three Rs.

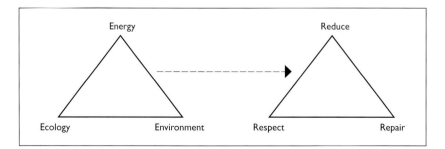

Fig 41
Three perspectives on eco-design: energy, environment and ecology.

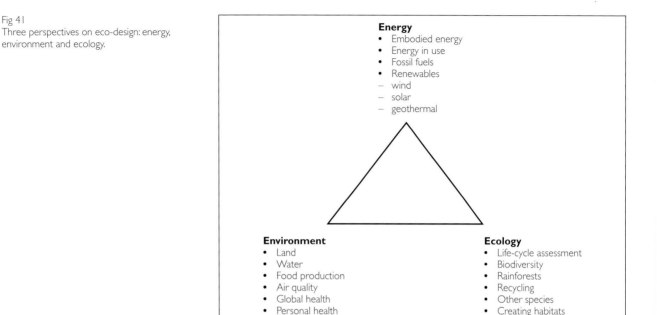

Energy
- Embodied energy
- Energy in use
- Fossil fuels
- Renewables
  - wind
  - solar
  - geothermal

Environment
- Land
- Water
- Food production
- Air quality
- Global health
- Personal health

Ecology
- Life-cycle assessment
- Biodiversity
- Rainforests
- Recycling
- Other species
- Creating habitats

KYOTO 1997: LIMITING CARBON EMISSIONS

In an attempt to limit production of greenhouse gases (GHGs), the Kyoto Protocol of 1997 established targets based on a system of 'carbon trading' between nations. This Emissions Trading System (ETS) allows one (typically rich 'developed') country to buy 'carbon credits' from another (typically poor, developing) country, offsetting these against investment in the development of clean technologies. Investors gain credits which allow the domestic market to buy international carbon emissions rights. Unfortunately the system, which has been ratified by over 100 countries (but excluding at the time the USA, Russia and Australia), is not ideal. For example, it has allowed the USA to purchase the former Soviet Union's carbon allowances, permitting the USA to pollute at twice the European average and at about 10 times the world norm.

Since Kyoto, various intergovernmental agreements have attempted to find consensus on limiting atmospheric CO_2 release: the climate change conferences

Typical CO_2 emissions in 2008 (based on living, working, transport and consumption) per person per year	
	CO_2 emissions in 2008 (tonnes)
USA	5.80
Europe	3.00
Japan	2.40
Russia	2.00
China	1.20
India	0.95
Data adapted from: www.eia.doe.gov/iea/carbon	

at the Hague (2000), Johannesburg (2006), Bali (2007), Poznan (2008) and Copenhagen (2009).

POZNAN 2008: CLEAN DEVELOPMENT MECHANISM

The ETS scheme was extended at the UN conference on Climate Change held in Poznan, Poland in 2008, by providing greater incentives under the UN Clean Development Mechanism for countries as well as international companies to pay for new projects in developing countries (such as hydro-electric schemes) in order to offset emissions at home.

Carbon offsetting encourages moves towards cleaner energy use rather than reduction as such. The effect may in the future require architects to be aware not just of the energy consumption of a building but also whether the energy is fossil fuel or renewables based. The global system of carbon offsetting and trading may in time filter down to parallel a similar system for towns and even buildings.

GLOBAL ECONOMIC DOWNTURN AND ITS CONSEQUENCES

Climate change will have a greater impact on the daily lives of the peoples of poor nations than on those who live in wealthy nations. The G8 (Canada, France,

Germany, Italy, Japan, Russia, UK and USA) leaders acknowledged their global responsibilities at Gleneagles in 2005 but took little meaningful action to help poorer nations adapt to altered climates. The creation of an infrastructure of basic services and public buildings is essential if Africa is to pull itself out of the current cycle of environmental and social decline. Sustainable development can only be achieved if aid is directed to the engineering infrastructure needs of water supply, roads and sanitation and the equally important building infrastructure provision of schools and health facilities. In both areas climate change and regional conflict elevates construction to beyond that of basic human rights.

Fig 42
Oslo Opera House, designed by Snohetta, is an investment in cultural capital, but its glacier shape hints at concern for global warming.

Thanks to the UN, the concept of sustainable development assumed a higher profile in the world economic order, which led to an inevitable rebalancing of national priorities. Not all nations, however, accepted the new imperatives, especially the USA, which resisted or diluted international agreements such as those signed at Kyoto in 1997, The Hague Conference on Climate Change (2000), Johannesburg (2002), Helsinki (2006) and Bali (2007). The USA's intransigence has been a particular problem for global ecological health. The USA is the world's largest consumer nation and, if all of the Earth's population used energy at the rate that the USA does, the world would run out of fossil fuels in under eight years.

Until the election of President Obama in 2009, the political focus of the USA was on sustainable development at the level of states rather than the federal government. Hence individual states such as California could adopt radical green laws while under successive US Presidents (up to Obama), there was a tendency to block international agreements such as Kyoto. However, four things have changed the political landscape over the past couple of years in the USA:

- the inauguration of President Obama in January 2009
- a growing awareness that global warming is a matter of national security
- a grass roots movement which has stimulated ecological awareness within the design professions and business community
- recognition that 'regulation' is a good thing after the collapse of the banking system in 2009.

Although it is now recognised that an unstable climate and scarce fossil fuels add to potential conflicts both at home and abroad, the main impetus for change has

33

come from ordinary Americans concerned at the price of fuel and deteriorating quality of life .

Soon after he came to power President Obama signalled a fundamental change in America's position on the environment. He not only acknowledged the problem of global warming and the link to CO_2 emissions, but also announced a willingness to embrace the post-Kyoto agreements. On the domestic front he said he wanted to harness new forms of energy (mainly renewables and clean coal technology) in order to create new jobs for those employed in ailing industries such as car manufacture.

Obama's inauguration speech committed 150 billion dollars over ten years to build a new clean energy future, creating, in the process, 5 million new jobs. His advisory team included the Nobel Prize winning physicist Steven Chu as Energy Secretary. Of the six priority areas identified for action, one included making buildings occupied by companies and government itself more energy efficient, another was in grants to families to improve the energy performance of houses, and another was in tax incentives to create greater energy efficiency.

In many ways Obama followed the lead of Europe in strengthening legislation, in providing incentives to foster the growth of green companies, and in linking welfare policies to energy efficiency ones.

At the time of writing, and in the wake of the global recession, governments across the world are implementing stimulus packages aimed at reviving their national economies. The world recession of 2009 has focussed political attention on job creation and the role of the green economy in this. Both Prime Minister Brown in the UK and President Obama in the USA have signalled the important role they see infrastructure investment, particularly in renewable energy and energy efficiency, playing in creating the switch from an industrialised old economy to a slimmer, greener one.

Various forms of green investment are under consideration – not just to create jobs for unemployed automobile workers but to re-fashion economies in new sustainable ways. The new 'green collar' jobs will be in wind and solar electricity generation, in public transport (particularly urban metro systems and high speed trains), in upgrading water networks, building hydro-electric dams for both water

Fig 43
Daylight and PV technologies used together at O'Hare airport, Chicago.

Fig 44
Use of renewable energy at Taos Earthship,
New Mexico, designed by Michael Reynolds.
Source: Sam Hughes

storage and power production, and in improving the energy efficiency of existing buildings. Obama wants government buildings to be the initial focus of this re-direction of resources and policy, tackling he says the poor energy performance of federal and state property, and then to address the poor infrastructure of 'cities across the land'.[3]

The USA has a lot of catching up to do compared to Europe and Asia. In many ways the current (2009) recession gives society time to take stock and to rebalance the equation of economic, social and environmental sustainability.

NOTES

[1]   For more information on United Nations initiatives see www.undp.org. See also Paul Jowitt 'Engineering civilisation from the shadows', *Civil Engineering*, vol 161, November 2008, pp. 162–8.

[2]   Adapted from www.direct.gov.uk/en/ environmentandgreenliving

[3]   Reported on CNN News, 10 February 2009.

2 Legislation and Regulations in Europe

The threats posed by global warming are severe and, given that levels of anthropogenic greenhouse gases (GHGs) have been rapidly increasing for around 250 years, urgent. By the time the full extent of the evidence for global warming first emerged in the 1980s, and came to the attention of world leaders via the United Nation's Rio Earth Summit in 1992, it was already clear that international action was necessary to stem the tide of ever-increasing carbon dioxide (CO_2) levels. International summits and global agreements are crucial as awareness-raising activities but are, essentially, impotent without the aid of cascading regional, country-level and – ultimately – local laws and regulations that impose requirements on (often unwilling, and even sceptical) individuals. California's pioneering CO_2-cutting legislation is a case in point – introduced in spite of the US national government's intransigence over international treaties.

Thus, although this book continues to acknowledge the ground-breaking work of pioneering architects such as Lord Rogers and Bill Dunster in the UK, Vandkunsten in Denmark and Dietmar Eberle in Austria, climate-related legislation is inevitable. The unfortunate truth, however, is that legislation and regulation are slow-moving vehicles for change, compared with the swift and

Fig 45
The masterplan for Shanghai, by the Richard Rogers Partnership, is an example of sustainable urban design.
Source: Richard Rogers Partnership

Fig 46
Eco-social housing at Skejby, Denmark, designed
by Vandkunsten.
Source: Vandkunsten Architects

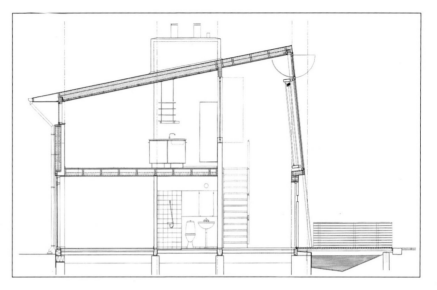

nimble (and preferable) option of individuals acting en masse to reduce the size
of their own 'carbon footprints'. For example, the Kyoto Agreement of 1997
committed its signatories to specific and binding cuts in greenhouse gas (GHG)
emissions. How these targets were to be met, however, was left to regional and
country-level governments to decide. In Europe, it took a further five years to
draft, agree and sign a piece of legislation (the Energy Performance of Buildings
Directive) that the (then) 23 member states could then 'transpose' into their
own legal framework – and a further three years (in the case of the UK) before
the changes actually began to impact on the work of architects and construction
companies.

This chapter presents an overview of the legislation introduced in Europe to help
combat climate change, and describes the measures taken in the UK to implement
the Europe-level requirements. It is important to remember, however, that there
are many other aspects of sustainable development and, although the focus of this
chapter is primarily on energy use, international, regional and local governments
are also busily tackling these wider aspects – planning policy, social cohesion,
international development, deforestation, urban regeneration and (not least)
global economic problems.

THE EUROPEAN LEGISLATIVE FRAMEWORK

In essence, European actions to cut GHGs employ three strategies: improve energy efficiency; phase in new (low-carbon) energy sources; and tax pollution, as follows.

The Energy Performance of Buildings Directive (2002/3)

The EU Energy Performance of Buildings Directive (2002/91/EC), which came into effect progressively across the members states from 2006 to 2009, has far-reaching implications for the design, construction and management of buildings. The aim of the EPBD is to promote the improvement of energy efficiency in buildings and to ensure convergence of standards across Europe. The building sector accounts for about 40 per cent of the EU's energy requirements (although the pattern varies among individual member states), with the Directive identifying construction as having the greatest potential of any sector to achieve energy efficiency.

Fig 47
Integer House, near Watford, designed by Cole Thompson, explores new sustainable glass technologies.

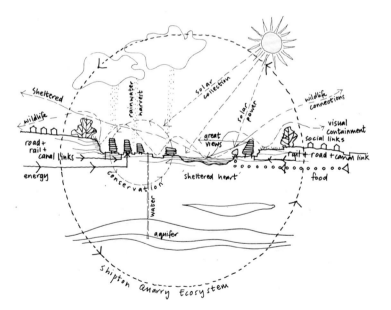

Fig 48
A new settlement for 6000 people, designed by Feilden Clegg Bradley at disused Shipton Quarry, Oxford.
Source: Feilden Clegg Bradley

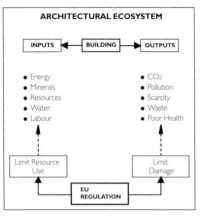

Fig 49
Architectural ecosystem and the role of EU regulation.

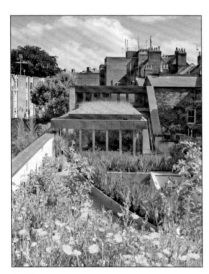

Fig 50
This house and office in London, designed by Bere Architects, sets high standards for low-energy and ecological design.
Source: Bere Architects

The two drivers behind the Directive were concerns over global warming (and particularly Europe's obligation under the Kyoto Agreement) and growing uncertainty over future energy security. With 70 per cent of domestic energy use being for heating, cooling and hot water requirements (and 50 per cent for non-domestic buildings) the EU signalled the importance of greater energy efficiency of buildings through the Directive. In fact, according the Green Paper *Towards a European Strategy for Energy Supply*,[1] the energy consumption of existing buildings could be reduced by 25–40 per cent by 2020 (compared with the 20 per cent as planned by most member states including the UK). And the European Environment Agency (EEA) has argued that, by 2030, savings of 50 per cent are possible via improvements in the design of new buildings and higher standards in the refurbishment of older property. By 2050 there is also the broad aspiration to reduce Europe's total CO_2 output by 80 per cent over current levels.

The EPBD, which applies to new and refurbishment projects:

- establishes a common basis for calculating energy performance
- sets minimum standards
- introduces 'energy performance certificates' (EPCs)
- requires heating boilers and air-conditioning plant to be inspected regularly.

The Directive falls a long way short of the target of carbon-neutral development across Europe. However, the display of energy ratings on buildings using the display energy certificates (DECs) or energy performance certificates (EPCs) for smaller buildings required under the Directive has done much to encourage awareness of energy efficiency in both publicly owned and private property.

The Directive also requires that all new housing, and older housing at the point of sale, will have to disclose the predicted energy performance to potential buyers. By making energy use calculations consistent (in the UK, by using the SAP method) and more readily understood, the Directive has encouraged builders to use higher levels of fabric insulation as well as controlled ventilation, condensing boilers, passive solar heating and intelligent glazing technologies.

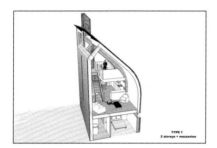

Fig 51
Sketch of the BRE-Kingspan energy
demonstration house, known as The Lighthouse,
designed by Sheppard Robson, which responds
to Level 6 of the Code for Sustainable Homes.
Source: Sheppard Robson

EU energy policies
☐ Cut CO_2 emissions by 8 per cent by
2010
☐ Double the contribution (to 12 per cent)
that renewable energy makes to
total energy demand by 2010 and to
20 per cent by 2020
☐ Improve energy efficiency by 18 per cent
(compared to 1995) by 2010

Whereas, in former energy assessment methods, poor energy performance
could be offset by increasing the size of air-conditioning plant, and poor insulation
standards by enhanced heat recovery, the EPBD heralded the implementation of
a common methodology for the integrated energy labelling of buildings, covering
aspects of heating, lighting, cooling, ventilation and heat recovery simultaneously.
Under the proposed methodology all the elements that consume energy in
pursuit of the environmental conditioning of buildings are integrated into a single
performance calculation.

Action on renewables

In March 2007 the EU finally agreed to adopt the European Renewable Energy
Directive. This commits Europe to achieving 20 per cent of its energy from
renewable sources by 2020. It is expected that about half of this will come
from photovoltaic (PV) systems (which convert sunlight into electricity) and
the remainder from other sources such as wind, biomass and hydro. The main
benefit of the Directive is the security it offers to the private sector to invest
in new technologies. It also provides an impetus to move from macro-scale to
micro-scale generation, thereby opening more possibilities for community and
individual building application.

The EU Emissions Trading Scheme

Carbon trading works by enabling energy intensive industries, such as power
stations and large manufacturing plants, to buy permits that will allow them to emit
carbon dioxide into the atmosphere. Companies can also buy unused permits
from other firms and are fined (at a rate of about 40 euros per tonne of CO_2)

Fig 52
RuralZed, designed by Bill Dunster Architects,
revives the English terraced house as the model
for energy efficiency. South is to the right in this
image.
Source: Bill Dunster Architects

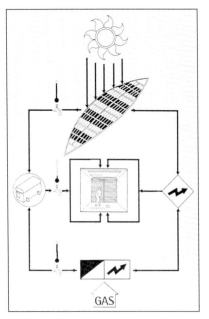

Fig 53
How fossil fuel and PV technologies work together at Duisburg Business Park, designed by Foster and Partners.

if they exceed their limits. Carbon trading makes the important shift from energy to carbon measurement, allowing renewables to make a more meaningful contribution.

Carbon trading is a clever idea because it creates a market in pollution. The 'polluter pays' concept, which was enshrined in EU law after the Maastricht Treaty, means that those companies which emit the most CO_2 are held accountable through the ETS mechanism. Making industries pay for their pollution should act as a brake on atmospheric contamination. In time the ETS will trickle down to smaller companies and hopefully will be adopted beyond the frontiers of Europe. The fear is that Europe's competitiveness will be lost under ever-expanding environment law.

The EU Emissions Trading Scheme (ETS) covers nearly 42 per cent of Europe's major manufacturing industries and represents one of the major tools for achieving the planned 8 per cent cut in carbon emissions across Europe by 2012. Although the EU hopes to persuade other nations to adopt a similar scheme as part of their commitment to Kyoto obligations, a fall in the price of the unused permits as a result of the economic decline in 2008 has limited the impact of carbon trading.

Many of the industries affected by the ETS are construction-related (cement and steel plants for instance), so there is an influence on the price of construction materials as well as on the price of the energy needed to keep buildings warm and fully functioning.

European environment policies after Maastricht
☐ Concept of 'sustainable development' adopted across Europe ☐ Environmental protection integrated with social and economic policy ☐ Consistent environmental laws between member states ☐ Control of cross-border pollution	☐ Consistent energy policy throughout Europe ☐ Action to maintain energy security ☐ Emphasis on renewable energy supplies ☐ European water framework ☐ Recognition of the cultural value of the European built environment

Fig 54
The challenge ahead is to balance the demands of pre fabrication with that of sustainability. Greenwich Millennium Village.

Main effects of global warming for design of buildings in UK
☐ Rise in temperature means reduced heating load over lifetime of building
☐ Temperature rise will lead to extra demand for cooling and air-conditioning
☐ Buildings will have to accommodate extremes in weather
☐ Flooding will pose unexpected problems
☐ Buildings will be expected to make significant contribution to CO_2 reduction targets

ACTION AT NATIONAL LEVEL

In 1999, the UK government identified four themes to unify its actions on sustainable development. Published in the report, *Achieving a Better Quality of Life: a Strategy for Sustainable Development in the UK*,[2] the four themes are:

- sustainable consumption and production
- climate change and energy
- natural resource protection and environmental enhancement
- sustainable communities.

At about the same time, the UK construction industry was also the subject of a government-backed review, chaired by Sir John Egan. The committee's report *Rethinking Construction* (often referred to as the 'Egan Report'[3]) sought to encourage the transfer of lean manufacturing concepts from the car industry to UK building construction. Although it was published a decade ago the report continues to have ramifications in the UK. At its heart, the concept of lean manufacturing is about achieving more with less and is, therefore, similar to the concept of sustainable design. The elimination of waste, the recognition of differential performance benefits over time (life-cycle costing), the need to respond quickly to changing environmental resources and human need are all characteristics of green design.[4] However, in spite of the structural similarities between new construction processes and sustainability paradigms, until recently there has been little evidence on UK building sites that 'green' is winning the ideological battle.[5]

A review of the UK's sustainable development strategy in 2002[6] highlighted that, although the UK construction industry at that time accounted for 7 per cent of GDP, it operates with small profit margins and has high levels of internal instability. Both facts, it noted, militated against investment in sustainable design and construction. The review also brought attention to the interrelationship between development and pollution, both at the site and in the manufacturing/ disposal process. Too little is known of the third-party effect of pollution through the occupation of buildings.

The UK government therefore began to develop policies[7] designed to:

- cut CO_2 emissions by 60 per cent by 2050

- keep water use within the limits of replenishment
- reduce biodegradable waste by 65 per cent by 2020.

The review also sparked investment in the UK encouraging social sustainability – in social housing, schools, libraries and hospitals (many based on Public Finance Initiative (PFI) procurement methods). This investment, aimed at 'improving the quality of life', also provided the opportunity to apply the principles of sustainable design and construction in specific projects. Some of these are discussed later and had the benefit of bringing to public attention via TV and newspaper articles the issues around green design.

In order to monitor its own targets, the UK government began publishing statistics in 2003 showing trends for a number of sustainability indicators,[8] following independent reports which had suggested that targets in key areas, such as renewable energy and waste recycling, were not being met. Failure to meet the targets was, in part, attributed to the lack of demand from end-users for sustainable design and the inadequate levels of financial support from government. Although there was a great deal of knowledge and rhetoric, there was little action on the ground compared to other countries in Europe. Part of this was attributed to the reluctance of the UK government either to fund demonstration projects or to use its own powers as a client to set an example. Under Tony Blair, Britain set a poor example of renewable energy investment or

Fig 55
The Greater London Authority (GLA) building, designed by Foster and Partners, uses stepped section for shading (right) and spherical shape for natural cooling.
Source: Foster and Partners

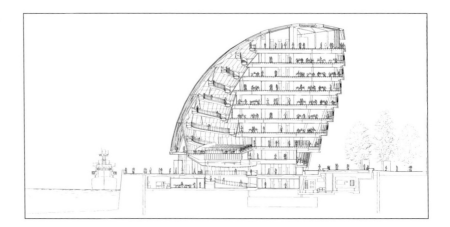

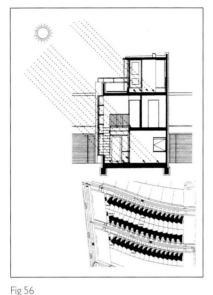

Fig 56
Passive solar housing in Almere, Holland,
designed by A and van Eyck and Partners.
Source: Van Eyck and Partners

Fig 57
Passive solar housing at Norrkoping, Sweden,
designed by Krister Wiberg.
Source: Krister Wiberg

Mapping green design onto UK government policy for sustainable development		
Principles	Sustainability	
	Economic: Maintaining capital and a productive workforce Environmental: Maintaining environmental functions Social: Maintaining social welfare and cohesion	
Strategy	Sustainable development framework	
	Social progress which recognises the needs of everyone Effective protection of the environment Prudent use of natural resources Maintenance of high, stable levels of economic growth and employment	
Indicators	National government	Local government
	Maintaining a stable economy Building sustainable communities Managing the environment and resources Sending the right signals	Prudent use of resources Protection of the environment Better health and education Access to services Shaping our surroundings Sustainable local economy Social/community enterprises
Design	National government	Local government
	Demonstration projects	Green housing Green transport
	Own buildings for occupation	Sustainable schools Sustainable hospitals
Building	National government	Local government
	Lean construction Prefabrication Less waste	Green collar jobs Maintaining local crafts Use of local resources
Source: After Ekins and Russell, 2000 and extended by author		

the construction of eco-villages compared to say Holland, Denmark, France or Sweden.

Changes to UK energy policy

The Energy White Paper of 2002[9] set out the framework for 'meeting tomorrow's challenges of a low carbon economy … through the promotion

Fig 58
(a) and (b) site plans; and (c) section and building plans of ecological social housing in Denmark, designed by Vandkunsten Studio. The practice won the Alvar Aalto medal in 2008.
Source: Vandkunsten

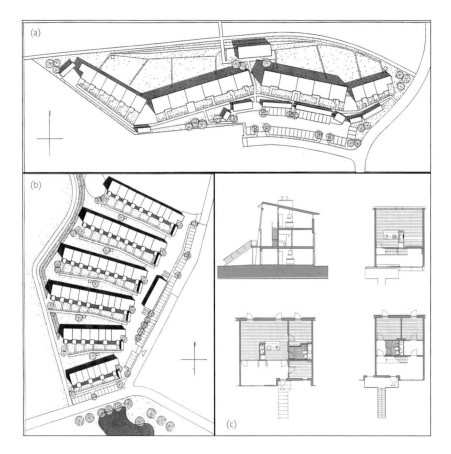

of renewables'. The political message in the White Paper was that of energy independence – making the UK less vulnerable to fossil fuel price increases, to fluctuating oil supply and political unrest in the Middle East. Since Britain is particularly well served by renewable energy resources (wind, wave, geothermal and solar), the government was signalling a massive investment in these alternative energy supplies.

In February 2003, following on the from Energy White Paper, the UK government signalled the introduction of a number of initiatives to improve energy efficiency and expand the use of renewable energy sources. In particular, it set a target of cutting the UK's carbon dioxide emissions by 20 per cent by 2020 and 60 per cent by 2050 with 'real progress in the period up to 2020'.

These changes had important implications for the practice of architecture. As part of the policy changes required, the government set up a 'Better Buildings Summit' in 2003 aimed at bringing key players in construction together to help develop strategies for achieving more sustainable practices. Topics considered by the task force included expanding the use of photovoltaics (PV) and local wind-generated electricity, combined heat and power (CHP), off-site construction technologies and taxation policy to increase the level of investment by the UK building industry in energy-saving practices.

The main emphasis of the new energy strategy was on local generation of electricity (rather than large, distant power stations) and carbon capture. Microgeneration of electricity using PV panels on the roofs of houses for instance could, according to the White Paper, result in new houses having zero emissions of CO_2 in 20 years' time.

However, with many of the UK's nuclear power stations (which currently provide 21 per cent of national electricity) being phased out between 2012 and 2015, there is increasing pressure on expanding local renewable energy generation.

By 2009, with an increasingly uncertain future for energy supplies and the need to speed up action on global warming (cutting carbon emissions by 80 per cent by 2050), the UK government (like many in Europe) signalled something of a reversal of its earlier policies – to focus on carbon capture at power stations (instead of local power generation), and to invest in a new generation of nuclear power stations.[10]

Even with unresolved issues such as nuclear waste and potential terrorist attack, politicians have returned to nuclear power as a 'safe' form on electrical energy and one which adds comparatively little to CO_2 emissions. Since electricity generated from fossil fuels carries a CO_2 burden of over twice that of other fuels, the decision makes some sense in terms of Kyoto obligations.

UK response to the Energy Performance of Buildings Directive, EPBD

UK government sustainable construction policies

Key priorities
- Benchmarking sustainable construction
- Reducing CO_2 emissions
- Improving productivity through better design (especially of the internal working environment) of non-domestic buildings
- Reducing resources used in construction by maximising recycling

Secondary priorities
- Conserving water
- Increasing use of renewable materials (timber, etc.) used in construction
- Treating and remedying contaminated land
- Reducing pollutants from construction processes
- Improve the construction industry's efficiency (by 30 per cent over 10 years)

As far back as 1999, the UK government stated that energy efficiency is the 'cheapest and safest way' of meeting the Kyoto agreements on reducing CO_2 emissions, and hence declared that buildings have a critical role to play. Consequently, the government determined that the Building Regulations would be progressively upgraded, and public sector buildings would be expected to act as examples of energy innovation for the private sector to follow. The design of schools, hospitals and universities would incorporate low-carbon technologies funded by fiscal measures such as the Enhanced Capital Allowances Scheme.

In order to implement the EU Energy Performance of Buildings Directive, the UK government made wide-ranging revisions to Part L of the Building Regulations in 2004, with a further raising of standards in 2006 and again planned in 2010.

To meet the rigorous targets of the Directive, the Part L aims to improve the energy efficiency of buildings by addressing both the design and construction elements (prior to 2000 only the construction element mattered). However, what the revisions of 2006 introduced was a common methodology for ensuring that the design actually delivers the energy savings predicted. This gives owners and tenants the evidence required to gain redress against the architect, system installer or builder for any failures in promised energy conservation. Further revisions to Part L are planned (in 2010 and 2015) to raise insulation standards still further, to encourage solar water heating and the use of photovoltaics. More immediately, the new Part L requires standards in building refurbishment to equal those in new buildings.

Amendments to Part L of the UK Building Regulations between 2002 and 2010						
	Standard wall U-value ($W/m^2 K$)	Ground floor U-value ($W/m^2 K$)	Window U-value ($W/m^2 K$)	Roof U-value ($W/m^2 K$)	Air-tightness at 50 Pa (air changes per hour; ach)	Boiler efficiency (%)
Building Regulations Part L 2002	0.35	0.25	2.00	0.20	No standard	93
Building Regulations Part L 2006	0.25	0.22	1.8	0.16	0.36	93
Building Regulations Part L 2010 (anticipated)	0.20	0.18	1.6	0.12	0.30	95

Anticipated effect on CO_2 emissions arising from changes to UK Building Regulations 2002–2010			
	Space heating CO_2 emissions (kg/yr)	Water heating CO_2 emissions (kg/yr)	Total CO_2 emissions (kg/yr)
2002 Building Regulations	813	746	1559
2006 Building Regulations	567	746	1313
2010 Building Regulations (anticipated)	397	706	1103

The technical guidance in support of the UK Building Regulations has also been upgraded to include matters such as air-tightness, avoidance of solar overheating, performance in use of air-conditioning and lighting controls, and thermal bridging. The standards for calculating insulation (U-values) have been brought in line with European standards making cross-border comparability easier while also raising standards.

As a general rule, changes in UK building law are generated in Brussels rather than Westminster. Although the British government has some independence, the broad sweep of energy conservation law is directed by the European Union. While Scotland, Northern Ireland and Wales have their own governments and hence local construction and planning legislation, it is EU directives that shape laws on the ground and ensure that political obligations (such as the Kyoto protocol) are met by member states.

As described above, the Directive also requires new buildings to carry an energy label, and existing buildings to be assessed at the point of sale or rent (more frequently for public buildings).

In 2008 the UK government signalled its intention to further revise the UK Building Regulations in 2010 (beyond the measures introduced in 2006) in order to comply with the Directive's phasing of greater efficiency measures. At around the same time, the UK Green Building Council unveiled its ground-breaking Code for Sustainable Homes,[11] which measures sustainability (not just energy efficiency) against nine criteria. Subsequently, the government announced its intention that all new housing should be zero carbon by 2016, in effect requiring Level 6 or above in the Code for Sustainable Homes (see chapter 3).

UK Climate Change Act 2008

In 2008 the UK government accepted that more significant cuts in greenhouse gases were required and introduced the Climate Change Act which set new legally binding targets. One was to reduce CO_2 emissions by at least 80 per cent from 1990 levels by 2050 and by at least 26 per cent by 2020 (subsequently revised to 34 per cent in the UK Budget of Spring 2009).

As well as targets, the Act introduced an obligation on governments and public bodies to report regularly on the risks associated with climate change. It also requires local authorities to display 'energy certificates' on its buildings over 1000 square metres in area and to report on the actions they are taking to address climate change to the Local Government Association (an umbrella body for UK local government).

The Act includes an obligation that, from 2010, all commercial bodies as well as public ones with electricity consumption of above 6000 MWh/year must apply emissions trading as an incentive cut emissions. Such legislation opens up new areas of work for architects in refurbishing existing buildings as well as requiring new skills in sustainable design for new construction.

By 2009 there was a marked change in emphasis in the UK, in spite of economic difficulties. Government departments, major companies, the professions and large numbers of consumers demanded greater energy efficiency and higher environmental standards at home and in the workplace. As Paul King, chief executive of the UK Green Building Council, has noted 'even in tough times, and perhaps particularly in tough times, customers will demand more in terms of energy efficiency, quality and productivity ... A built environment that is sustainable – economically, socially and environmentally – is the only one worth investing in now'.[12]

Fig 59
Dugald Stewart Building, University of Edinburgh, designed by Bennetts Associates, makes a note on campus about low-energy design.

Fig 60
Author's apartment in Copenhagen where the thermal capacity of exposed concrete compensates for large glazed areas.

A different perspective: Regulations in Denmark

After leading the world in green initiatives in the 1980s (and developing, in the process, innovative energy-related companies such as Vestas, Velux and Rockwool) Denmark subsequently left the leadership to others – mainly neighbours Sweden and Germany. However, in 2008 the Danish Prime Minister announced the development of a 'green market economy' and issued revised building regulations up to 2015. These he hoped would put Denmark back at the forefront of sustainable design: '… spurring further the nation's green technologies'. (See chapter 9 for further information on Danish design and construction techniques.)

Danish Building regulations for Housing 2008–2020		Danish Building Regulations for Non Housing 2008–2020	
Year	Standard for total energy consumption in kWh/m²/yr	Year	Standard for total energy consumption in kWh/m²/yr
2008	70	2008	95
2010	50	2010	70
2015	35	2015	50
2020	25	2020	35

NOTES

[1] *Towards a European Strategy for Energy Supply*, available at www.ec.europa.eu/energy/efficiency

[2] DETR, *Achieving a Better Quality of Life: a Strategy for Sustainable Development in the UK*, DETR, London, 1999.

[3] John Egan, *Rethinking Construction*, The Construction Task Force, DETR, London, 1998.

[4] G.B.S. Penoyre and S. Prasad, *Constructive Change*, RIBA, 2000.

[5] E. Vedung, 'Constructing Effective Government Information Campaigns for Energy Conservation and Sustainability: Lessons from Sweden', *International Planning Studies*, 1999, Vol. 4, pp. 2–7.

[6] Department for Environment, Food and Rural Affairs, *Achieving a Better Quality of Life: Review of Progress Towards Sustainable Development*, DEFRA, London, 2002.

[7] See www.defra.gov.uk/sustainable development

[8] Sustainable Development Commission, *UK Climate Change Programme; A Policy Audit*, 2003.

[9] DTI, *Energy White Paper: Our Energy Future – Creating a Low Carbon Economy*, DTI, London.

[10] The government's Committee on Climate Change report *Building a low-carbon economy*, which is pushing the idea of 'carbon capture'. See www.theccc.org.uk

[11] Source: www.planningportal.gov.uk/england/professionals/en/1115314116927.html

[12] The quote is from Paul King, Chief Executive, UK Green Building Council, in publicity material for the EcoBuild conference and exhibition (www.ecobuild.co.uk).

Essay – Natural Capital: The New Economics?

THE IDEA OF 'CAPITAL'

The UN Environment Commission of 1987, chaired by Gro Harlem Brundtland, is best known for its definition of sustainable development (see page 25), but the Commission's report, *Our Common Future*,[1] included another concept that is beginning to bed itself into the consciousness of the 21st century – the notion of 'capital', that is, global resources that need to be husbanded.

The normal measure of 'capital' is that of economic capital expressed as stocks and shares, as gold and as currency. This is the measure used by governments, by companies and by individuals to assess their wealth and economic performance. Unfortunately, it makes little allowance for other forms of 'capital' or of the interactions of one form of capital on another.

What is needed is a way of joining up the measures of economic capital with the imperatives of other 'capitals', especially environmental and ecological. After all, unlimited growth of population and consumption is an impossibility on a planet of limited resources.

'Natural capital' is a form of accounting that recognises the value of all environmental and ecological systems. It seeks to quantify the worth of forests, natural ecosystems, land, oceans, water and air. Natural capital is a technique developed to measure and assign value to biodiversity and natural wealth, just as stocks and shares give value to companies. The basis of natural capital is that of production from nature expressed in the form of harvests (on land and from oceans), of clean air and water, of renewable energy such as the sun and wind, and of the power of nature to renew damaged ecosystems. The currency of natural capital is divided into four categories – natural resources, habitats, species and genetic diversity. Hence, what natural capital seeks is a balancing of the human construct of economic capital by the 'carrying capacity' of natural systems. It allows the impact of the world industrial economy to be set against that of global ecology and natural resources, using a form of accountancy employed in economics.

Fig 61
Skyhouse Project – a fresh approach to sustainable urban living, designed by Marks Barfield Ltd.
Source: Marks Barfield Ltd

Thus in the 'new economics' there are three main types of 'capital', each based on the triple bottom line of social sustainability economic sustainability and environmental sustainability:

- social capital
- economic capital
- environmental capital.

SOCIAL CAPITAL

Social capital has been well understood, as a concept, for some time, but in the context of sustainable development it is used to relate skills and education to the agenda of environmental resource use. Society needs individuals who are trained and equipped to understand the new agenda; and in particular it needs architects, engineers and builders who can create useful social products (buildings) using the minimum of resources, so that future generations can have their share. To achieve this requires a new approach to education in the construction industry and new values to be adopted by society (including building clients). It also requires a recognition that society is itself a resource, and that the good design of buildings such as schools and housing helps to achieve social cohesion. Cultural value, social value and design skill are interconnected in the concept of social sustainability.

ECONOMIC CAPITAL

Economic capital is the clearly understood concept of financial resources, and has been at the political heart of world order for at least 100 years. Businesses use their share value, an indicator of their economic capital, as a measure of success, while governments can make certain adjustments to the performance of the economy by controlling interest rates. The amount of economic capital depends on resource exploitation (land, people, resources) and so, of course, the concept of sustainable development challenges its foundations. For most of the 20th century economic systems worked well – they were relatively transparent and comprehensible. But the global financial crisis of 2008/9 highlighted the hidden dangers of placing too much emphasis on a system that was not as transparent as it appeared. One benefit is that regulation is back in fashion – not just in financial services but in all fields.

ENVIRONMENTAL CAPITAL

Environmental capital is the term used to quantify all the resources of the Earth. It embraces fossil fuels, water, land and minerals, as well as a series of potentials or capacities, for example agriculture, fisheries, forestry and renewable energy. The term also covers negative values such as pollution, contamination and desertification. The UN's 1987 report by Brundtland brought the idea of environmental capital to political attention, especially in the context of future, rather than present, needs.

OTHER TYPES OF 'CAPITAL'

- **Technological capital** is the knowledge and design base that allows us to turn raw materials and other resources into useful human products (cars, buildings, etc.). It therefore has much in common with economic capital and is a form of capital with a strong basis in science and in design. In fact, the two (science and design) are essential to the realisation of technological capital in an architectural sense. However, as our natural resources diminish, our design and scientific skills need to expand. Technology is never static, especially at a time of environmental stress. New skills and technologies are required for sustainable development. And those technologies not only need to be lean and smart, they must also be environmentally benign and socially acceptable. How architects are to employ technology and help the construction industry to develop new sustainable technologies is the challenge ahead.
- **Cultural capital** recognises the knowledge, skills and creativity locked into socio-cultural systems. It embraces a wide range of capital on which the modern world depends – the state of knowledge expressed in the various sciences, creativity and design skills, technology, the arts and humanities. Education has a key role to play in handing on the skills across generations; research in expanding the knowledge base; the arts in expressing contemporary life in all its complexity; and the professions in serving society with skill and integrity. Cultural capital is in some way what the profession of architecture

Fig 62
Design is a cultural statement which addresses many agendas. Selfridges, Birmingham, UK, designed by Future Systems.

Fig 63
PassivHaus student accommodation in Vienna designed by Baumschlager Eberle. The student rooms have sliding copper shutters and triple glazing, and achieve an energy efficiency of $15\,kWh/m^2/yr$.

Fig 64
Integral solar shading and photovoltaic (PV) cells
at Copenhagen Energi Office.

stands for. It is also what bodies such as the Architects Registration Board
(ARB) and the RIBA seek as their overarching mandate, i.e. the assurance that
an architect will be up to date in knowledge, skilled in design and management,
and ultimately answerable to society at large.

■ **Ecological capital** is a branch of environmental capital and includes habitats,
species and ecosystems. It has tended to be outside the terms of reference
of other capital measuring systems or annexed to environmental capital.
Yet ecological capital is the basic life system to which the human species is
intimately attached and upon which we all depend. The UN Earth Summit
at Rio in 1992 brought biodiversity to political attention, paving the way
for the introduction of the concept of ecological capital. Today, ecological

Fig 65
Planted roofs provide important wildlife habitats
and are quickly colonised by birds and insects.
Source: Erisco Bauder

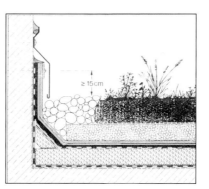

Fig 66
This ivy-clad wall in Paris gives the apartments
behind climatic protection on an exposed gable.

capital remains the most fragile of the systems listed and is largely ignored by governments, companies and individuals alike. The arguments surrounding the genetic modification of crops and changing agricultural productivity following global warming are, however, symptoms of a growing awareness of ecological capital.

COUNTING THE COSTS

The main forms of capital are part of a complex network of interactions necessary to achieve a sustainable future. They broadly mirror the three dimensions of sustainable development – environmental, social and economic – but differ in their emphasis on the cultural importance of design and, in particular, architecture. The concept of 'capital' is a useful means of understanding the architect's role and especially the importance of buildings and cities as inter-generational assets.

The 2008/9 global economic crisis demonstrated the dangers of placing too great an emphasis on one form of capital (economic) over the others. The many governments that signed international sustainable development treaties committed – on paper, at least – to give due weight to other forms of capital. The danger now is that, in the scramble to regain economic stability, the other equally important forms of capital will be ignored.

NOTE

[1]   Gro Harlem Brundtland, *Report of the World Commission on Environment and Development: Our Common Future*, 20 March 1987. See www.un-documents

Section B
Tools and techniques

3 Measuring Success at the Building Scale

The 21st century has seen the rise of eco-modernism, a movement that combines the intellectual strength and disciplines of modernism with growing sensitivity towards nature. The shift has seen the development of new tools to aid the designer, new regulations to protect the planet, and new outlooks for the architectural and development professions.

Several techniques have been advocated to achieve a better balance between town and country and between architecture and nature. One such system is 'carbon accounting' (sometimes known as 'carbon footprinting'), whereby CO_2 emissions are balanced by the conversion back into oxygen by forests, as discussed in chapter 1. Under this system, for every house, half a hectare of deciduous forest is needed; for a supermarket, perhaps 40 hectares. If this ratio is not sustained, the carbon becomes locked into the upper atmosphere where it contributes to global warming. The idea of carbon accounting emanated from the 1997 Kyoto Conference, but it is a flawed system because the rich countries such as the USA can buy the carbon credits of the poor ones (e.g. Mexico). In other words, it allows the wealthy to carry on polluting and holds the poor in a cycle of debt.

Indicators and some energy modelling software tools (e.g. Ecotect) allow the complexity of sustainability and the complexity of architecture to be presented in a understandable fashion: they present the architect with choices at the design stage allowing one criteria to be set against another; and they are a useful tool in client discussion at the development brief stage. However, indicators and assessment tools are no substitute for deeper understanding of the issues involved. The key principles behind sustainability still need to be understood and decisions need to be underpinned by core values.

LIFE-CYCLE ASSESSMENT

Life-cycle assessment (LCA) is one tool that could help to deliver better design insights and value judgements. The LCA process brings ecological principles into the development process, and it is used to evaluate the environmental performance of buildings from the cradle to the grave. It measures the ecological costs of resources such as energy, or of a manufactured product such as a brick, which are then evaluated against environmental criteria. For a building, LCA brings into focus the complex impacts of construction, use and decommissioning of buildings and their component parts.

The technique has two main benefits: it can be used to guide architects and facilities managers over the lifetime of the building; and it can help to identify potential cost savings by reducing the building's exposure to future environmental legislation or maintenance problems.

LCA helps with identifying choices at the design stage. It also encourages thinking from that of 'cradle-to-grave' to 'cradle-to-cradle' (see page 10). Since most of the energy and fiscal costs occur during the lifetime of the building, rather than during construction, LCA clarifies the relationship between initial cost and full cost over a period of 50 years (or more), and between initial environmental footprint and impacts over subsequent decades. It also provides a basis for deciding on refurbishment strategies and timescales. For example, with rising energy costs, it might be more cost-effective to accelerate the cycles of upgrading, to have a speedier-than-planned switch from fossil to renewable energy sources. Likewise, with material scarcity, LCA allows the switch from landfill to recycling to be justified. Thus LCA is an environmental tool but it has useful design attributes and can be employed as a costing tool.

Fig 67
The life-cycle impacts of a brick.

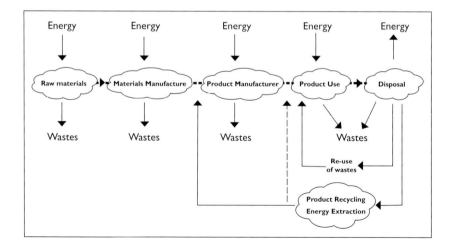

Fig 68
Traditional brick and tile works in Morocco.

A working definition of LCA

LCA identifies the material, energy and waste flows associated with a building over its entire life in such a fashion that the environmental impacts can be determined in advance.[1] The flows described are from the extraction of raw materials for use, reuse, recycling or disposal. Normally, there are five main choices at the end of a building's functional life:

- to reuse the building for a new purpose making necessary adaptation and upgrading
- to reuse parts of the structure, materials and decorative features in new construction
- to break down the materials and reuse in new construction as aggregates, or, for example extract energy or minerals from the building materials
- to demolish and dispose of it in landfill.

So, under this scheme, reuse is preferable to recycling (because of the energy costs of reforming a material), and recycling is preferable to disposal. Disposal is a last resort, because landfill sites are increasingly scarce, landfill taxes are rising, and the methane production and other off-gassing from landfill sites contributes to global warming (although on the other hand it is occasionally possible to extract energy from waste or to compost organic waste).

What LCA highlights is the opportunities that exist at the end of a building's life, and it allows these benefits to influence choices made by the designer at the beginning of the process.

Too often architects ignore the demolition opportunities and costs at the design stage, leaving that problem to another generation. In the future the disposal costs and recycling potential will need to be itemised perhaps as a condition of approval to build at all.

As well as the end of life issues that LCA illuminate, the tool also allows better informed choices to be a made during the life of a building – when and how, for instance, to upgrade finishes, service systems and the installation of, say, photovoltaic (PV) panels. Since LCA is informed by fiscal , ecological and sometimes community costs, the choices allow for the integration of environmental, social and economic parameters.

Life-cycle costing

A development of LCA is life-cycle costing (LCC) which looks at the cost of a building over its full design life (usually taken to be 50 years, but could be up to 100). In actual fact, LCC is the net value of the design, construction, operation and maintenance costs calculated over the full lifetime of the building.

Rather than focussing on environmental impacts and their life-cycle consequences, LCC puts into the equation the operational costs (heating, lighting, ventilation) and the building maintenance costs (servicing of air-conditioning units, etc.). As such, it is responsive to rising oil prices and the cost of upkeep of mechanical plant, and potentially provides a basis to measure the enhanced productivity of the building.

LCC is thus a sophisticated tool that measures price and asset value over the full life cycle, rather than the initial cost of construction. Increasingly, LCC includes the staffing costs for the occupying company – which opens the door for 'well-being' as a factor of good design to be included in the asset value calculation.

Architects, like many construction professionals, are under pressure from clients and others in the supply chain to reduce the adverse ecological impact of their buildings. Growing environmental awareness has led to a more demanding public (clients and building users) who expect better environmental performance without additional cost. Using LCA means that the capital cost (i.e. the actual construction cost) can be seen in the context of a building's overall lifetime cost, allowing cost, environmental value, maintenance, recyclability and reuse to be considered jointly.

LCA therefore has three advantages as an assessment tool:

- it brings time into the equation, allowing impacts and recycling loops to be readily comprehended from cradle to grave
- it allows energy, ecological and environmental impacts to be analysed and set in the context of social and economic benefit
- it is a holistic tool, which bridges design services, manufacturing, construction and building maintenance.

The pros and cons of LCA

LCA differs from other environmental auditing systems by measuring impacts away from the site.[2] Not only are all the ecological factors over time considered, but also those over a wide geographical area.

Take the example of a brick. There are many environmental impacts of a brick, both during its life and spread over a large area (extraction, baking, transport, use, reuse, etc.). LCA puts these into an easy-to-understand framework that architects can readily grasp at the design stage. It also avoids the potential problem of shifting adverse impacts from one area to another, and thus making the development appear benign – a problem that can happen with high-tech green buildings that source their materials from around the world, often from places with lax environmental legislation.

LCA also reinforces the impetus towards recycling existing buildings rather than demolishing them. The emphasis on life-cycle costing – including costs for lifetime pollution, demolition and disposal – promotes the idea of whole building reuse. In straitened economic times reuse is expedient, but it is also more sustainable to recycle than to manufacture. The building stock needs to react to changing circumstances and here LCA is a useful tool in making the case for conservation as against demolition. It also helps with anticipating change in, for instance, the switch from fossil fuels to renewables. For instance, over the lifetime of a typical new building fossil fuels will become either depleted or too expensive to use; then the building will need to generate its own life support system. Adaptation for new energy technologies will involve the 'soft' parts of an existing building – the roof before the wall, the windows before the solid masonry, the pipework before the structure. Over the past generation existing buildings have been upgraded with super-insulation, new boilers and windows; over the next the changes will involve photovoltaics and solar collector panels, wind turbines, ground-source heat pumps and water catchment. These will alter beyond recognition the look of many of our familiar urban structures. LCA is an indispensible tool in making the case for sustainable change.

However, life-cycle assessment is at its best when it is being used to examine elements of construction (steel, concrete, ceramic tiles, paints, etc.) and developing precise statements of the ecological impact over time for each. Unfortunately, buildings are more complex than that, involving materials used in unison, and the life-cycle benefit of one element of construction may be at the detriment of another. For example, painting steel reduces the ease with which it can be reused; and bricks bedded in a cement mortar cannot be recycled as readily as those using lime mortar. So although LCA is useful in theory, in practice there are sometimes knowledge or methodological difficulties.

The Dutch have overcome this problem by using Eco-Quantum,[3] a system that assesses the life cycle of whole units of construction such as glazing systems (glass, frames, mastic), structural walls (bricks, mortar, foundations) and interior partitions (plasterboard, framing, paint). There are four parts to an Eco-Quantum audit:

- extraction of raw materials, waste
- impact on health, toxicity, global warming
- life-cycle assessment of equipment and appliances
- transport and material impacts in use.

Whether LCA or the Eco-Quantum technique is used, the goal remains the same: to be better informed about the ecological impacts involved during the life of a building. These are not decision-making tools but decision-aiding ones.

THE IMPORTANCE OF INDICATORS

As the issues to be addressed have become more wide-ranging, the tendency has been to use indicators rather than to measure every possible impact. Indicators are a useful assessment tool because they provide a guide to the bigger picture.

There are two types of indicator:

- as an indication of the attainment of a goal
- as an indication of fluctuations in a system.

Both types are used in the construction industry – the first at the design stage and the second as a monitoring tool once the building is occupied (such as the PROBE Studies based on post-occupancy evaluation[4]).

For example, a good indicator of energy efficiency at the design stage is the measure of units of energy expected to be consumed per square metre (normally expressed as kWh/m^2). The same figure can then be used to measure performance on completion and modify the building services management system as needed. But the source of the energy is not taken into account, so a further indicator might be necessary, such as the percentage of energy generated by renewable means. This could well change over the occupation of the building, so that CO_2 emissions would be reduced compared with initial expectations. The same indicator (energy), therefore, could be a useful guide to the designer, to the client and user, to those who manage the building by providing a measure for performance enhancement, and to government as a target for national CO_2 reduction.

Health is another useful indicator – the health both of construction workers (there are many health risks from different construction materials and techniques) and of building occupants whose health can suffer as a result of poor environmental design.

Local biodiversity is sometimes used, but as an indicator it is not without problems. For example, the full ecological picture from excavation, production, construction, use and disposal of a building material is difficult to measure. In brick manufacturing, for instance, there is the ecological impact of clay extraction,

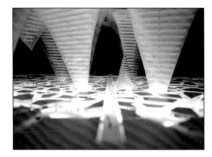

Fig 69
Indicators allow the environmental impact of projects to be assessed at various points in the evolution of a design. This hotel in the UAE is by BIG Architects.
Source: BIG Architects

but with good management and design, valuable wildlife habitats can be created, perhaps exploiting the cleansing of 'grey water' from local industry or housing areas. What is important here is to consider the full life cycle and to use sample species for measuring environmental impact rather than complete habitats, which are necessarily complex.

Many assessment techniques, such as the Building Research Establishment Environmental Assessment Method (BREEAM) in the UK and the Leadership in Energy and Environmental Design (LEED) programme in the USA, increasingly recognise the complexity of choices or decisions required – and both techniques are discussed in more detail below. As an environmental assessment tool for offices and other building types, BREEAM has moved from concentrating almost solely on energy issues to widen its scope to reflect the multifaceted nature of ecological choices. In the process, other topics have emerged as influential, such as water conservation and occupancy health.

To avoid being swamped by statistics, the designer needs a simple toolkit for assessment based on readily understood principles and values. These already exist, but few are sufficiently simple to provide a useful guide, especially at the sketch design stage (when key decisions on the environment are made). The problem with BREEAM and other toolkits is that they often come into operation only once the fundamentals of footprint and location of the building have been decided. there is a need for simplicity in initial assessment and the use of multipliers to give priority to certain values. Since not all projects need to give equal weight to energy considerations, the addition of multipliers allows adjustments to reflect political and client values or the priorities that may flow from the nature of the site, building function or occupant need. In Europe the multipliers would be different to those in the Middle East, Australia or Africa where water assumes greater importance. The author has developed two simple self-assessment checklists for use by architecture students. The first (shown opposite) applies weightings to a series of sustainability assessment criteria and could be used to measure the impact of any building being studied; while the second (on page 68) looks at wider design issues as well as sustainability, and is specifically aimed at students' own design projects.

Self-assessment sustainability toolkit for architecture students				
Theme	Topic	Score	Multiplier	Sub-total
Energy	Orientation		×4	
	Climate and shelter		×3	
	Super-insulation		×3	
	Glazing area		×3	
	Passive solar gain		×3	
	Passive solar cooling		×3	
	Renewable energy		×4	
	Heat recovery		×3	
Materials	Waste minimisation		×2	
	Local sourcing		×2	
	Reuse (of buildings)		×3	
	Recycling (of parts)		×3	
	Embodied energy		×2	
	Maintenance		×2	
Resources (land)	Brownfield site		×2	
	Density		×3	
	Avoidance of flood plains		×2	
Resources (water)	Low-water appliances		×2	
	Grey water recycling		×2	
	Rainwater collection		×2	
	SUDS		×2	
Access	Disabled		×2	
	Public transport		×2	
	Cycling		×2	
	Walking		×2	
Health	Natural materials		×2	
	Natural ventilation		×2	
	Natural light		×2	
	Stress		×1	
	Contact with nature		×1	
Total				

Fig 70
Self-assessment form for the integration of
sustainability and design.

SUSTAINABLE DESIGN PROJECT SELF-ASSESSMENT FORM

	Assessment Criteria	Max Points (per Criteria)	Student	Student Peer	Tutor
I	**Site Planning 1:1250 / 1:500**				
(a)	Architectural merit in site organisation and broad approach	15			
(b)	Specific merit in strategy to achieve a significant level of sustainability in design	15			
2	**Scheme at 1:200**				
(a)	Interpretation of opportunities in brief What merit does the design have as a piece of architecture?	15			
(b)	Environmental strategy for scheme as a whole	15			
3	**Detail design at 1:50 and larger scale**				
	Appropriateness of materials structure, envelope and level of understanding of sustainable construction and imagination used in its application	20			
4	**Quality and depth of supporting explanation**	20			
	Total	**100% Max**			

Comments

The Sustainability Assessment Model

There are several assessment tools available to help predict the sustainability of a project. Some are energy-focussed; others take a broader view. Among the techniques that adopt a wider perspective is the Sustainability Assessment Model (SAM), developed by Inchferry Consulting and the University of Aberdeen.[5]

SAM assesses the project over its full life cycle under four headings. The headings map onto the 'triple bottom line' of sustainable development – environmental protection, social progress and economic prosperity – but with the addition of 'resource availability':

- **Resource use impacts** – an assessment of the intrinsic and inherent values of the resources employed, especially their security, cost and environmental impacts. This allows decisions to be made between different construction materials (steel, concrete, glass), between different energy sources (oil, gas or renewables), and between different forms of capital (nature, social and intellectual).
- **Environmental impacts** – four assessment criteria: pollution; ecological footprint and impact on biodiversity; nuisance (noise, smell and visual); wastes. These are weighted and measured to form indicators.
- **Social impacts** – the social and community benefits, the direct and indirect jobs generated, and the health and safety impacts.
- **Economic impacts** – the benefits arising from the products or services provided, the contribution towards productivity, asset accumulation and economic growth.

The four main headings are broken down into 22 key indicators, which are then measured and given a score. Each project (or alternative design) then has a 'signature' that can be compared with best practice in the type and subsequently modified.

Such tools are versatile and relatively easy to use. They allow designers, clients and regulators to understand the complex impacts raised by a typical project. Also, since the indicator can be represented graphically, SAM provides a visual picture of the likely impacts, raising awareness of sustainable development issues.

Like LCA, it is a tool that can also be used to measure the decommissioning of a building or to assess the sustainability impacts of adaptation versus demolition.

Other sustainability assessment tools can be developed for particular types of building project, for example, for tourism, schools, higher education, health buildings, etc. Each will have common generic characteristics but with a weighting of indicators or the addition of extra ones to reflect specific impacts. For example, with tourism visual impact may be given particular attention, with hospitals the impact on social welfare and health, with education the impact of teaching and learning.

GENERIC ENVIRONMENTAL MANAGEMENT SCHEMES

Architects and engineers are more familiar with the management systems developed to measure the environmental impact of buildings at the design stage than with the more broadly based systems. However, both have a part to play under specific conditions. For example, the environmental management system developed under ISO 14001 is useful in terms of operating an office to good ecological principles, or in terms of choosing a contractor or supplier with sound environmental practices. However, it is not helpful in assessing the ecological impact of a specific project. So it is important to apply both the building-specific auditing tools (such as BREEAM in the UK or LEED in the USA) and the generic ones. Of the latter probably the most useful is the Environmental Management System (EMS) approach. This normally involves five actions which are externally audited (though the data gathered is not normally made available to third parties)[6]:

- develop an environmental policy
- set objectives and measurable targets
- implement the objectives and targets
- monitor performance and take remedial action as necessary
- review the policy systematically.

The Eco-Management and Audit Scheme (EMAS) is, however, the preferred model in the European Union. Both LCA and EMAS share a common basis, but under EMAS the environmental performance is required to be publicly reported, as well as externally audited.

Three requirements of registration under EMAS	Content of environmental statement under EMAS
☐ Establish an environmental management system ☐ Produce an environmental statement ☐ Have both system and statement independently audited	☐ Description of company's activities ☐ Assessment of significant environmental issues ☐ Statistical summary of emissions, pollutants, impacts, etc., on environment ☐ Other factors pertinent to environmental performance ☐ Timescale of monitoring ☐ Name of accredited environmental officer

No matter what environmental auditing scheme is adopted, the objectives remain much the same. For an architectural practice, EMAS provides the measures needed to decide how to reduce environmental impact directly and indirectly through the choice of contractors or suppliers. For a manufacturer of building products, LCA and eco-labelling help to identify areas where energy can be saved, waste reduced, pollution prevented and, as a consequence, money or liability saved.

Design practices and manufacturers can both benefit from the improved public image that follows from an implementing an environmental auditing scheme. However, with all auditing systems there is the tendency towards a 'tick box' culture. It is easier sometimes to measure an impact than to design out an adverse consequence. Having made the environmental prediction two things need to follow: first, correction to the design to improve performance; second, monitoring of the project through its design gestation period to ensure compliance.

Eco-labelling

Eco-labelling is another useful tool for the designer, especially for product selection. Like EMS and EMAS, this is an EU-led initiative. It seeks to make all environmental claims by manufacturers conform to the same evaluative criteria. Eco-labels are intended to guide purchasers or specifiers and share some characteristics of LCA, although eco-labels are always product-specific.[7]

Eco-labels cover certain product types used in the building industry such as paints, ceramic products and light bulbs, and are assessed on the basis of an independent audit carried out to common EU standards.

ENVIRONMENTAL ASSESSMENT TOOLS FOR SPECIFIC BUILDING TYPES

Although the generic tools discussed above have their uses, a growing interest in understanding the environmental impact of buildings by clients, regulators and users has demanded the development of building-type-specific assessment tools. The new awareness of ecological and energy issues stems from the fact that poor design may damage the environment for many decades and disadvantage occupiers in terms of their health or their pocket. There is also growing demand for benchmarking projects of similar type, for example schools or offices, and setting these against 'best practice' at home and overseas. With climate change threatening to accelerate, many who commission buildings wish also to be confident that their investment is in sound environmental design.

The principles behind all environmental assessment schemes are much the same. There needs to be a list of criteria (with appropriate definitions) against which to assess the design, a weighting system, a reporting system which allows buildings to be compared, a grading system which ranks performance, and a public display which communicates the sustainable or green credentials. The latter has commercial value. Increasingly, assessment at the design stage is being matched by monitoring of the building once occupied.

There are many tools available to assess the environmental performance of particular building types, but most share a common basis. Those developed in the UK have come mainly from the Building Research Establishment (BRE) and cover common building types – housing, schools and offices. Although they were initially concerned primarily with energy conservation, the criteria employed have been expanded to embrace a wide range of environmental, ecological and health issues. The most widely used tool is the Building Research Establishment Environmental Assessment Method (BREEAM) which provides the methodological basis for most environmental assessment tools used worldwide including the US-based LEED.

Different building types pose different problems, have different climatic constraints, different cultures and different political priorities. Some countries believe that existing building law is sufficiently demanding to not require separate assessment schemes, arguing as in Denmark's case, that green design is what architects do as a matter of course.

BREEAM

This was the world's first environmental weighting system, which began as 'BREEAM for offices' in 1990 and remains the most commonly used by UK designers for offices and other buildings. It is comprehensive, yet simple to use and results in a scoring system that allows different design strategies to be compared before construction begins. The aim is to raise standards, particularly of energy consumption, above the regulatory minimum. The measures span global atmospheric pollution down to local impacts, including those that affect human health. The different factors are weighted but embrace, among other things:

- CO_2 emissions with quantified benchmarks
- healthy building features
- air quality and ventilation
- minimisation of ozone depletion and acid rain
- recycling and reuse of materials
- ecology of the site
- water conservation
- noise
- risk of legionnaires' disease
- hazardous materials
- material choices
- lighting
- management of the building.

As with all environmental assessment tools, BREEAM is useful both to the designer and to the client. The benefits to the construction industry as a whole are numerous:

- developers can promote the high environmental performance of their buildings and thus increase sales or raise letting values
- designers can quantifiably demonstrate the environmental achievements of their work
- owners or landlords can audit the property from an environmental point of view with the aim of making cost savings
- employers can reassure employees that their working environment is healthy and of high environmental quality.

Fig 71
The new BDP office in Manchester received an
'excellent' BREEAM assessment, and helps with
wider social and economic regeneration.
Source: BDP and Brian Edwards

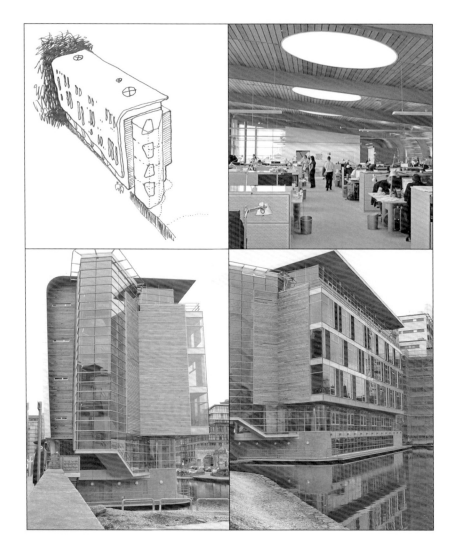

Fig 72
Sectional details of the new BDP office in
Manchester. The façade is active (rather than
sealed) in achieving a high level of energy
efficiency.
Source: BDP

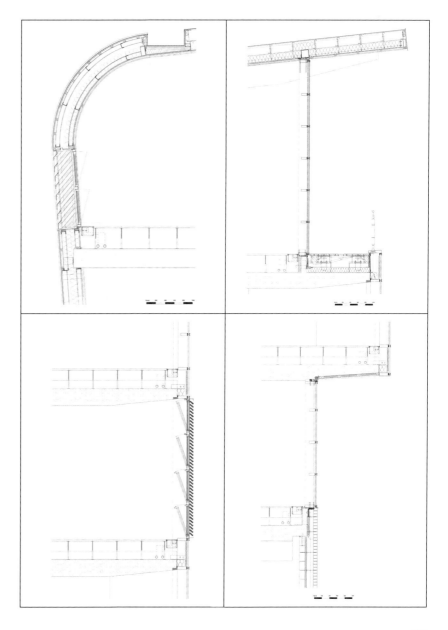

Potentially, these benefits could lead to a better legacy of built assets, healthier office environments (and, hence, a more productive workforce), and reduced adverse environmental impacts at a global level. Developers in particular have used high BREEAM scores to promote their buildings, appealing to the widening environmental concerns of consumers. To date in the UK over a hundred thousand buildings have been BREEAM certified. There are six ratings for the assessed building – outstanding, excellent, very good, good, pass and unclassified. Such has been the success of BREEAM for offices that versions of BREEAM are now available for healthcare buildings, schools, industrial buildings, retail development and homes.[8]

BREEAM in Use

One of the problems with the existing building stock (where energy efficiency should be focussed) is that gathering and evaluating environmental performance information is complicated. There are so many design variables and subsequent alterations that it is hard to pin down the most cost-effective measures to improve performance. Thermal imaging is useful, particularly in highlighting thermal bridges, but hardly provides the comprehensive tool that surveyors and architects need. 'BREEAM is Use' is a new tool that evaluates operational aspects of the building and performance in use, and compares this with the potential performance of the building against best practice. It is designed to use existing data on energy and other aspects of environmental performance (for example Energy Performance Certificates required under EU Energy Performance in Buildings Directive) and highlights areas of potential improvement in both management of the building and opportunities for physical upgrading.

The aim of 'BREEAM in Use' (introduced in 2009) is to better inform those who occupy buildings of their carbon footprint, allowing them to enhance and demonstrate improvement against credible measures. It also allows for property assets to be evaluated against future environmental legislation – providing a measure of quality assurance in the expanding arena of sustainable development.

LEED

Started in 1998 and run by the US Green Building Council, LEED is the main environmental assessment tool used in the USA. It is more relaxed than other tools and provides no weighting on the six categories of impact measured although the different points available gives a useful guide. The six categories, each with their own sub-divisions covering aspects of design and construction, are:

- sustainable sites
- water efficiency
- energy and atmosphere
- materials and resources
- indoor environmental quality
- innovation an design process.

Typical environmental assessment systems by country		
Country	Assessment method name	Key features and differences
UK	BREEAM	Most widely used system worldwide Comprehensive Available for range of building types
USA	LEED	Business focussed Relatively relaxed auditing system Available for range of building types
Holland	Eco-Quantum	Elements of construction based Energy focussed
Sweden	EcoEffect	Ecological basis Health focussed
France	ESCALE	Benchmark based Environmental profile not score
Norway	EcoProfile	Indoor climate based Bar-chart presentation
Australia	Green Star	BREEAM based Water and CO_2 priority
Gulf States	BREEAM Gulf	Water conservation and CO_2 priority Ecology of coastal areas

The scheme provides strong linkage between environmental and economic benefits and encourages a form of integrated design which promotes client collaboration in the design and management of the building. There are four levels of LEED certification – platinum, gold, silver and certified.

BREDEM

This is the environmental assessment system developed by the BRE for domestic buildings. The BRE Domestic Energy Model (BREDEM) is a software package designed to calculate the heating load of different housing configurations based on gains, losses and boiler systems. It takes into account locational and latitudinal factors, insulation levels (in walls and roofs), air-tightness, window area and orientation. It is an energy (rather than environmental) design tool, but it can be adapted to shed light on comfort levels and humidity, as well as energy used in transport. It is not as comprehensive as other design assessment tools (such as BREEAM) and is sometimes cumbersome to apply, but it is particularly useful in calculating passive solar gains. For a simpler manual tool, the BRE produces Method 5000 but, again, it avoids ecological and wider environmental issues.

BREDEM is a speedy and cost-effective modelling tool for assessing the energy performance of dwellings at the design stage. SAP, the UK government's Standard Assessment Procedure for Energy Rating of Dwellings is a version of BREDEM. SAP allows different types of house designs to be compared against likely energy use for heating, lighting and hot water supply. Its calculations are based on standard expectations of usage levels unlike BREDEM which makes adjustment for expected lifestyle differences. As such, BREDEM is more sophisticated than SAP but less comprehensive than the Code for Sustainable Homes (described below).

Code for Sustainable Homes

The Code for Sustainable Homes (CSH), introduced in 2008, has become a mandatory element of permission to construct new housing in the UK. The Code measures sustainability (not just energy efficiency) against nine criteria, is aimed at both pre- and post-construction evaluation, and sets minimum standards in two key areas – energy and water use and offers guidance on others. Credits can be traded between categories (except energy and water) to provide flexibility for designers and developers. The nine categories are:

- energy and CO_2 emissions
- potable water
- surface water run-off
- materials
- waste
- pollution
- health and wellbeing
- management
- site ecology.

Of the credits available for each category 36 per cent are awarded in the area of energy, signalling the importance of domestic energy consumption in meeting Kyoto obligations. Bearing in mind that more than a quarter of UK total energy consumption is in housing, the introduction of the Code and the distribution of the 29 credits in the energy area should change attitudes among volume house builders.

Some of the energy credits under CSH are for predicted emissions reduction rather than 'energy conservation' measures. This is to encourage the shift towards renewable energy exploitation and to target areas of high emissions such as electric lighting and poor performing white goods.

The calculations in CSH are based on SAP 2005 methods, and aim at percentage improvements on the UK 2006 Building Regulations, Part L. The Code levels – which, like BREEAM, are publicly available and displayed at point of sale or lease – set energy performance improvement targets from Level 1 (10 per cent improvement over current Part L) to Level 6 (full 'zero carbon').

At present Level 1 is the regulatory standard but this is expected to rise as developers become familiar with the methodology and its supporting technologies. Level 4 is a realistic target and is roughly comparable to PassivHaus standard. Several major UK house builders and research institutes have sought to test the new Code by building demonstration houses at Level 6. These have included low-carbon demonstration houses built on the BRE Innovation Park at Watford, UK, by Kingspan, Barratt and others.

As the cost of meeting Level 6 is likely to add about 15 per cent to the cost of the house, it is more realistic to seek Level 3 or 4 standards.

Fig 73
Barratt Green House at the BRE Innovation
Park in Watford, UK, designed by Gaunt Francis
and Glass Canvas.
Source: Gaunt Francis and Glass Canvas

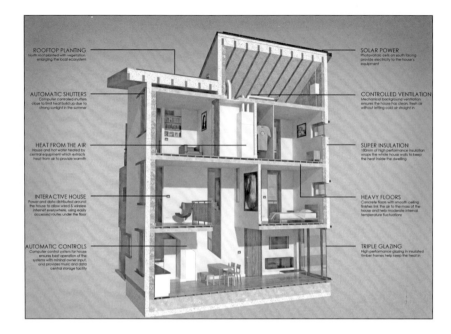

ROOFTOP PLANTING
North roof planted with vegetation
enlarging the local ecosystem

SOLAR POWER
Photovoltaic cells on south facing
provide electricity to the house's
equipment

AUTOMATIC SHUTTERS
Computer controlled shutters
close to limit heat build up due to
strong sunlight in the summer

CONTROLLED VENTILATION
Mechanical background ventilation
ensures the house has clean, fresh air
without letting cold air straight in

HEAT FROM THE AIR
House and hot water heated by
central equipment which extracts
heat from air to provide warmth

SUPER INSULATION
180mm of high performance insulation
wraps the whole house walls to keep
the heat inside the dwelling

INTERACTIVE HOUSE
Power and data distributed around
the house to allow wired & wireless
internet everywhere, using easily
accessed routes under the floor

HEAVY FLOORS
Concrete floors with smooth ceiling
finishes link the air to the mass of the
house and help moderate internal
temperature fluctuations

AUTOMATIC CONTROLS
Computer control system for house
ensures best operation of the
systems with minimal owner input,
and provides music and data
central storage facility

TRIPLE GLAZING
High performance glazing in insulated
timber frames help keep the heat in

Fig 74
RuralZed, by Bill Dunster Architects, is designed
to achieve Code for Sustainable Homes Level 6.
Source: Bill Dunster Architects

The main actions needed to meet the mid-table energy and water requirements of CSH	
For energy	**For water**
☐ Reduction in air permeability	☐ 4/2.5 litres dual flush WC
☐ High efficiency condensing boiler	☐ Flow reducing taps
☐ Reduction in thermal bridging	☐ 6–8 litres/minute shower flow rate
☐ Improved thermal efficiency of building fabric to U-value of 0.2 $W/m^2 K$	☐ smaller, shaped bath
☐ Inclusion of renewable energy technologies	☐ 13 litres maximum volume dishwasher
☐ Use of orientation, passive solar design and high thermal capacity structure	☐ 49 litres maximum volume washing machine

Source: Based on lecture by Steve Sharples titled from 'BREEAM to LEED' given at the Royal Danish Academy of Fine Arts, School of Architecture November 12, 2008

NOTES

[1] This definition is adapted from the Environmental Technology Best Practice Programme guide ET257: *Life-cycle Assessment – An Introduction for industry*, 2000, p. 2.

[2] Ibid., pp. 2–3.

[3] EcoQuantum is at www.lca.jrc.ec.europa.eu/lcainfohub/tool2

[4] See, for example, W Bordass and A Leaman, 'Probe: How it happened, what it found and did it get us anywhere?' conference paper prepared for *Closing The Loop: Post-Occupancy Evaluation: the*

Next Steps, Windsor, UK, 29 April–2 May, 2004.

[5] *Energy and Environmental Management*, January/February 2004, pp. 10–11. See also www.inchferry.co.uk

[6] Good Practice Guide 200, *Energy and Environmental Management*, Environmental Best Practice Programme, DFTR, London, 2000, p. 7.

[7] Brian Edwards, *Green Buildings Pay*, 2nd edn, E&FN Spon, London, 2003, pp. 207–9.

[8] Further useful information is available at www.breglobal.com

Section C
Resources for construction

4 Energy

Energy conservation is a central concern in the quest for sustainability, and is of particular concern to architects working in the UK where, in 2008, the government under Prime Minister Gordon Brown signalled an 80 per cent reduction in carbon dioxide (CO_2) emissions by 2050. The burning of fossil fuels for buildings and their construction is responsible for about half of all energy use in Britain. Heating, lighting and ventilation require oil, gas or coal to be burnt either at the building or in a power station. It is the relationship between the combustion of fossil fuels and CO_2 emissions that is crucial, not 'energy' as such. If society could generate all of its power needs from renewable sources there would be no problem. In the UK, the main sources of CO_2 emissions are:

- heating, lighting and ventilating buildings (responsible for approximately half of all emissions)
- transportation of goods and people (a quarter)
- industry, agriculture (a fifth)
- building construction (around 5 per cent).

These proportions are not static and depend on the price of energy, the state of the economy, effects of legislation, global commodity prices and changing climate. For example, buildings in the UK are currently responsible for around 47 per cent of the nation's CO_2 emissions and falling (due mainly to the effects of 2005 changes to building regulations and the growing use of tools such as BREEAM). In 1990 the figure was 50 per cent.

Fig 75
Energy use in UK: (a) today; and (b) in the future.

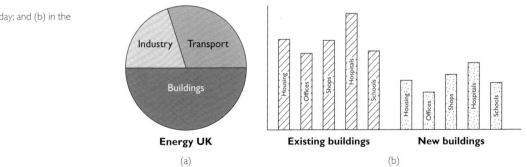

85

THE ENERGY CHALLENGE

Buildings present a particular challenge when it comes to energy efficiency. Many were designed when energy was abundant and the science of global warming was not developed. Their architects and engineers assumed that unlimited energy was available for heating, lighting, ventilation and lifts. In the commercial sector, these buildings were commonly fully air-conditioned and were deep in plan, thereby distancing much of the interior from natural sources of light, solar energy and ventilation. In the domestic sector, old patterns of dense city living (apartments, terraced housing) were replaced by detached and semi-detached dwellings. As a consequence, cities became widely spaced and unable to support public transport. Also, heat loss from one home was not the heat gain for another, as it would be in an apartment. With this dispersal went the separation of land uses. Journeys were necessarily made by car, adding to the overall carbon emissions. In many industrialised countries, such as the UK, USA and Australia, transport had, by 2000, begun to account for nearly 30 per cent of all greenhouse gas emissions.

What is needed is more consistency between climate planning, socio-economic planning, land-use planning, building design and life-style planning. Consumers can demand more in terms of energy efficiency, but leadership has to come from politicians. There is no shortage of words on global warming and climate change – in fact it is one of the most legislated areas of public life. What is needed is action that makes the link between government and the individual. Unless architects become involved at the urban level, the big decisions on the future shape of cities will be determined by city planners and urban geographers.

FUTURE ENERGY OPTIONS

There are three main options available to reduce levels of greenhouse gases (GHGs), and break free from reliance on diminishing reserves of fossil fuels: nuclear power; renewable energy; and carbon capture. Nuclear energy, promoted initially as a clean energy source, has its own well-publicised environmental problems. Carbon capture – the process whereby CO_2 is extracted from exhaust gases at the point of energy generation (i.e. at the power

Global reserves of fossil fuels

Oil	25 years
Natural gas	40 years
Coal	200 years
Lignite/Coal sands	300 years

station) and stored instead of being released into the atmosphere – is currently gaining favour in the UK, because, from the government's point of view, it is easy to implement and regulate, and could therefore quickly halt the escalation of atmospheric GHGs.[1] However, storing compressed CO_2 under the earth (for example, in the spaces below the sea once occupied by natural gas) is an unproven technique and in essence is, like nuclear waste, simply storing up the problem for future generations to resolve. Renewable energy, however, has much potential, to the extent that the UK government has set the following targets:

- 10 per cent of all energy from renewable sources by 2010 (current level in UK in 2009 is 5 per cent and 8 per cent for EU)
- 20 per cent of all energy from renewable sources by 2020
- 50 per cent of all energy from renewable sources by 2050 (EU target is 60 per cent).

Carbon sequestration or 'offsetting'

Since the late 1990s, There has been a growing interest in 'carbon sequestration' or 'carbon offsetting'. The concept is a valuable means of viewing the link between development and the carrying capacity of the land which supports it in terms of energy, but it has been misused by some commercial organisations, who have set up sequestration schemes as a way of appearing to be 'green' while carrying on their energy-hungry businesses as usual.

The idea is based on the fact that trees and forests to convert CO_2 back into oxygen (via photosynthesis) at a rate of about 1 m^2 of forest absorbing one kilogram of CO_2 per year. Although the science is imprecise, the theory says that about 15 mature trees are required to convert the carbon emissions over a year of a typical car, and 40 trees would be needed to do likewise for a house. Much depends, however, on the size and type of tree and the energy efficiency of the CO_2-producing element. The conversion is based on an equation whereby

160 m^2 of trees are required to balance 1000 kWh of energy consumed in heating, 900 m^2 for every 1000 kWh of electricity used, and 1200 m^2 for every 1000 litres of petrol combusted.

Typically, it means that every household requires roughly two acres of woodland to convert its CO_2 emissions back to oxygen. Using these figures, however, it quickly becomes clear that the energy requirements of London alone exceed the capacity of all the forests of the UK put together to achieve effective CO_2 conversion. Even if all of the UK was forested, it is unlikely that the national output of CO_2 would be balanced. In fact it would take a forest of about five times the land area of the UK to create effective carbon conversion at today's level of emissions.

This, of course, is the basis of ecological footprinting, and it neatly illustrates the reason why we have such a problem.

RELATIONSHIP BETWEEN FOSSIL FUELS AND RENEWABLE ENERGY

The cost of fossil fuels influences the rate at which market forces drive the change towards renewable energy use. With high oil prices there is an acceleration in the development of wind and solar technologies, but when oil prices fall (as in 2009) so too does investment in renewables. That is why other mechanisms are employed such as taxation, international carbon emission agreements and construction law. However, in the long term the depletion of fossil energy supplies will lead to ever increasing prices and the shift to cleaner energy technologies. Since buildings are very long-lived and the infrastructure of cities (railways, roads, urban patterns) even longer, architects need to think long-term about energy choices and the design consequences. After all some of the basic choices made at the design stage – such as the orientation of the building, the plan depth, window-to-wall ratio – have long-term consequences for energy consumption.

Buildings designed today on the assumption of infinite fossil fuel availability face an uncertain future by about half way through their design life. With rising energy use by India, China and Brazil, comes sooner than expected scarcity and faster than expected rise in the price of energy for heating, lighting, ventilation and transport for those in the developed world. In theory, this accelerates the momentum towards alternative supplies (such as renewables) but it also amplifies the problem of the interrelationship between building design and energy. Whereas in the past buildings could adapt to different energy sources (from say coal to gas or oil to electricity) in the future such adaptation will need to cross over between fossil fuel sources and renewable ones.

Flexibility between fossil fuel and renewable energies has profound implications for design, particularly if the renewable sources exploited involve a mixture of wind, solar and geothermal. Here the spatial and geometric parameters for maximum utilisation are strict and imprinted into the footprint of the building at the design stage.

The particular problem with electricity

Delivered energy via electricity produces, on average, about two and a half times as much CO_2 as would be released if gas or oil was used instead. This is partly caused by the fact that burning coal to generate electricity (as was common in the UK until relatively recently, and is still common in other countries, particularly China) is an inefficient process. But even if gas- or oil-fired power stations are used, there are still inefficiencies in the process, and losses during transmission. However, since an increasing amount of electricity is provided by exploiting renewable energy sources such as wind and solar, the 'carbon efficiency' of electricity production is improving, to perhaps twice the CO_2 level as primary fuel sources by 2010. Because electricity has to be used for artificial lighting and for powering fans used in cooling. ideally, it should not be employed for low-level uses such as space heating, unless it is derived from a renewable source.

Generally speaking electricity consumption is rising in industrialised countries while energy for heating is falling. In Denmark, for instance, electricity consumption in housing since 1975 has risen by over 10 per cent while energy consumption for space heating has fallen by 65 per cent.

Since electrical energy is indispensible, buildings should ideally be designed to generate their own electrical power, particularly in building types such as offices, which require energy during the day for computers. In this situation, photovoltaic (PV) panels make environmental sense, although with the current price of imported electricity the economic argument is difficult to sustain. In other building types such as schools or universities, the use of new energy technologies such as solar or wind generated electricity sends an important message to decision makers of the future. Where there is no grid connection as in parts of Africa, renewable energy is the only means available for generating electricity.

Since there is a great deal of wasted energy (usually in the form of steam) as a result of conversion from oil, gas or coal at the power station, the trend is towards exploiting this 'wasted' energy for district heating. This is common in Sweden, Denmark and Germany, where power stations produce electricity plus heat for warming houses, schools and workplaces in the immediate neighbourhood (up to 6 kilometres away). In Denmark 52 per cent of homes are served with district heating from combined heat and power (CHP) plants; in Europe as a whole the figure is 18 per cent; and in the UK 8 per cent. With CHP stations, the CO_2 emissions per unit of power are reduced to around 1.8 that of primary energy sources when both heating and electrical demand are considered together.

Since electrical consumption is increasing faster than space heating, architects need to consider the totality of energy needs rather than parcelling them up into energy for heating, lighting and ventilation. As insulation levels and air-tightness improve, and as window areas decrease under the impact of stricter building regulations, the interaction between lighting and energy consumption becomes critical. There is the risk that under new building laws aimed at reducing fabric heat losses there will be a corresponding increase in the use of artificial lighting with consequences for the level of electricity use.

The case for renewables

'Renewable' energy can be used to heat, cool or ventilate buildings instead of fossil fuels. The main sources of useful renewable energy for buildings are solar, wind and geothermal resources. At a macro-scale, wave, hydro and tidal power are also available, but are not always sufficiently exploited. Until recently, the ready availability of fossil fuel sources has been a deterrent to the wider exploitation of renewable energy in the architecture and urban design realm. One trend noticeable at present is the shift from macro- to micro-scale application of renewable energy, thereby involving more building-related installations.

The combination of relatively secure long-term supplies (25–100 years, depending on fossil fuel type), low taxation and cheap prices has, until recent times, created complacency among consumers, developers and designers. However, the threat of global warming and fuel scarcity, coupled with the concept of 'peak oil' (i.e. that most of the accessible source of fossil fuels have now been depleted) has shifted the focus to unexploited, cheap and readily available renewable energy sources. Both the CO_2 targets agreed within the Kyoto Treaty and incentives provided by the EU have played their part in the growing interest among architects in renewable energy. Consumers have also begun to link energy consumption with the wider question of healthy lifestyles, because renewable energy has particular advantages at a physical and psychological level.

Potentially, renewable energy could satisfy all of humankind's energy demands. The total energy of the sun far exceeds that required for human use. In his book *An inconvenient truth and the crisis of global warming*,[2] Al Gore argued that all of the USA's energy needs could be met within ten years with a switch to renewable technologies. However, with a current level at only 3 per cent, Gore and

Fig 76
Integration of various new energy, environmental and constructional technologies will re-shape architectural aesthetics for the 21st century.

incumbent President Obama have a lot of ground to make up compared to other nations, particularly those in Europe.

The problem with the exploitation of renewable energies is not the basic supply but how to distribute, store, convert and apply solar, wind, geothermal and hydro energy into a form useful for heating buildings, driving machinery and the countless other tasks which are now performed by burning fossil fuels.

Renewable energy can be exploited for use in buildings in a variety of ways. It can be:

- extracted elsewhere and delivered through conventional delivery channels
- extracted at or near the site of the building and delivered conventionally or unconventionally
- extracted via the fabric of the building (walls, roofs and underground).

To take advantage of these possibilities, it is important to consider potential renewable sources at an early design stage. Sites for development can be

Fig 77
Madrid's eco-boulevard, designed by Ecosistema Urbano, exploits renewable energy, rainwater harvesting and microclimate moderation in an integrated package incorporating local food production and community interaction.
Source: CINARK

selected on the basis of their access to renewable energy supplies – sun, wind, water power, geothermal, etc. A south-facing slope offers obvious benefits in terms of exploiting solar power just as a windy location provides the chance to develop local wind-generated electricity. After site selection, there are other design decisions that can help to maximise the exploitation of renewable energy. Orientation, building footprint and location on the site all allow for effective and cost-efficient harvesting of solar, wind and other sources of natural power. So, the first principle of renewable energy is to consider available sources and the method of exploitation at the briefing and sketch design stage (RIBA Plan of Work Stages A, B and C). Too often, renewable energy is considered only after the crucial decisions that affect its exploitation have been made. This is particularly true of passive solar design, where the geometric constraints are most marked.

MAIN TYPES OF RENEWABLE ENERGY

Although there are many renewable energy sources, only the most easily exploited in buildings will be considered here.

Solar radiation is the basis of photosynthesis and the primary source of renewable energy. Solar power helps to create vegetation, which can be used as a fuel either directly or extracted from energy crops such as oil seed rape. More commonly, solar power is used passively in buildings to provide space heating, ventilation and lighting. Solar power is also used actively to heat water in roof-mounted collectors and to generate electricity with the use of photovoltaic (PV) cells. Since the sun drives the Earth's climate, solar power is also locked into wind and wave power. Sun power is also stored in geothermal sources and in fossil fuels.

Passive solar

Passive solar energy is commonly used in buildings, but its full potential is rarely exploited. South-facing glazing provides useful space heating, creating about 20 per cent of the energy needs of a typical house. With enlarged windows to the south, the addition of conservatories or atria, and some ducting of the warmed air to the colder parts of the building, passive solar gain can provide nearly 40 per cent (or 2000 kWh/yr) of the primary energy heating needs of a typical house in the UK. For this to be most efficiently achieved, the solar energy

Fig 78
Photovoltaic (PV) and passive solar heating at the Doxford Solar office, Sunderland, UK, designed by Studio E Architects.
Source: Studio E Architects

Fig 79
Section through Doxford Solar Office.
Source: Studio E Architects

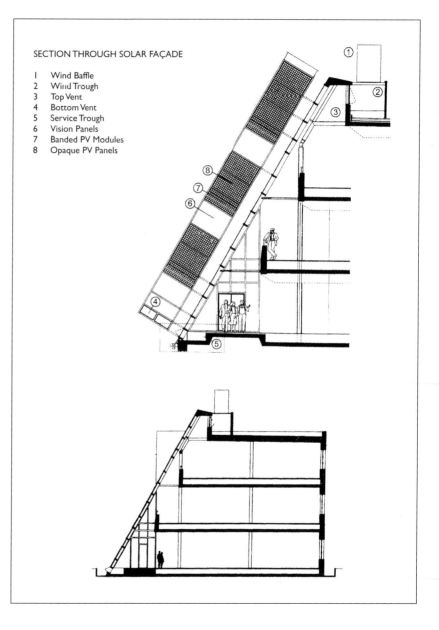

SECTION THROUGH SOLAR FAÇADE

1 Wind Baffle
2 Wind Trough
3 Top Vent
4 Bottom Vent
5 Service Trough
6 Vision Panels
7 Banded PV Modules
8 Opaque PV Panels

needs to be stored in a building fabric of high thermal capacity, and the building should be well insulated and relatively air-tight. Simple measures such as southerly aspect, differential window area between north and south, and high levels of insulation can achieve a great deal of benefit at little extra cost. Necessarily, public rooms are placed on the south side and utility areas (kitchens, bathrooms, small bedrooms) to the north.

Passive solar design is exploited in the design of many building types. Schools frequently exploit its principles by placing highly glazed classrooms to the south, which are then vented at high level to a central corridor or circulation street. The plan maximises solar gain while the cross-section exploits stack-effect ventilation by using a stepped ceiling and high-level vents. By such simple measures, schools in the UK can save about 25 per cent of the energy normally used in space heating. In offices, passive solar design is employed by the use of atria and perimeter glazing to provide convective cooling currents which help to avoid the use of air-conditioning. Typically, modern commercial buildings are designed on the mixed-mode principle of passive solar, mechanical or fan-assisted ventilation, restricting air-conditioning to hot spots such as photocopying rooms. As with schools, these buildings employ hybrid systems of heating and cooling, producing in the process interesting new building typologies.

Solar energy is also used for lighting, and most designers combine passive solar design with the maximisation of daylight. Artificial lighting is a major source of energy use in buildings, sometimes approaching the energy consumption of space heating. Lighting can account for about one-half of all electricity consumed in a building. The cheapest way to reduce energy used in lighting is to take full advantage of daylighting. To achieve this, room depths should not exceed 7 m from an outside wall, and consequently building plans should be about 14 m in depth (possibly 15 m with an internal corridor exploiting 'borrowed' light).

Daylight penetration can be improved by the use of daylight shelves positioned on the outside of the building. Correctly designed, they can increase the level of daylight inside the building without glare or sharp contrast in the distribution of light from the window to the interior. Daylight shelves also frequently double up as solar shades, thereby reducing unwanted solar gain and the problem of sunlight penetration on work surfaces or computer screens. Such external shelves can also provide a window-cleaning gantry for building maintenance.

Fig 80
Flat-plate solar water heater at the Arizona Earthship.
Source: Sam Hughes

Fig 81
Tubular solar water heater at Bo01, Malmo, Sweden.

The energy efficiency of existing buildings can be improved by increasing the level of natural light. This often involves opening up the roof of deep-planned buildings, sometimes incorporating an atrium which allows light to spread to lower levels while also addressing ventilation. However, there are complex interactions between daylight, heating, solar gain and fabric heat loss that need to be addressed in an integrated fashion. For students and practitioners there are software tools available such as 'Ecotect' which predict these things and produce colourful drawings of the building under different conditions. However, in the design studio context it is important that the underlying building physics is understood by the student and sometimes this is better relayed through hand sketches and physical models. The calculations and computer modelling available today is highly sophisticated and helps focus attention on the energy performance of the building as it evolves in the studio.

Active solar systems (solar collectors)

Active solar systems employ flat-plate water heaters and evacuated tube collectors. Solar water heaters are normally placed on south-facing inclined roofs with the heated water taken directly into the hot water storage tank, which is usually positioned in the roof space. A few square metres of solar water heater can provide up to two-thirds of the hot water requirements of a typical household in the UK.[3] A typical house in England requires 3–4 square metres of solar panel at a cost of about £800 per metre, providing about 50–60 per cent of water heating needs over a typical year and with evacuated tube system about 60–70 per cent. South-facing roofs are best, but installations are effective up to 45 degrees east or west of south.

Outside the UK, community-based solar district heating systems are to be found. Here, solar collectors heat the water stored in large thermal (often underground) tanks during the summer, which, because of their size, retain much of the heat during the winter. This pre-heated hot water is then piped to adjoining buildings, where it can be heated further before use either in radiators or as domestic hot water.

Active solar systems are also being employed to convert sea water into potable water in dry desert regions by the sea. Here condensation is trapped as part of reverse heat transfer and collected for use in irrigation and domestic use.

Expansion in renewable energy use in EU between 1995 and 2010		
Type of energy	1995	2010
Wind (gigawatts)	2.5	40
Photovoltaics (PV) (gigawatts)	0.03	3
Biomass (measured in million tonnes of oil equivalent)	45	135
Geothermal (heat pumps) (gigawatts)	1.3	5
Solar thermal collectors (million m²)	6.5	100

Photovoltaics (PV)

Solar energy is increasingly being exploited in buildings through the use of PV panels which convert sunlight directly into direct current (DC) electricity. Their use is becoming more common as the cost of PV technology falls and confidence in its effectiveness rises. PV use globally is increasing by about 10 per cent every year, with costs falling, initially by 12 per cent a year and currently by around 5 per cent a year.

There have been many showcase projects, such as the athletes' village at the Sydney Olympic Games, which had 665 houses heated, lit and ventilated almost entirely with electricity generated by rooftop PV panels.[4] Other showcase demonstration schemes include the Doxford Solar Energy Office near Sunderland, designed by Studio E Architects. Here, PV panels generating 70 kW are integrated on a large south-facing glazed wall which also employs passive solar technologies. Energy modelling of the building suggests that energy consumption will be 85 kWh/m² per year, producing 'a saving of one-third over typical offices in the region'.[5] More recently PV technologies were widely used at the Beijing Olympics in various structures as well as in the athletes village, and by Renzo Piano at the Academy of Sciences Building in San Francisco.

Issues and choices

The key issues architects need to consider when contemplating the use of photovoltaic technologies in buildings are:

- How much will it contribute to the energy load?

- Is PV technology cost-effective over the lifetime of the building?
- Are the site and use appropriate?
- Is the technology reliable?
- Can PV technology be integrated into the design and other service strategies?
- How much does using PV panels reduce overall cladding costs?

As a consequence of its benign nature and current government inducement, PV technology is attractive to clients and the public at large. With PV panels there are no emissions, no noise and no waste (except at the end of their lives). There are environmental costs in manufacture, but since most of the materials are recyclable – glass, aluminium, silicon – these are not considerable. Also, because of the modular nature of most PV systems, it is possible to start small and add further PV modules later. In Europe in the period 2002–8 annual growth in the use of PV technology was 48 per cent, with most of the expansion in the area of architectural application, i.e. integration with buildings. Also, since PV systems are more efficient when they operate at low temperatures, much of the growth has been in sunny northern locations. To a degree, the temperature efficiency compensates for the loss of solar radiation away from the equator. China currently accounts for 22 per cent of worldwide use of PV technologies.

The main advantage of PV technology is the way that direct sunlight (or just daylight, if it is bright enough) is converted into electricity. This means that lights, computers, TVs, microwave ovens, electric cookers and refrigerators can be powered without resorting to imported energy. In commercial applications where much of the energy load is electricity used for interior lighting and equipment there are obvious advantages.

However, the main problem with exploiting all renewable energy sources within buildings is the intermittent nature of the supply (sun and wind) and the difficulty of storing the generated electricity. This is why it is important to ensure integration of the energy strategy with the design and day-to-day use of the buildings. In offices, for example, where lights are usually employed during the day, PV technology allows energy from the sun to be converted to electricity at the point of use. Hence, natural supply and human demand are in close proximity (unlike fossil fuel systems). Any PV-generated electricity that has not been consumed in the building can be fed into the national grid, which acts as an 'energy store'. At times of low generation (at night or on cloudy days) the

PV technology can be used in buildings via:
- ☐ Sloping roofs
- ☐ Flat roofs
- ☐ Façades
- ☐ Within atria
- ☐ As part of solar shading devices
- ☐ Integrated into roof tiles or bricks

Fig 82
Integral solar shading and photovoltaic (PV) cells at Copenhagen Energi Office.

building user can buy back the electricity at a discounted rate. Hence, the efficient operation of a PV system requires access to the grid, otherwise expensive and space-consuming batteries are required for storage.

Before PV electricity can be used, either in the building or fed into the grid, it needs to be converted from DC to AC supply. This requires an inverter, which adds to the cost of installation and is more frequently the source of system failure than the PV panels themselves. Modern PV panels have a module efficiency of 15 per cent – that is, they convert 15 per cent of the primary energy of the sun directly into electricity. As a rough guide, 8–10 m² of PV modules generate 1 kW of electricity all the time over a year, or put another way, the annual output in the UK is 750–800 kWh/kWp (i.e. kW hours per kW peak (kWp)). However, output is reduced by shading, poor orientation and poor installation – hence the need to consider PV technology as a fundamental design issue as against a later 'bolt-on'. The peak output in the UK in high summer is 1.2 kW/m² of panel (or 9.6 kW in total with 8 m² of panels), a level far in excess of energy demand at the time in a typical domestic building.[6]

Cost of PV technology

In the UK the cost of a typical domestic solar water system is £3000–£5000 while a PV system generating a similar level of electrical energy costs £7000–£10,000 per kWp. Prices have changed considerably: for a small commercial building such as a petrol filling station, the capital cost in 2001 of producing around 6000 kWh/yr of electricity from PV panels was £35,000,[7] giving a payback period of 12 years. Roof-mounted PV systems are normally more expensive than façade systems over their lifetime, and since about 30 per cent of the capital cost is construction or installation based, there are economies in scale.[8]

However, the advantage of the PV system is that the type of power generated – electricity – is essential for most modern appliances. Bearing in mind that PVs can convert around 20 per cent of light into usable electricity, whereas 45 per cent can be utilised for space heating and 30 per cent for water heating, the ideal answer is to employ a hybrid system, as at Sainsbury's eco-store in Greenwich, designed by Chetwood Associates. One benefit of PV installation is that in the summer when a great deal of electricity is generated, this can be used to power electric vehicles which act as an energy store along with the grid.

Fig 83
Low-energy community building with PV roof canopy at BRE Innovation Park, UK, designed by Willmott Dixon.

Fig 84
Sainsbury's supermarket, Greenwich, UK, designed by Chetwood Architects. Green issues were set out in the brief, making integration possible from the outset.
Source: Chetwood Architects

PV and passive solar technologies used together provide an ideal system, especially when integrated with other 'green' energy systems such as woodchip boilers or geothermal energy.

There are, however, disadvantages at present, which grants from government, fuel costs and technological innovation may alter in the future. Solar electricity is two or three times the cost of fossil fuel power at the point of use. Relatively low oil prices mean that PV is (at present) disadvantaged. However, the creation of a large market in Japan for PV technology as a result of central and local government procurement policy has led to mass production by companies like Sharp. This in turn has driven down prices and improved both the efficiency and reliability of solar technologies. By 2050 it is possible that at current levels of technological innovation, PV will be employed in large solar electricity power stations, making nuclear and oil-based stations obsolete. Even in the domestic sector, PV installations will be competitive by 2020 (at current oil prices), and as an expanding market reduces unit costs, it may well be cheaper than oil and gas for non-domestic applications even sooner.

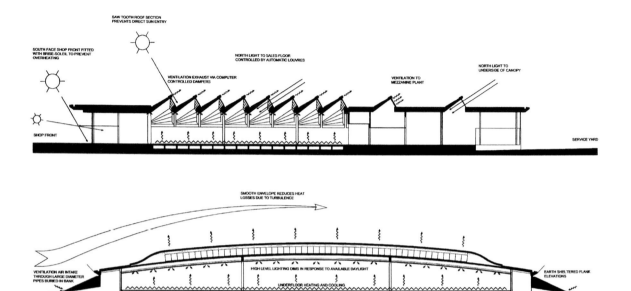

Fig 85
Sections: Sainsbury's supermarket,
Greenwich, UK.
Source: Chetwood Architects

At the moment, the payback time for the energy consumed in the manufacture of PV panels (i.e. the embodied energy) is recouped by the energy generated after five years of use. Over the typical lifetime of a PV system (put notionally at 20 years) four times more energy is produced than consumed in manufacture. And since this output is clean energy as against an input of 'dirty' energy (in manufacture) the wider environmental benefits are obvious. As a consequence companies which were oil-based, such as BP and Shell, now market themselves as 'energy companies' complete with a division manufacturing PV panels.

The need for design integration

With their ultra-modern aesthetic, photovoltaic panels are well suited to high-tech applications. Their ability to respond to sky conditions, their sheen and glamour (compared to other renewable energy applications) mean that many clients are happy to pay the extra cost of installation. PV panels on a roof or tilted façade reflect favourably on a company, signalling a concern for the environment.

Fig 86
BRE Kingspan House designed by Sheppard Robson at BRE Innovation Park; and showing details of active roof generating electricity and hot water for the building. Notice the central skylight for daylighting and ventilation.

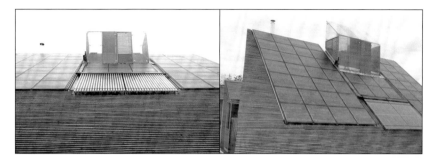

This combination of aesthetics and prestige, added to the fact that most governments have grants available to help expand the market, suggests that PV will outstrip other renewable energy technologies over the next generation.

The emphasis on energy, especially photovoltaic applications, has placed greater attention to the roof as an architectural element. Many see the roof as the 'fifth elevation',[9] the form and orientation of which is as important as the vertical elevations. Architects need to ensure that the technical aspects of PVs and the shape, orientation and angle of roofs are well integrated. The ad hoc effect of poor integration undermines the aesthetic potential of PV panels. With office buildings integration can readily be achieved, but with individual houses the effect can be less satisfactory. PV panel sizes are rarely in scale with domestic roofs, especially when a number of panels are required for efficient energy generation. As a consequence, some manufacturers (such as Redland) are developing roof tiles with integral photovoltaic cells.

Fig 87
PV panels at the Vauxhall bus interchange in London, designed by Arup.

Typical performance of roof-mounted PV system (2003)	
Module efficiency	15%
System size	1.5 kW
South-facing roof at 30°–40°	System provides 50–60% of total energy use
Cost of PV modules	£6/W of energy generated
Cost of PV roof tiles	£9/W of energy generated
Breakdown of total cost	60% is cost of PV panels
	40% is cost of inverter and wiring
Source: Energy Saving Trust	

Disadvantages of PV systems	
□ Sunlight is intermittent □ Electricity is difficult to store □ System design is specific to location and building use	□ Control and maintenance add to cost □ Costs are high at installation, low in use (opposite to traditional energy systems)

Source: Northumbria Photovoltaics Application Centre

In the high-tech design arena, the concept of seamless engineering should be the ultimate goal. The dramatic curved forms of many modern buildings suit PV use, because the sun is always moving and changing its altitude: panels set at different angles can achieve optimum efficiency at different times of the day or the year. Also, since the glass of PV panels can be tinted in different shades, their colour and surface texture can be modified to produce an art-glass effect popular with many architects today (for example, at the TuArena in Tubingen, Germany). A kind of sexy integration is the key, with the needs of PV technology driving the basic shape, form and look of the building.

The UK is behind much of the world in PV application. This is partly the result of lack of government incentives and the availability or price of alternative energy sources. It is also a cultural issue – Germany and Japan see themselves as high-technology countries, where to invest in PV engineering is a statement of national or corporate identity. In parts of Europe such as Sweden, PV installation on houses is encouraged by discounts on mortgage interest rates or direct government grants.

Wind power

Wind power is one of the fastest growing energy technologies in the world. It can be exploited to generate electricity offshore, on land and at the building itself. Installation and maintenance costs have fallen to the point where it is now viable to use this technology at the site or on the roof of buildings. Various new technologies and windpump designs are available – some generate electricity directly, others are used for ventilation or for pumping water. Although wind energy has been demonstrated commercially over a wide range of geographical conditions, the UK is particularly well placed to exploit it. Sufficient wind is available in the UK to power turbines for about 85 per cent of the year, making the UK one of the best places in Europe for wind power.

The principle of renewable energy from wind is similar to solar power. Electricity generated can be fed into the national grid and bought back on windless days. It can also be used directly to provide the power for lighting and electrical goods (though special circuits are needed). Normally, wind energy is turned into electricity and fed into large power grids, but it can also be used in small grids serving an individual building (house, school, supermarket) or a village community. Here surplus electricity is fed into the national grid after local demand has been met. In remote areas, community-based wind power systems offer a degree of independence from grid suppliers and are much more energy efficient and cost-effective than conventional generators fed by oil.

Wind energy is particularly important when fossil fuels are not available (e.g. on islands) or when electricity supply is intermittent. It is also useful as a complement to solar energy on the assumption that windy grey days occur when the sun is not shining. PV and local wind-generated electricity provide a wider range of self-sufficiency than solar power alone. However, unlike solar energy, which peaks when demand is at its lowest (in the summer), wind energy is most available when demand is greatest (in the winter). Wind turbines vary from small domestic appliances capable of generating 5 watts to large turbines with outputs of over 1.5 MW. Most commercial wind turbines are around 400 kW in capacity, and wind farms tend to operate most efficiently with several smaller turbines (300–500 kW) than one or two large ones. The same is true of buildings, where several micro-turbines are more effective than a single larger wind turbine.

Wind turbines can be used:

- offshore in large wind farms (capacity 1.5 MW per turbine)
- on land in rural areas (capacity 0.5–1 MW per turbine)
- near building and small communities (capacity 5–500 kW per turbine)
- on buildings (capacity 1–5 kW)

Note: as a rule 1 kW installed of wind energy produces 2500 kWh annually.[10]

Offshore wind farms
Concern over the environmental impact of land-based wind farms has encouraged the development of offshore facilities. The UK government wants half of the 3500 planned wind turbines over the next decade to be erected offshore,

Fig 88
Large-scale wind farm in Yorkshire producing electricity for 9000 homes.

and half on land. Although the offshore sites are not without impact (on migrating birds and fishing) they offer clean energy without upsetting local communities. An example is the Noah Hoyle Offshore Wind Farm, developed by a consortium of National Wind Power and the Danish turbine manufacturer Vestas, which began producing sufficient electricity for 50,000 homes in 2003. Further large offshore wind farms exist at Scroby Sands, 6 km into the North Sea near Great Yarmouth in Norfolk and in the Thames estuary. These and 15 other planned offshore wind farms are expected to produce 5.4–7.2 GW of electricity.

In 2004, the UK government was expecting the construction of offshore wind farms to create 20,000 jobs in the UK, thereby compensating for the loss of jobs as a result of decommissioning of nuclear power stations.[11] However, this has not yet come to fruition, partly due to public concern over the environmental issues surrounding large wind turbines. By 2009, however, many of the barriers were beginning to fall. Even the Royal Society for the Protection of Birds, formerly a vociferous campaigner in the offshore wind debate, has recently unveiled a turbine at its Rainham Marshes visitor centre, Essex,[12] although the RSPB still opposes wind farms on Lewis and Harris.

As a general rule, one large offshore wind farm (of about 30 mega-generators) produces electricity for 50,000–60,000 homes and creates about 200 jobs locally (installation and maintenance) and 400 further afield (turbine manufacture). Hence, there is an economic argument in addition to the environmental one, with major turbine manufacturers arguing that 20 per cent of the UK's energy could readily be generated by the wind.

Micro-turbines

As an alternative to large-scale production there has been a growth in micro-wind turbines suitable for building-related application, as turbines fitted to the roof not unlike a TV mast. Unlike large wind-powered systems the surplus energy is not normally fed into the national grid but installers are eligible to receive government subsidies in the form of Renewable Obligation Certificates (which are tax deductible). Some systems now incorporate micro-turbines into the ridge systems of buildings, sometimes altering the profile of roofs to maximise wind potential. Such systems require average wind speeds to be above 6 m/s to be cost-effective. As with PV technology, designers need to work closely with specialist manufacturers to ensure that aesthetic and engineering demands are met.

At the building level, micro-turbines are beginning to make an impact, although they face two main difficulties. The first concerns the relatively unstable wind conditions in urban areas compared to rural or offshore. Wind turbulence results in more expensive turbines which, being smaller than conventional types, already suffer from cost disadvantage. Normally building-mounted turbines are under 5 kW capacity and cost from £3000–5000 per kW installed giving a payback period of about 15 years with a life expectancy of perhaps 20 years.[13] The second problem is that of obtaining planning permission. Although the rules in the UK were relaxed in 2008, there are size limits on permitted development and restrictions for buildings in conservation areas, national parks etc. Because efficiencies increase with scale, the controls on wind generator building development run counter to achieving energy targets nationally.

OTHER RENEWABLE ENERGY SOURCES

Combined heat and power

Combined Heat and Power (CHP) takes the waste heat from electricity generation for use in adjoining properties. CHP occurs as large-scale community based installations and increasingly at the level of individual buildings. In Europe CHP accounts for 20 per cent of electricity generation (over 50 per cent in Denmark) but under 5 per cent in the UK, suggesting that this is an area of future growth.

CPH works by distributing the waste heat from electricity generation, normally in the form of steam, to local houses, schools and commercial buildings. With well-insulated pipes which are usually laid under the road, the district heating can extend for 8 kilometres.

There are three main benefits of CHP:

- It can utilise waste products in the combustion chamber and therefore contributes to reducing the demand for landfill sites.
- Being small in operation compared to large-scale power stations, CHP can be located close to urban areas, and in countries like Sweden and Denmark, new communities (such as that at Albertslund near Copenhagen) are planned

around new CHP power plants. This encourages a sense of ownership and integration between energy consumption and supply.

■ It can be used in large buildings with consequent benefits for energy efficiency.

The main disadvantages of CHP lie in noise, disturbance due to delivery of fuel source, and pollution. Placing a power station in a village, for example, may make energy sense but the wider environmental consequences are considerable.

In building-operated CHP systems, the waste heat which stems from electricity generation is used for space and water heating. Normally there is a gas or oil boiler linked to a generator which produces electricity and heat simultaneously. The technology is fairly widespread in large buildings such as universities and hospitals, but it is increasingly being used by architects in individual houses.

The best conditions for small CHP application are where there is a large demand for electricity, ready access to the grid for selling surplus capacity, long periods of occupation so that the waste heat can used effectively, and well-integrated building services and architecture. As with other renewable or emerging energy technologies, CHP should not be 'bolt-on' but planned at the outset. Design integration is essential with CHP at both urban levels and in application at the building scale.[14]

Leicester Community CHP Project

Leicester was the first UK city to win support from the government's Community Energy Programme aimed at expanding the use of CHP. Funded in 2004 through the Climate Change Levy (administered by the Energy Saving Trust), the Leicester project was steered by De Montfort University's Institute of Energy and Sustainable Development. The CHP plant supplies heat and power to university buildings, four local authority housing estates and 16 public buildings, using locally grown energy crops, mainly willow. A government grant of over £5 million towards a project costing £70 million underwrote the viability of the initiative. Monitoring of the project is overseen by De Montfort University and the Energy Saving Trust.

Fuel cells

An emerging technology which looks set to transform energy production is that of fuel cells. These work in a fundamentally different way to photovoltaics, fossil fuel combustion systems and normal lead-based batteries. Fuel cells rely on electrochemical technology and employ hydrogen gas mixed with oxygen to generate electricity. Hydrogen fuel, obtained from natural gas, methanol or petroleum, is combined with liquid oxygen to produce electricity, with heat and water vapour being the by-products.[15]

Potentially, fuel cells can provide electricity with minimal emissions and no moving parts – hence the technology is nearly as benign as photovoltaics. At present, however, hydrogen is made from fossil fuels – normally natural gas – but the technology is under rapid development at present, with some claiming that renewable energy could replace fossil fuels as the raw material in the future.

A fuel cell consists of two electrodes separated by a polymer membrane electrolyte. A thin platinum-coated catalyst layer on each electrode allows the hydrogen fuel to disassociate into electrons and protons, then the electrons generated are conducted into an external electrical current.

Individual fuel cells generate about 0.6 V, which is used directly or stored in a battery. According to the Building Centre Trust, hydrogen fuel cells will be in common use in 20 years' time for a wide range of uses from urban transport to lighting of buildings.[16] Rather than produce carbon dioxide as a by-product, the hydrogen cell produces only hydrogen dioxide – water.

Geothermal energy

Using a simple ground source heat pump (GSHP) it is possible to provide heating and cooling for a building by exploiting the energy stored underground (geothermal energy). In the UK, for instance, the below-ground temperature is fairly constant at 9°C–13°C. GSHPs can extract this heat, either via horizontal or vertical 'collectors' respectively exploiting near-surface warmth derived from sunlight, or deeper heat from molten rock well below ground level. Geothermal energy can be employed to offset seasonal variations by acting as a heat reservoir in the winter and a heat sink in the summer. As such, it reduces primary energy consumption for winter heating and summer cooling. Although the system offers benefits for all building types it is most useful for buildings such as offices and shops where cooling is routinely required.

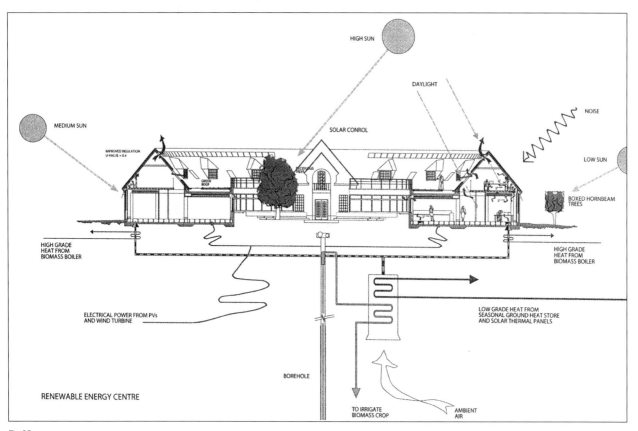

RENEWABLE ENERGY CENTRE

Fig 89
Geothermal energy at Renewable Energy
Centre, designed by Studio E Architects.
Source: Studio E Architects

There are two main types of GSHP – a closed-loop system and an open one. The first circulates an antifreeze liquid through a loop of plastic pipes laid in the ground either horizontally or vertically. Generally, horizontal coil systems are cheaper than deep-bore applications and soft soil is preferable to hard rock. A trench is normally dug into which the pipe is laid and then backfilled with heat-conducting aggregate. The second GSHP method uses groundwater from a supply well or river course, which is passed through a heat pump to extract the available energy, and which is then used for heating or cooling the building.

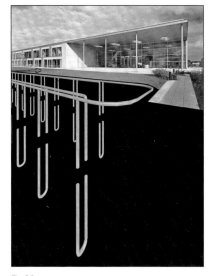

Fig 90
Geothermal energy at Roche Building, designed
by BDP.
Source: BDP

GSHP schemes are usually more cost-effective than other renewable energy systems (such as photovoltaics and micro-wind generators) and are relatively emission-free. Since the technology avoids using high-tech gadgetry, maintenance costs are fairly low and reliability high. Compared to typical domestic heating systems, GSHP can reduce carbon dioxide emissions by between 40 per cent and 60 per cent. A typical GSHP installation for a new house using a horizontal loop system of 80–100 m is about £10,000.[17] However, a land area equal to about twice the footprint of the building is required for horizontal loop systems – limiting the use of the technology in built-up urban areas.

There has been a significant increase in the use of geothermal technologies over the past decade and costs have stabilised. Their use is, however, mainly restricted to new construction in rural areas and in this sense the technology has only limited application in the search for sustainable development. Like all renewable energy technologies, there has to be adequate space for exploiting the new energy source. Costs increase quickly when GSHP applications are used as part of upgrading an existing building or installing a system in a built-up area. However, with a new building on a large area of semi-rural ground such as a school or local medical centre with a generous area set aside for car parking, geothermal technologies make a great deal of sense both environmentally and financially. The pay back period with current energy prices is around eight years.

Vertical GSHP technology allows more restricted sites to utilise the technology. However, the boreholes are normally between 50 m and 200 m deep and about 10 m apart. Drilling at such depths is expensive and certain rock types are not suitable; in addition high-capacity heat pump compressors are required adding to cost compared to horizontal systems.

Geothermal heating: design considerations	
☐ Existing underground services must be located accurately ☐ Efficiency depends upon heat transfer rates. Solid ground is more effective than porous, and damp conditions better than dry ☐ Horizontal pipe systems are cheaper than vertical ☐ GSHP should be sized to meet 60–70 per cent of total energy requirements,	so a secondary heating/cooling system is required to meet extreme conditions ☐ Watertightness is essential for the piping to avoid loss of antifreeze ☐ Non-toxic antifreeze is essential with closed-loop systems ☐ Good quality groundwater is essential with open systems

Biofuels

Biofuels are another renewable energy source gaining in popularity. They are either specially grown timbers or energy crops, or fuels based on waste of various kinds (municipal, agricultural or forestry). Energy crops are currently diversifying agriculture in the UK, providing fresh sources of energy and changing the ecology of the landscape.

Although biofuels provide energy through anaerobic digestion (producing methane) or combustion (producing heat) they are not without environmental disadvantages. Because they tend to be produced locally from farming or waste collection, biofuels are best used in community-based power stations or directly in buildings. At its simplest, biofuel technology consists of wood-burning stoves, but it is also commonly employed in district combined heat and power (CHP) plants, which exploit the waste heat in electricity generation for district heating, and, less commonly, in gasifier units, which exploit the high temperatures of gas combustion.

The integration of locally grown biofuels (such as coppiced willows), CHP plants and buildings provides an ecologically benign system for the future. In Denmark, for instance, the mixture of biofuel and waste-powered CHP installations, plus extensive coastal wind farms, provides the country with nearly 80 per cent of its primary domestic energy needs.

However, biofuels do emit carbon dioxide and methane, which are the main gases leading to global warming. Providing the fuel source is local and well-managed, the fact that the plants extracted CO_2 from the atmosphere during their growth can mean that some systems are regarded as 'carbon neutral' – wood-burning stoves using local fuel, for example.

Politically, the main advantage of biofuels is energy security, particularly so where locally grown biofuels provide new business to farmers and hence the rural economy. However, in an effort to develop large-scale agri-businesses based on biofuels, land once used for growing food crops is being converted to growing energy crops, with the side effect of rising food prices, particularly in parts of Africa and South America. Here international pressures are leading to farmers growing palm oil for export rather than maize for local consumption.

As reserves of oil, gas and coal become depleted, there will be growing pressure to convert world economies from fossil fuels to biofuels. According to the BP report *Putting Energy in the Spotlight*,[18] China is the largest consumer of coal worldwide and the second largest of oil and gas. Although at the time of writing heavy fuel oil is around 50 US dollars per barrel, with Canadian oil shale (a heavy polluter) trading at 38 US dollars, global scarcity will force nations into biofuel dependency unless other renewable technologies can be developed in the meantime. India and China are expected to double their demand for fossil fuels by 2025 with a predicted trebling of prices at today's levels. Under such pressures biofuels may emerge as a major global source of energy, adding to subtle climate changes and rural poverty.

Woodchip technology

Wood fuel has about 80 per cent of the calorific value of coal and represents Europe's main source of renewable energy. Approximately 40 per cent of domestic heating in Denmark and Austria is via efficient wood fuel stoves, and 20 per cent of primary energy production in Finland is derived from timber. Wood fuel comes in the form of logs, chips and pellets – the latter being made of compressed sawdust derived as a by-product of other timber processes. Since timber derives from renewable sources (if properly managed) and returns oxygen to the atmosphere during the growing phase, it is an important element in any strategy for sustainable development.

Wood fuel can be used to produce heat or, via combined heat and power (CHP) technology, both heat and electricity. It has the advantage of being useful as a fuel at a variety of scales from the individual house to a school or as district heating. Timber production and processing is also relatively labour-intensive, having the secondary benefit of producing employment locally.

When burned as a fuel, timber releases into the atmosphere the carbon dioxide it absorbed during the growth stage. This means not only that timber as a fuel is carbon neutral but also that the forests from which it is derived are carbon dioxide stores, thereby helping to stabilise the global atmosphere. Compared to other fuels timber is low in net emissions, producing only 5 per cent of the CO_2 life cycle emissions (g/kWh) of gas, about 3 per cent of those of oil and 2 per cent of those of coal.[19] Added to this, wood fuel is low in sulphur and nitrogen (the main sources of acid rain). It produces ash at

1–2 per cent of dry weight of timber, which can be composted or used as a fertiliser.

Whereas oil, coal and gas are international products, creating employment sometimes thousands of miles away from source, timber fuels encourage a stable rural economy. People are employed in the forests, in wood processing, in community-based power plants, and in boiler manufacture and servicing. The employment chain becomes part of the sustainability network which architects and developers will be reinforcing by specifying wood fuel. Also, since much wood fuel derives from forest thinnings, the product of combustion is part of the waste chain of other industries. It is prudent to ensure that community-based wood fuel heating schemes (or CHP) are developed in partnership with forest owners. If there is a common interest (social and environmental as well as economic) between consumers and forestry companies the enterprise will have a better chance of succeeding.

In much of Europe and parts of Canada wood fuel is widely employed in biomass district heating schemes (BMDH). These are normally located in villages of up to 5000 people or self-contained inner city communities of similar size. The usual pattern is to have a small number of BMDH plants on a circuit providing hot water to nearby houses. Each plant will generate 4–10 MW of power, the smaller amount being sufficient for about 500 inhabitants. Often larger buildings such as schools, factories or offices will have their own wood fuel heating plant, with many of them exporting their surplus heat to the community system.

District heating networks are usually twin pipes (flow and return) set about 600 mm below ground in a sand trench. The pipes are highly insulated, usually in foam, and able to withstand a temperature of 120°C. Since water conducts heat and reduces the insulation of the sand trench, there is normally an underground drainage pipe and filter mat. Water (and steam) is usually circulated at 12–16 bar pressure, leading to transmission losses of as little as 10 per cent per kilometre length. It is also commonplace for district heating networks to employ both biomass fuels and conventional fuels. This mixed energy economy means that oil or gas can be employed to even-out peaks in demand when wood fuel on its own is unable to cope. As a general rule, the biomass share of total output should approach 70 per cent.

At the level of individual buildings, wood fuel is normally employed as part of underfloor heating schemes. Woodchips are fed into a pellet boiler to produce hot water, which is circulated in double or triple tubing placed directly beneath the floor finish but above an insulating layer of foil-faced insulation. Where wood fuel is locally available in high volumes (as logs, chips or pellets) it is cheaper to install and run than conventional oil or bottled gas boilers.[20]

RENEWABLE ENERGY AND TAXATION

Under the Emissions Trading Scheme[21] (ETS), carbon liabilities account for as much as 40 per cent of the market capitalisation of some companies. This suggests that these companies are vulnerable to the tightening of government taxation to promote energy efficiency; and such taxation may limit their economic growth and stock market valuation. Companies that rely heavily on fossil fuels will find themselves increasingly heavily taxed as the government seeks to meet European Union emissions trading obligations. The UK's Climate Change Levy (the result of Kyoto Protocol agreements embedded since 2002 into EU law) represents a major force for change, especially for companies such as PowerGen, BP and Shell, whose businesses are largely fossil fuel based.

It is hoped that the UK Emissions Trading Scheme will result in investment in new cleaner technologies (such as renewable energy and fuel cell development) and the construction of more green buildings. Emissions trading allows one company to buy the carbon credits of another with the result that energy efficiency will figure in annual company reports. Given that the EU ETS began in 2005 with around 11,500 companies participating, there is likely to be pressure on companies to reduce their dependence on fossil fuels. As these businesses comprise most of Europe's household names, new energy taxes will be a major driver of change in energy supply.

New laws, particularly from Europe, have activated change in energy production as well as its use in buildings. In fact, of the nine new EU environment policies introduced after the Maastricht Treaty (1992) three deal specifically with energy use and security. Here the emphasis is on renewable energy technologies – sun, wind and the hydrogen fuel cell. It is expected over the next generation that the fuel cell will have considerable impact on energy use not just in buildings but in replacing internal combustion engines and making obsolete highly polluting lead–acid batteries. Powered by a combustion of natural gas, photovoltaics and liquid petroleum gas, vehicles running on fuel cells are starting to make inroads into formerly conservative markets. Individual fuel cells with a capacity of 1–25 kW can be stacked to produce the energy required to power a typical home. Since housing accounts for more than a quarter of all energy use in the UK, the benefits are obvious.

NOTES

[1] See, for example, www.forumforthefuture. org/greenfutures/articles/UK_first_ carbon_capture

[2] Al Gore, *An Inconvenient Truth*, Rodale Inc., 2006. See also *Earth in the balance: Ecology and the Human Spirit*, Viking, 2008.

[3] Source: www.energysavers.gov/water_ heating

[4] Brian Edwards, *Sustainable Architecture*, Architectural Press, Oxford, 1999, p. 117.

[5] The quote is from David Lloyd Jones, *RIBA Journal*, June 2002, p. 62.

[6] Northumbria Photovoltaics Application Centre, 2003.

[7] *The Architects' Journal*, 10 May 2001.

[8] *Architecture Today*, Vol. 190, July/August 2008, p. 75.

[9] Randall Thomas, *RIBA Journal*, June 2002, p. 62.

[10] Source: ODPM, *Low and Zero Carbon Energy Sources – Strategic Guide* (Interim Publication), January 2005.

[11] *Energy and Environmental Management*, January/February 2004, p. 7.

[12] Source: Wind of change at RSPB Rainham Marshes, News Release, 1 May 2009, www.rspb.org.uk

[13] Office of Deputy Prime Minister, *Low or Zero Carbon Energy Sources – Strategic Guide* (Interim Publication), January 2005, p. 35.

[14] Ibid; this report provides useful overview of many alternative energy sources and their uses.

[15] Penny Lewis, 'Renewables', *Prospect*, March 2004, p. 33.

[16] See www.buildingcentre.co.uk/energy/ research

[17] *EcoTech*, Issue 8, November 2003, p. 20. See also Office of Deputy Prime Minister, *Low or Zero Carbon Energy Sources – Strategic Guide* (Interim Publication) January 2005.

[18] Peter Davies, Putting Energy in the Spotlight, BP Report, London, 2005.

[19] See www.thecarbontrust.co.uk

[20] Cliff Beck, Highland Birchwoods, personal communication, 24 November 2002.

[21] Source: The EU Emissions Trading Scheme http://ec.europa.eu/environment/ climate/emissions/index.en.htm

5 Water

The attention given to energy conservation over the past few years has deflected attention away from concerns about water. The construction industry has started to come to terms with global warming but has yet to face up to its responsibility with regard to water conservation. Water is potentially as important as energy and, globally, water scarcity is a problem as pressing as energy supply. Unlike energy, water impacts directly on health and food production and, although there is a link between fuel, poverty and health, the connection is by no means as direct as that with water. In Africa, most of Asia and even parts of southern Europe, water is the most pressing resource crisis: it is tomorrow's oil.

Fig 91
Typical water stressed settlement in North Africa.

Around one eighth of the world's population (884 million people) do not have access to safe water.[1] Unsafe water is the world's biggest killer and, as well as disease, poor sanitation leads to lack of human dignity and quality of life. Since many children spend a great deal of time gathering water for their families, inadequate water provision leads to poor education and a spiral of poverty. Also, in poor parts of the world the cost of water is greater than in affluent countries, with bottled water costing about 10 times that of municipal supplies. Families can spend 20 per cent of their income on water, and as the water-table drops (due to excessive extraction of groundwater supplies), this percentage is expected to rise.

Global water stress
□ 97.5 per cent of the earth's water is saltwater. If all the world's water fitted into a bucket, only one teaspoonful would be drinkable □ 2.5 billion people do not have access to adequate sanitation (almost two fifths of the world's population) □ 1.4 million children die every year from diarrhoea caused by unclean water and poor sanitation (approximately 4000 deaths per day; one child dies every 20 seconds)
Adapted from WaterAid statistics: www.wateraid.org/uk/what_we_do/statistics/default.asp

---

Water use – some facts

☐ Agriculture accounts for over 80 per cent of the world's water consumption
☐ The average European uses 200 litres of water every day
☐ The average North American used 400 litres of water every day
☐ The average person in the developing world uses 10 litres of water every day for their drinking, washing and cooking
☐ On current trends, humans will use 40 per cent more water then they do now over the next 20 years

Drinking water
☐ In a typical building only 4 litres of the 150 litres of water per person consumed per day is used for drinking
☐ An old lavatory uses at least nine litres of water per flush; modern low-flush models use as little as three litres
☐ In the UK, flushing accounts for 35 per cent of domestic water use (about 50 litres per person per day)

Soft drinks
☐ 2.5 litres of water are required to make 1 litre of soft drink
☐ 0.5 litres of oil are required to make 1 litre of soft drink

Adapted from WaterAid statistics (www.waterair.org/uk/what_we_do/statistics/default.asp) and Richard Nicholls 'Designing for water conservation', in Brian Edwards Sustainable Architecture: 2nd edition, 1999, Architectural Press, Oxford

---

WATER: POVERTY AND HEALTH

Why water matters in the 21st century
☐ Essential for public health
☐ Essential for agriculture
☐ Increase in human population puts stress on water supply
☐ Climate change is altering patterns of rainfall
☐ Rising living standards means a rise in water demand per person
☐ Water use also means energy use (in supply and in waste)

Architects working outside the UK need to take water as seriously as they do energy, and those working in Africa, parts of Asia and Latin America will find that water engineering and domestic plumbing are often intractable problems. Water, not oil, is the priority – first, creating clean unpolluted supplies and, second, providing sanitation either in the form of community latrines or domestic toilets.

In countries such as Kenya, Tanzania, Sudan and Rwanda architects need to address the infrastructure of water before they can approach the task of designing buildings. Non-governmental organisations (NGOs) such as Oxfam and Water Aid provide advice and funding for digging wells, laying pipes and supplying remote rural communities, but it requires architects, engineers and mechanics on the ground to install the equipment and supervise the work. A modern well can be dug in Uganda for under £1000, and with clean water comes health, education and more effective farming. Hence, water is the key to a chain reaction of benefits for some of the most impoverished regions of the world.

The main water-related diseases are cholera, dysentery, typhoid, schistosomiasis (also known as bilharzia or snail fever), hookworm and trachoma. These cause death, stunted growth or blindness, and are the result of either contaminated water or lack of water leading to poor sanitation through insufficient supplies for hand washing. Hence, the answer is not just to provide clean supplies of water but to provide the basic sanitation of toilets, wash basins and sewerage systems to ensure a healthy lifestyle. Although engineers are involved mainly in the supply of new water infrastructure, architects have an important role to play in providing public buildings such as schools, which can be models of energy and water efficiency for other buildings. Architectural education in the developed world could do more to prepare its young professionals for practice in the developing world, where water is more pressing than oil, and where sanitation matters more than comfort.

Water is the key to overcoming the poverty trap which holds millions of people to subsistence farming in large areas of rural Africa. Not only are the residents impoverished by lack of water and the expanding grip of AIDS, but their demands on other resources, such as timber to boil what water is available, stress the environment further. Hence, poor water leads to poor health, and overlarge families to compensate for premature death, which in turn leads to forest and scrub clearance. The cycle is one of growing poverty, desertification and political instability. In such an environment three conditions are required to meet future challenges: good governance, infrastructure investment including buildings, and new skills in renewable technologies.

The situation is often as bad in large Asian cities. In Dhaka in Bangladesh about 3 million people live without the simplest drainage or sanitation. Many of the new homes for the inward-migrating rural poor (often driven from ancient farming areas by rising sea levels) are built on parts of the city which were formerly rubbish dumps.

These facts demonstrate the scale of environmental stress caused partly by global warming and partly by the lack of proper planning of infrastructure in rural Africa and urban Asia. This is why of the ten UN Millennium Development Goals, three specifically mention infrastructure, and by implication better water provision.

WATER USE IN THE UK

In the UK, the wet maritime climate provides a relatively assured supply of domestic, agricultural and industrial water; yet we take water too much for granted.

Recent floods in the UK (and Europe) confirm, however, the unpredictability of our water resources: there have been eight drought years in the past twenty years, and although 2000, 2004 and 2007 were wet years, the trend is towards less rainfall in the south and east, and more in the north and west. Climate change, the result of the fossil fuel/global warming equation, is clearly altering rainfall patterns. As the planet gets warmer, the distribution of rain varies both within continents and within countries. Global warming means more global rain, but it falls in the wrong place. The extra precipitation does not reach the centre of continents, which are becoming hotter and drier. The UK is on a water divide, with some parts wetter and some drier, but all areas are having to face up to change in the water regime.

Water consumption in the UK	
☐ 150 litres per person per day but subject to increasing legislative constraint ☐ 51 per cent of extracted water goes to public water supply	☐ 36 per cent to power generation ☐ 13 per cent to agriculture ☐ Architects influence directly or indirectly 50 per cent of water use in UK

Water use in a typical household in the UK		Water use in a typical office building in the UK	
Activity	% of total	Activity	% of total
Washing and hygiene	40	WC flushing	43
Toilet flushing	30	Urinal flushing	20
Laundry	11	Washing	27
Washing dishes	6	Canteen	9
Gardening	4	Cleaning	1
Drinking	4		
Miscellaneous	5		

Changing rainfall patterns are only part of the problem. People in the UK now consume more water per household than ever before and there are more premises demanding water (housing, offices, schools, supermarkets) – around half of all water use in the UK occurs in buildings.

There is growth in the consumption of water per person and, as a consequence, per building. Just as with energy, buildings are responsible for about a half of all consumption and architects and designers have to take the water issue on board as an environmental imperative.

Water conservation is no more difficult to achieve than energy conservation. Although cost is a major impediment, not just of the equipment necessary for collection and recycling but also for the extra space and structure required, the

Strategies for water conservation	
Technological	Reduced-flow taps
	Self-closing taps
	Low-flush toilets
	Compost or vacuum toilets
	Waterless urinals
	Sensors for urinal flushing
	Showers rather than baths
	Small, shaped baths
	Low-water-use domestic appliances
Grey water systems	Recovered wastewater (recycled water)
	Rainwater collection at site
Engineering design	Pervious paving to feed groundwater supplies
	Landscape design to soak up rainwater
	Soft water catchment to 'sponge' rainfall peaks
Management	Monitor use (metering)
	Price rise
	Leakage detection
	Education

reality is that with rising water bills attention to water conservation makes financial sense. However, while for many institutional clients water bills are too low for expensive conservation strategies to be worthwhile, significant economies of water use can be achieved with modest measures (such as reduced-flow taps).

Although many urban sites do not have sufficient space for reed beds, and any collected water from roofs may be too contaminated by air pollution for use in the building except for toilet flushing and the like, there are still water-saving options that could be explored, such as the relationship between renewable energy and rainwater conservation. For example, wind energy could be used for pumping water and solar energy for cleansing it. If this were to happen, buildings would be genuinely holistic in their approach to sustainability, integrating strategies for energy and water saving.

The principles of water conservation are similar to those of energy conservation (or any other resource, for that matter). There are four stages:

- harvest renewable or local sources
- reduce the level of usage
- reuse primary supplies
- recycle the wastes.

Domestic water harvesting

Water consumption in the UK rose by 75 per cent between 1960 and 2002 with annual rainfall decreasing by about 8 per cent over the same period. In southern England the supply situation is particularly acute, especially over the summer. A simple answer is to use domestic roofs to collect water, which is then stored in a basement. About 200 litres of water per day are consumed by a typical person, so around 600 litres per day are needed for a typical household. With the UK's rainfall pattern, a storage tank of about 200,000 litres is required to meet expected demand over a year. Using a simple sand filter and pump the stored water can then be used for flushing toilets (the main water use in a typical house), washing machines, garden irrigation, showers and baths. Mains supply will still be required for drinking water and cooking but, by diversifying water sources, there is reduced demand on the water grid, and domestic consumers will face lower water bills.

In theory, water self-sufficiency is achievable. However, there are four main problems:

- Water storage tanks are large, heavy and take up valuable space that could be used for other purposes. Storage is viable only in new construction where basements can be constructed for storage. In existing buildings, the weight of stored rainwater is prohibitive.
- Rainwater may not be of potable quality (water is strictly regulated under EU and UK law). Quality depends on catchment surfaces (lead and copper are clearly unsuitable), the storage method and the biological treatment. Often, the water needs to be boiled before drinking or subject to ultraviolet light (radiation cleansing). This adds to cost and, importantly, CO_2 production, demonstrating the link between water and energy use.
- The cost of water self-sufficiency is expensive in construction terms. The capital outlay may not be recovered quickly, especially when the invisible costs are computed. However, with water bills rising (in well-designed modern houses, the water utility bill is often higher than the energy bill) over the lifetime of the building, the initial cost will be recovered. At the Hockerton Energy Village near Newark in Nottinghamshire, designed by Robert and Brenda Vale, considerable efficiency was gained by putting water high on the environmental agenda at the briefing stage.
- The building will need to be designed to exploit water catchment. This will entail large gutters, the ability to access the system at key points (to clear leaves, etc.), and the use of roof pitches which do not add excessive velocity to the flowing water or unduly slow down its path to the tank. As a consequence, water conservation, just like energy conservation, has aesthetic ramifications.

Reducing water demand

Water consumption can be reduced by adopting simple design and management measures. By dividing water into potable and non-potable use, it is possible to gain the benefit of harvesting, reusing and recycling water without any associated cost or health problems. This strategy includes water-use reduction, employing simple measures such as low-flush or dual-flush toilets. A useful measure for all public buildings is to use sensors in public toilets to avoid urinals flushing when not in use (e.g. Birchanger Green Service Station on the M11). In the domestic setting, dual flush systems respond to the different flushing needs of toilet uses and can reduce domestic water consumption by 40 per cent.

Typically, a dual flush toilet is operated 4–5 times a day on low flush and once on full flush per person occupation.

Changes to UK Water Regulations			
Appliance	1986 Water Bye-laws	1999 Water Regulations	Code for Sustainable Homes
WC	7.5 litres/flush	6 litres/flush	4/2.5 dual flush
Washing machines	150–180 litres/cycle	120 litres/cycle	49 litres/cycle
Dishwashers	7 litres/place setting	4.5 litres/place setting	3 litres/place setting
Showers	None	Meter if more than 20 litres/min	6–8 litres/minute maximum flow
Source: Environment Agency, UK and Code for Sustainable Homes (CSH) 2008			

Use reduction is also encouraged by water metering, which provides an immediate measure of water usage as a benchmark from which improvements in water efficiency can be made. Typically, meters reduce water use by around 20 per cent, and more for poorer households. It is also worth remembering that reduced water use means less waste, and less waste requires less energy to process sewage.

Benefits of water conservation in buildings	
☐ Lower water charges ☐ Groundwater supplies conserved for future generations ☐ Reduced stress on water supply infrastructure	☐ Reduced pressure to build reservoirs ☐ Reduced use of hot water (saving energy) ☐ Reduced use of water in supply and sewerage systems (saving energy)

At Hockerton – a pioneering self-sufficient development of five homes, in Nottinghamshire, central England – high-grade (i.e. drinking) water needs are met in part by the collection of rainwater from conservatory roofs, which is then stored and mineralised (passed through light and carbon filters) before use. The shared storage tanks assume 5 litres are per person per day and provide sufficient drinking water capacity for two-thirds of the year. Typical water use in the UK

Fig 92
The Hockerton Energy Village in Nottingham, designed by Robert and Brenda Vale, integrates a number of sustainable design principles.
Source: Hockerton Energy Village Trust

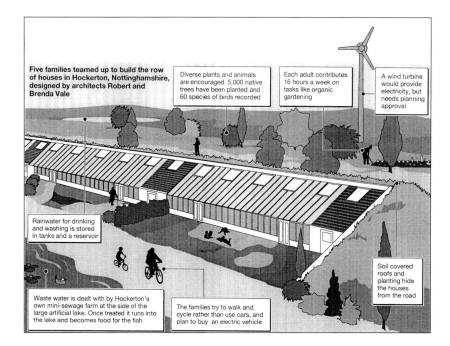

Five families teamed up to build the row of houses in Hockerton, Nottinghamshire, designed by architects Robert and Brenda Vale

Diverse plants and animals are encouraged. 5,000 native trees have been planted and 60 species of birds recorded

Each adult contributes 16 hours a week on tasks like organic gardening

A wind turbine would provide electricity, but needs planning approval

Rainwater for drinking and washing is stored in tanks and a reservoir

Soil covered roofs and planting hide the houses from the road

Waste water is dealt with by Hockerton's own mini-sewage farm at the side of the large artificial lake. Once treated it runs into the lake and becomes food for the fish

The families try to walk and cycle rather than use cars, and plan to buy an electric vehicle

is 150–200 litres per person per day; at Hockerton, low-grade water needs (i.e. toilet flushing) are met by a reservoir served by drainage from other roofs, roads and surrounding fields. Here, the water is fed through a sand filter before use. The reservoir stores 150 m^3 of water which provides the village with a secure 100-day supply for flushing toilets, clothes washing, and so on. Water conservation is made viable by the use of flow restrictors, low-water washing machines and, for garden irrigation, the use of soiled water.

RECYCLING OF WATER

Water is commonly recycled as low-grade water but not as high-grade (drinking) water because of the possible health hazards. Recycling allows cleansed water to be put back into effective use – for irrigation, recreation, amenity, and ecological diversification. Typically, recycling consists of passing low-soiled water (i.e. with no solid wastes) into a reservoir via reed beds or other biological cleaning

Fig 93
Grey water recycling at Bo01 in Malmo using
canals and ponds between the buildings.

processes. The water has to pass slowly through the system for the bacteriological
breakdown to occur. The usual set-up in domestic development positions the
reed bed after the septic tank. In commercial development, the reed bed is
positioned after the water separation in the building and before the most polluted
water is taken to public sewers. For recycling to work, there needs to be a highly
active ecosystem – one that is not threatened by groundwater contamination.
The Green City of Tomorrow, known as Bo01 in Malmo, Sweden, demonstrates
how this kind of system operates, where the organic waste is taken to the local
power plant and water run-off finds its way to the local canal system via reed beds
and willow thickets.

Grey water recycling

Reed beds work by cleaning the soiled water biologically. The roots of reeds (and
other plants) supply oxygen to the naturally occurring bacteria in the water, which
then digest any pathogens present. Faecal coliforms are broken down with the
residual matter, supplying nutrient-rich water to a lake (as at Ecolonia in Holland,
masterplanned by Lucien Kroll[2]), which can then provide a habitat for wildlife or
a resource for a fish farm.

Fig 94
Section through the Barclaycard Building,
Northampton, UK, designed by Fitzroy
Robinson and Partners to show environmental
systems.
Source: Fitzroy Robinson and Partners

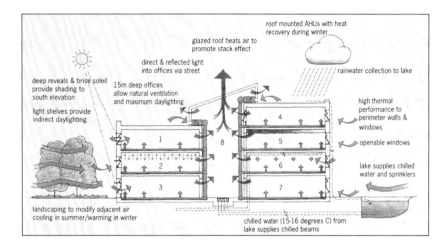

At the Barclaycard Building in Northampton, designed by Fitzroy Robinson and Partners, the cleansed water is used as part of the chilled ceiling system.[3] In this example, water is taken from a lake on the north side of the building (where it remains cool), passes through pipes in the ceilings, and is returned, warmed, to the lake only to be naturally chilled again. Like all robust water systems, the loop is complete and balances the needs of the building with those of the wider ecosystem.

SUSTAINABLE URBAN DRAINAGE SYSTEMS (SUDS)

SUDS is a drainage system that seeks to reduce water run off into drains. The principle is simple: using porous paving, perforated pipes, soft rather than hard ground cover, and high levels of planting at tree, shrub and ground level, water is encouraged to filter into the natural subsoil rather than be channelled into drains. Not only does this help with the ecology of sites, it helps maintain ground water supplies which, in many countries (e.g. Denmark) makes up 80 per cent of national water resources. SUDS leads to less engineering of the urban drainage network, thereby reducing cost. It also means that more water is absorbed naturally, and in periods of heavy rainfall, the ground acts more effectively as a sponge for surplus water. One further benefit is the reduced stress on a city's

Fig 95
The regeneration of docklands in Malmo, Sweden, uses natural rather than engineering flood control.

sewerage system and a corresponding reduction in energy consumption since sewage requires water treatment.

Although SUDS is mainly a technique applied on and beneath the ground, the principles apply at the building level as well. Surfaces that can absorb water for a period such as planted roofs and ivy covered walls, allow for water evaporation, which improves the urban microclimate and reduces run-off into drains. Sustainable urban drainage design applies the principle of ecology to areas where engineering was once dominant.

Paving around buildings is frequently impervious, with rainwater taken quickly to land drains via concrete drainage channels. A better solution using SUDS is to allow the moisture to replenish groundwater supplies by, for example, bedding paving on a sand mix, by using soakaways as opposed to storm drainage, and by using ponds to catch excess water run-off. These are quite different approaches from most water engineering solutions adopted today. Even when buildings are constructed on flood plains, they rarely adopt natural solutions for absorbing rainfall peaks, such as reed beds, meandering watercourses, irregular river banks, riverside tree planting and overflow areas. Instead, design solutions are predominantly concrete, contained, sealed and engineered in a protective rather than responsive manner.

THE NEED FOR INTEGRATION OF ALL RESOURCES

There is embodied energy in water – that is, considerable amounts of energy are invested into getting clean, potable water into our taps. Much of the world's water supply comes from fossil-fuel-driven desalination plants. Where this happens, embodied energy can represent half of the water content by volume (i.e. it takes half a gallon of oil to produce a gallon of desalinated water). Water is a valuable resource in drought-stricken areas such as the Middle East, and has frequently been the underlying reason for regional conflicts. In the Gulf region, water provided by desalination carries ten times the embodied energy as water delivered by tap in the UK.[4]

Even if we in Europe do not face such challenges, it is prudent, given the life of buildings (50–150 years), to plan to accommodate future changes in rainfall or

Fig 96
Rainwater captured for cooling and irrigation at Alexandria Library, Egypt, designed by Snohetta.

consumer use patterns. Both input (rainfall trapping) and output (water use) strategies are needed, but more crucial still is the importance of combining energy and water design as a coherent package. This is largely what happens at Hockerton in Nottinghamshire, where a heat pump, which exploits air warmed by the conservatory, heats the communal water supply, providing preheated water to the five dwellings. The system takes advantage of the capacity of large volumes of stored water to stay warm for a long time, resulting in an overall energy saving of 75 per cent.

Similar systems operate in Denmark, where large tanks of water (often collected rainwater for domestic non-potable use) are stored partly underground but roofed in glass to maximise the chances of the sun warming them through what is known as 'passive solar gain'. This preheated water is either distributed by pumps to adjoining houses or taken to small CHP plants. In either case, the efficiency gained from integrating energy and water strategies is considerable.

It is also the design approach behind the Mistral Building, Reading (architects Foster and Partners) which applies a balanced approach to all resources, from energy to water, and materials to drainage. Such ideas have begun to find their way into the many eco-towns which have begun to appear in China and

Fig 97
The Mistral Building, Reading, designed by Foster and Partners.
Source: Foster and Partners

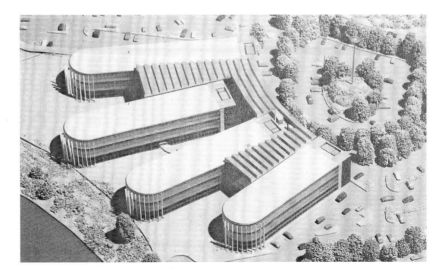

elsewhere. Another good example of integrated energy and water resource use is Alexandria Library in Egypt which adapts traditional approaches for the modern world.

There is one other benefit of addressing water as a design challenge. Recycling water is a more visible medium of resource conservation than energy. It can be tracked, felt, seen and reused more directly than energy. As such in buildings such as schools and universities, water conservation demonstrates sustainable practice in a tangible way, making sustainability visible (unlike aspects of energy conservation) for the decision makers of tomorrow. Buildings that do not confront the water, waste and recycling agenda are not facing one of the overriding design challenges of the 21st century.

NOTES

[1] Source: www.wateraid.org/uk/what_we_ do/statistics/default.asp

[2] Brian Edwards, 'Ecolonia', *Architecture Today*, No 67, April 1996, pp. 10–15.

[3] Brian Edwards, 'Green goes mainstream: Barclaycard headquarters', *Architecture Today*, No 80, July 1997, pp. 20–30.

[4] Mark Standen of BRE is quoted in *The Architects Journal*, 30 October 2008, p. 36.

6 Materials and Waste

Materials used in building construction have a huge environmental impact – in extraction, processing, transport, use and disposal. This impact exists at the global, regional and personal levels, affecting climate and biodiversity on the one hand, and the health of people on the other. Natural resources used in construction (roads and buildings) account for about half of all resource consumption in the world. Architects and engineers cannot claim to be sustainable practitioners without addressing the complex and sometimes contradictory demands of building materials. To help designers and maintain common standards across Europe, the new Essential Requirement 7 'Sustainable use of natural resources' was included in revisions to the EU Construction Products Directive, which came into force in 2009. This requirement is particularly useful in the area of aggregates.

In general, there are four main considerations when selecting building materials or construction products: embodied energy; performance over lifetime of building; appearance; salvage-ability.

No single methodology exists to guide those who specify the wide range of construction materials which make up a typical building. Frequently, the concept

Fig 98
Slate used as a facing material and rain screen for low energy housing in Madrid.

Fig 99
Demolition of concrete buildings provides the opportunity to reuse waste as aggregate in new building and to recycle the steel reinforcement.
Source: George Mills

of 'embodied energy' is employed, i.e. the energy used during the extraction, manufacture and transportation of the material or product. But over the life of a building the embodied energy of the materials represents only around 10 per cent of the total energy consumed by the building in use.

However, the concept of embodied energy does highlight the high energy transport costs of bulky materials (stone, aggregates, brick, concrete products) and the high energy processing costs of some commonly used lightweight materials (steel, aluminium). It also informs choices over the selection of renewable energy products such as PV panels which have particularly high embodied energy coefficients.

Fig 100
Brick offers many benefits for sustainable housing construction, as here at Accordia in Cambridge, UK. The architects were Feilden Clegg Bradley Studios with Alison Brooks and MacCreaner Lavington Architects.
Source: Tim Crocker

Comparison of embodied energy by construction material	
Material	Embodied energy (kWh/tonne)
Concrete	500
Steel	7000
Aluminium	28,000
Copper	18,000
Glass	2000

CHOICE BASED ON EMBODIED ENERGY

Using the concept of embodied energy it is possible to derive three reliable guidelines for selecting green, sustainable construction materials and products:

Fig 101
Eco-house in Australia, clad in aluminium for ease of recycling and buildability. Designed by Lindsay Johnston.

1. **Source heavyweight materials locally**: Stone, aggregates, bricks, etc. should be specified from quarries or manufacturers located near the construction site. This saves on energy use in transportation and reduces the overall environmental impact (disturbance, noise, pollution). Ideally, materials will be made on site (such as sun-baked bricks commonly produced in Africa and the Middle East as part of the construction process) or sourced within a reasonable radius (10 km). Apart from the reduced environmental damage, this approach will revive local building traditions and employ local

Fig 102
Experimental timber and rammed earth
multi-storey housing known as Atypi for
Christinia, Copenhagen, being developed by
School of Architecture, Royal Danish Academy
of Fine Arts.
Source: Christina Capetillo

people, allowing the development to be seen as belonging to the local
community.

2. **Source lightweight materials globally**: Most embodied energy relates to
   transport costs but this is not the case for lighter materials. In the case of
   aluminium, for instance, the bulk of its embodied energy is the result of the
   manufacturing process, with a ratio of about 5:1 in the amount of energy
   consumed per unit weight of aluminium. Embodied energy is also high in

other lightweight materials such as PVC. However, it must be remembered that, once the energy has allowed the manufacture to take place, society has a stock of material resources that can then be used, reused or recycled (see below). This represents a 'capital reserve' trapped in buildings which can be released at the end of the building's life. During their life, lightweight materials also perform a useful energy service which reduces the embodied energy load. For instance, aluminium used in conservatory construction can help trap solar energy, giving a valuable payback, and over time more than cancels out the cost of its embodied energy. Similarly, aluminium used as an external louvre can effectively shade a building, reducing, in the case of an office or school, the cooling load. So, in considering embodied energy it is important to understand the full lifetime energy equation, and to remember that this varies according to building type, orientation and location.

3. **Recycling potential**: Life-cycle assessment (see chapter 3) has highlighted the complex picture of cradle-to-grave environmental impacts. Taking energy as a single issue, the impact of a material depends on initial energy costs (input costs) and the final energy costs (output costs). There is embodied energy at the beginning but also embodied energy at the demolition stage of a building's life. Two actions are needed: first, to ensure that the potential for reuse and

Fig 103
This stainless steel façade with integral ventilation and glazing offers high environmental performance and provides for salvageability. BDP Office, Manchester.

Fig 104
The stone and timber in this school in Tibet, designed by Arup Associates, can be recycled. Notice the bolted fixings.
Source: Arup Associates

recycling influences the material choices made at the beginning by designers; and, second, to ensure that any residual embodied energy is extracted before the material is placed in a landfill site. Residual energy may be extracted via burning, perhaps in a waste incinerator plant, producing electricity, or via composting (where the energy breaks materials down into useful chemicals or by-products). Resources that go into the manufacture of a building material can be retrieved and converted back into a useful product at the end of the building's life. This is true of plasterboard, concrete and, of course, steel. The easiest ways to achieve energy saving in construction materials are to design for reuse (of the whole building or its parts) and to detail for recycling (discussed below).

CHOICE BASED ON FUTURE AVAILABILITY

Energy is a useful measure of sustainability when selecting construction materials, but it is not the only one. There are other impacts to consider, such as air and water pollution (both commonly the result of building material manufacture), damage to the visual, ecological and cultural landscape (of quarrying or felling of forests), and the scarcity of future supplies. The Brundtland definition of sustainable development (see chapter 1) introduced the concept of 'futurity', that is, considering the resource needs of future generations. This immediately brings to mind fossil fuel energy supplies, but it applies equally to metals (copper, lead, zinc), to hardwood timber sources, and to water. The latter is not normally considered a pressing environmental issue but, as discussed in chapter 5, concerns over water supplies and pollution are growing; indeed, one of the main sources of global water pollution is buildings, especially the manufacture of materials and the construction process. Eventually, the global construction industry may wish to develop an embodied water methodology (similar to energy) or at least to recognise the pollution impacts of the manufacturing processes involved in making building materials.

There are long-term future supplies of sand, stone and softwoods.[1] Global scarcity does not exist in these areas, and hence they should be selected in preference to metals, plastics and hardwoods. This will lead to a particular aesthetic and architectural style (a kind of updated vernacular architecture) and, when combined with globally sourced high-tech lightweight materials, the

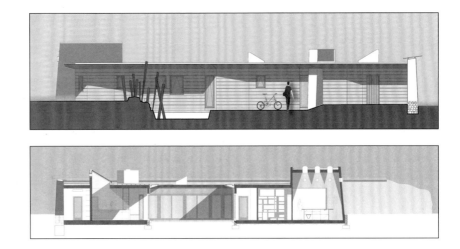

Fig 105
Section through cob wall house near Worcester, UK, designed by Associated Architects.
Source: Associated Architects

Fig 106
Healthy low-tech materials of slate and timber used at the Active House in Denmark, designed by Aart Architects.
Source: VKR Holding

combination has the potential to generate energy-efficient, resource-friendly and responsive buildings. The marriage of local sourcing of commonly available bulky materials and international sourcing of specialised lightweight ones (such as photovoltaic panels or intelligent glazing systems) will be the basis of architecture in the 21st century. High and low tech will co-exist in the same building rather than being hostile neighbours along a street.

DESIGNING FOR WASTE REDUCTION

All forms of construction provide opportunities for waste recycling, reuse or reduction.

Reuse is a term normally employed for a material that is given a new life without substantial remanufacture (e.g. a reused steel beam). Recycling is when a material is reprocessed into a new product of the same material type. Aluminium and copper are both commonly recycled, with over two-thirds of all new copper consisting of recycled old copper. The degree of recycling depends on world commodity prices – aluminium is currently cheap and abundant, providing a disincentive to recycle. Copper, on the other hand, is relatively expensive and there are measurable limits to the world supply of copper ore. So, whereas only 40 per cent of aluminium is currently recycled, 75 per cent of copper is. Irrespective of market forces, architects should select materials on the basis of their recycled content because recycling is less energy demanding than the full process of extraction, processing and manufacture.

Structural steel offers the obvious advantage of reuse, either as new structural members or by recycling old steel at the foundry. However, the protective coatings employed and the method of fixing can be a significant inhibitor to reuse. Aluminium offers similar advantages, although all the metals have high embodied manufacturing energy costs and some use dirtier processes than others. The architect could help the environment by specifying new steel with a high recycled element or requiring steel or aluminium from manufacturing plants that employ 'clean-burn' fuels.

Structural concrete offers an alternative range of potential benefits. Concrete is very long lasting (if correctly specified), and hence concrete buildings lend themselves to recycling either in whole or as a structural frame. Concrete does not normally require a finish, so there are fewer health risks and, being environmentally stable, it offers climatic advantages over some other forms of construction. In addition, concrete can be recycled to form high-quality aggregate, although the costs are relatively high and there are often noise and dust problems. From the point of view of 'industrial ecology' – the ability to use waste from other industrial processes and to recycle itself – concrete offers benefits that the green architect can exploit. In particular, the 300 million tonnes of materials quarried each year in the UK to provide the aggregates and cement for concrete could be reduced if architects specified a percentage of waste (such as glass fibre or fuel ash) in the aggregate. Also, by specifying locally produced concrete products, the embodied energy costs of transport would be greatly reduced. At the Earth Centre in Yorkshire, 2000 tonnes of recycled concrete was used in the convention centre, designed by Feilden Clegg Bradley with Bill Dunster. Also, it should be remembered that, in the UK, all of the reinforcement in concrete is from recycled steel scrap.

Timber construction is often regarded as the best environmental option. However, it has limited application for a wide range of building types where size, height, fire risk and climatic factors reduce timber's overall penetration into the construction market. Where timber is widely used – in housing and similar smaller projects – it provides considerable potential for reuse. Also, being an organic material with

Fig 107
Natural materials left untreated at BRE Kingspan
House, BRE Innovation Park, Watford, UK.

high energy content, after use it can be burned as a fuel or allowed to compost. However, the preservatives and protection required to safely use softwoods (such as pine and spruce) pose health risks to construction workers and the wider environment. Although hardwoods (such as oak and beech) require little or no protection, fixings should be employed to allow for ready dismantling at the end of the building's life. Timber waste forms a large percentage of typical construction skips because of the amount of on-site cutting normally employed.

Brick construction offers endurance and satisfactory appearance over long time-scales. Brick buildings are relatively healthy (no additional finishes) and can be readily recycled at the end of their lives and easily repaired during them. The individual brick can also be reused if the building is dismantled but only if lime mortar (rather than cement) is employed. If the mortar joint is stronger than the brick then the only recycling option is as low-grade aggregate. Although the embodied energy component of bricks is relatively high, their ability to provide structural support, high thermal mass, maintenance free finish and recycling means that whole bricks rarely end up in landfill (although brick waste does).

The embodied energy can be reduced by using unbaked bricks. This is a technique commonly used in the Middle East, Mexico and has a long tradition in China where it was employed for the construction of the Great Wall. Experiments have been undertaken in the UK to test the appropriateness of unfired bricks in the domestic sector in the British climate. The results are encouraging and suggest a growth in application where low carbon footprints, humidity control and healthy conditions are particularly sought.[2] However, the limiting factor appears to be the structural strength of load-bearing walls since the compressive strength of bricks or clay is reduced as moisture levels rise, especially when used in conjunction with lime mortar.

WHICH IS GREENER: STEEL OR CONCRETE?

Architects face a dilemma when choosing a construction material, a fact highlighted by an examination of the use of steel in construction.

Steel is often seen as a poor relation to concrete because of its high embodied energy and poor performance with regard to thermal capacity and fire. However,

Fig 108
Life-cycle impacts of steel construction.
Source: Corus

Fig 108
Life-cycle impacts of steel construction.
Source: Corus

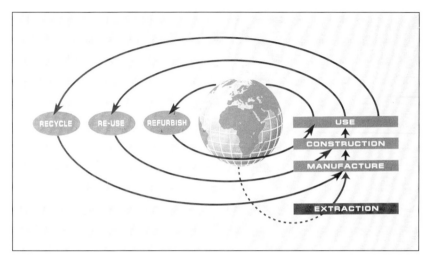

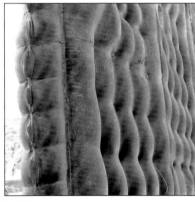

Fig 109
Fabric-formed concrete offers the advantage of mimicry of nature's organic forms and offers potential to reduce the cost of concrete in developing countries. (See detailed view overleaf.)
Source: Anne-Mette Manelius

since steel can be recycled indefinitely, thereby allowing the embodied energy to be traded across generations, and the thermal capacity benefits of concrete are sometimes overrated (except for office buildings), steel may, in fact, be a wise green choice. To be sustainable, the design of steelwork should be such that it can be readily dismantled (i.e. bolted not welded connections) and of uniform length for reuse.

The BRE Green Guide Ecopoint system[3] provides a useful scoring system of different common construction materials. The Ecopoint ratings allow materials and products to be compared; the lower the score the more benign the material. Ecopoint assessment is based mainly on two factors: the energy and CO_2 emissions during manufacture; and the depletion of mineral resources. Hence, concrete with its high energy input in cement production benefits from the almost infinite natural supply of the component materials (limestone, chalk, sand, gravels, water). However, what really matters in architecture are the operational impacts of the material selections over the lifetime of a building in areas such as energy, acoustics, fire risk, flood risk, maintenance, adaptability and appearance. Taking the broad view, concrete offers a wider range of benefits than most other structural materials and, although the manufacture of concrete is responsible for around 2.5 per cent of UK CO_2 emissions, its strength, thermal capacity and sculptural qualities make concrete popular with many green architects.

The embodied energy of steel is many times higher than that of concrete (unreinforced) but only about a quarter of that of aluminium. But embodied energy needs to relate to the weight/strength potential of the material and to its ability for subsequent material reuse. Both steel and aluminium have high energy costs in manufacture but relatively low recycled energy costs. A lot more can be done structurally with a tonne of steel than with a similar weight of concrete, and, as many architects will testify, a great deal more tectonic construction can be achieved as well.

It is said that most of the steel needed for the future already exists in the form of existing buildings and other structures. New steel manufacture is needed merely to top up the supply we already have. So embodied energy is not as critical as many claim, as long as the design provides the facility for reuse (of the member) or recycling (of the material). In fact, nearly 50 per cent of all new steel today consists of recycled material, as does around 70 per cent of aluminium.

Fig 110
Notice the simple stitching of the fabric form work, which allows for reuse.
Source: Anne-Mette Manelius

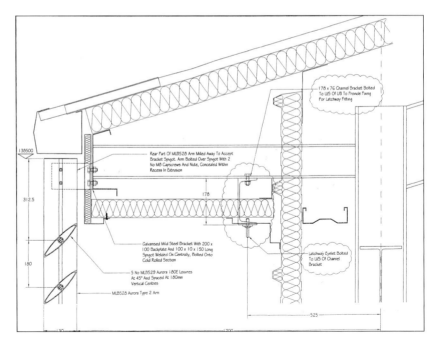

Fig 111
Example of steel bolted construction at IPI Building, University of Bradford, designed by Rance, Booth and Smith.
Source: Rance, Booth and Smith

Running the aluminium or steel manufacturing process through a full life-cycle assessment generates some interesting outcomes. First, embodied energy is relatively insignificant as a proportion of total energy used in a building. The amount of energy needed to produce a building (manufacture, transport and erect) is only a fraction of that consumed by the building in heating, lighting and ventilation during its life. Typically, embodied and in-use energy have a ratio of about 1:10 in buildings (unlike washing machines, where the ratio is 1:2).

Also, some manufacturing plants use hydro or geothermal power, thereby adding further to the complexity. The life-cycle assessment also highlights the transport energy costs, which are largely related to weight. Steel, being lighter than concrete, requires much less transport energy, and the same is true for aluminium. So an inverse equation appears: the higher the embodied energy, the lighter the material and the lower the transport costs. Other materials like concrete may have low embodied energy (in manufacture) but high energy transport costs. So weighty materials (such as concrete, bricks, etc.) should be locally sourced. But even here there are complexities; heavy materials are often carried by ship (over long distances) and rail (over shorter ones) and lightweight materials carried by plane. Most of the UK cement plants are served by rail resulting in 60 per cent transport energy saving over road.

There are other impacts, too. Steel consumes far less water than concrete and its manufacture is less of a pollutant in water systems. At most steel manufacturing plants, water is held in a closed system and is used and reused in a cycle; while the manufacture of concrete requires extraction and aggregate washing, which affects both water quality and quantity.

Faced with such contradictions, architects can almost be forgiven for choosing the material mainly on aesthetic grounds. As mentioned earlier, the complexity of sustainability and the complexity of architecture can be difficult to reconcile.

A typical steel building weighs about half that of a concrete one. Weight is a useful rough measure to assess general environmental impact. Pollution, dust, nuisance and noise are generally weight related – the heavier the building, the greater the environmental damage. The trick with environmental assessment is to reduce pollution, not transfer it, and to see environmental impacts as total systems with feedback loops. The three stages in the life of a material or building – manufacture, use and disposal – all have their impact interactions.

Recently, manufacturers have developed a system of cheap, flexible, low-maintenance steel-framed housing for use in developed and developing countries. Steel offers advantages over brick, timber or concrete homes on cost, speed of construction and recycling potential. Steel is increasingly employed as an ecologically sound high-tech material capable of generating sophisticated climateresponsive buildings.

Some of the best recent buildings from an ecological point of view are mongrels not thoroughbreds – they use steel and concrete or steel and bricks. The choice of materials is made on the basis of what is 'appropriate' rather than 'consistent'. At Doxford, near Sunderland, Auketts with Studio E Architects have designed three-storey modern business units with load-bearing brick perimeter walls (for thermal performance and appearance), a steel frame (for flexibility and speed of construction), pre-cast concrete floor/ceiling panels (for thermal cooling capacity) and photovoltaic facades (for local electricity generation). The result is material diversity with enough energy complexity to ensure sustainability.

Fig 112
Mixed material façade at City Square, St Gallen, Switzerland, which offers environmental and energy flexibility.

WASTE

Waste from construction accounts for about a third of all waste going to landfill sites in the UK. Although trends suggest a reduction in this percentage as a result of increasing levels of recycling, construction and demolition waste is one of the areas of priority identified in the government's sustainable construction initiative and is included as an issue to be addressed under the Code for Sustainable Homes (see chapter 3).

Architects can contribute to waste reduction in four broad ways:

- Design out waste: For example, by specifying materials that do not need to be cut on site. The use of standard components and modular construction reduces the need for modification and, hence, waste. However, the need to address packaging becomes more important as prefabrication increases. Architects should seek to specify the waste chain as well as the production chain and insist that the building site has skips for different types of waste. The legislation on waste is increasing rapidly and the recent introduction of site waste management plans (SWMPs) for UK projects over £300,000 means that on-site separation of waste streams will enhance the potential for reuse or recycling. Smaller projects may not, as yet, be covered by the requirement for SWMPs, but the approach should be adopted by any contractor concerned about sustainability.
- Specify reused, recycled or reclaimed materials. Designing using reused components, structural members and materials can reduce costs but may add to the complexity of site operations. Questions need also to be asked about the performance and reliability of recycled construction products. However, it is increasingly common for materials such as bricks to be recycled for use in new construction, and old concrete is frequently broken down to form new construction aggregate. Architects could help to expand the market for recycling by specifying reused or reclaimed materials.
- Design buildings to be easily dismantled at the end of their life. This requires attention to the type of fixings employed and the finish given to materials. By bolting rather than welding steel junctions, by screwing rather than nailing timber and by using lime rather than cement mortar, a whole range of recycling possibilities is opened up with little extra design thought.

- Design buildings that are inherently flexible and capable of reuse at the end of their functional life. Since the structural life of a building is usually longer than its economic life (100 years as against 50), architects should design for functional change. Reusing the whole building obviously saves on waste and helps maintain visual, social or cultural continuity. However, reuse of the whole structure requires attention to the quality of construction and the robustness of materials over long periods of time. In the UK, the pressure to build cheaply under government initiatives such as the Public/Private Finance Initiative can militate against long-term benefits. Waste is too rarely part of the financial equation which dictates the design of buildings.

Waste disposal is both an environmental problem and a health issue. Waste exhausts the availability of new resources, it contributes to global warming via the release of methane, and it is a source of pollution of the air, water and soil. Local pollution around waste disposal sites can have adverse impacts on the health of nearby residents, on agricultural productivity and on local biodiversity. Given that half of all waste is the result of the activities of the construction industry, the professionals have an ethical responsibility to address the issue.

Over the next generation, waste will become as important as energy to construction professionals. Under the Waste and Emissions Trading Act 2003, the UK government made a commitment to reduce levels of landfill in 2020 to 35 per cent of that in 1995. This demanding target, required to meet the standards set by the EC Landfill Directive, puts pressure on all member states to address the problem of waste generation and disposal.

Faced with rising sea levels, the debate has shifted recently from landfill to land-raising. As the UK begins to run out of holes in the ground in which to dispose of waste, some are contemplating using urban waste to create either whole new islands in flood prone areas or to raise the general ground level in anticipation of future flooding. It is an idea that stemmed from action following the flooding of the Elbe river valley in northern Germany in 2007. By raising ground levels by a metre, society may be able to buy itself out of the predicament it will face after the next one-hundred years of global warming. Waste in the future (although there will have to be adequate safeguards) may become an asset in the battle against the encroaching sea.

The four Rs – reduce, reuse, recycle and recover

If the current world population of 6 billion people increases to 10 billion by 2050 as predicted, the human race will have four times the environmental impact that it has today. This frightening prospect is based on the assumption that the World Trade Organisation's expectation of 2 per cent global economic growth per year will be realised in spite of resource shortages or sink limits (the ability of natural systems to absorb pollution). The world's ecosystems are already under great stress, and society needs to adopt a strategy which brings improvement in living conditions without global disaster. Quality of life can be maintained, but only through the application of the four Rs – reduce, reuse, recycle and recover – which are embodied to a large degree in site waste management plans.

Environmentalists have long advocated the three Rs, but the fourth – recover – was added more recently because so much of the human habitat needs to be repaired and recovered from abuse or contamination. This is especially true of cities, which have become the global focus of pollution and waste. Because the construction industry is mainly concentrated in urban areas, it carries a particular responsibility to address the agenda of brownfield sites.

Brought together as a package, the four Rs help to focus on the interconnectedness of the options available. Good ecological design consists not in considering issues in isolation but in combining them into a systemic whole. Typically, an architect will have to employ elements of each R in a brownfield project and will need to balance the Rs according to cost, programme and time constraints. However, by bringing each part together, the building will enjoy the consequent environmental benefits. A mixed use of environmental measures is infinitely preferable to the chasing of single green goals.

Reduce
Society has to reduce the demands made on all non-renewable resources – fossil fuels, water, mineral ores, agricultural land and geological deposits. A reduction in consumption means that supplies will be available for future generations. It also provides extra time to develop alternative supplies. For example, by conserving energy, we reduce the demand made on the finite reservoir of fossil fuels (oil, gas, coal) and we give ourselves more time to develop renewable sources of energy.

Fig 113
Reusing whole buildings offers many
environmental benefits.

Fig 114
New building for the Freitag shop in Zurich
made from recycled steel containers.

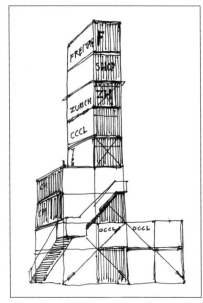

Society needs a culture of reduction, not ever-growing consumption. The consumer-led economy may benefit share prices and create global employment but it strips the environment of its resource capital. As we have already seen, there is at present a conflict in the world economic system between economic capital and natural capital. Architects and engineers need to strive towards creating a better balance in buildings between resource use and performance. 'Less is more', the famous aphorism coined by German Modernist architect Mies van der Rohe should refer to reduced material and energy use, and more comfort and value. A strategy of reduction, supported by stricter building regulations for existing and new buildings, is a necessary condition of global ecological well-being.

Reuse

Once a building or city is created it becomes a capital asset. Within its bricks and concrete lie resources and human investment which should be reused over generations and across changing building use priorities. This means that the buildings should be robust in form and construction, should be socially valued (and hence desirable objects to reuse), and should be well located. Reuse of the whole or recycling of parts is preferable to total demolition. After all 40 per cent of the cost (financial and environmental) of the building resides in its primary structure. Where the whole building cannot be reused, the elements of construction from which it is made should be designed so that they are capable of reuse.

An interesting example is the refurbishment of a 1920s warehouse in London to become offices for the architectural practice of John Thompson and Partners. A number of actions were taken to improve energy efficiency, to exploit renewable energy sources, provide better cross ventilation, trap rainwater for toilet use, add a green roof to improve urban biodiversity – all achieved using the existing structure and floors of the old warehouse. PV panels are used to shade the top floor windows, creating power for the air-conditioning. The aim is to practise what these architects preach and to demonstrate the environmental potential locked in existing structures.[4]

Reuse, as opposed to recycling, requires the architect or designer to address the design task differently. Conventionally, the architect forms a building plan to suit the precise needs of a brief. The building matches the brief in the specifics of

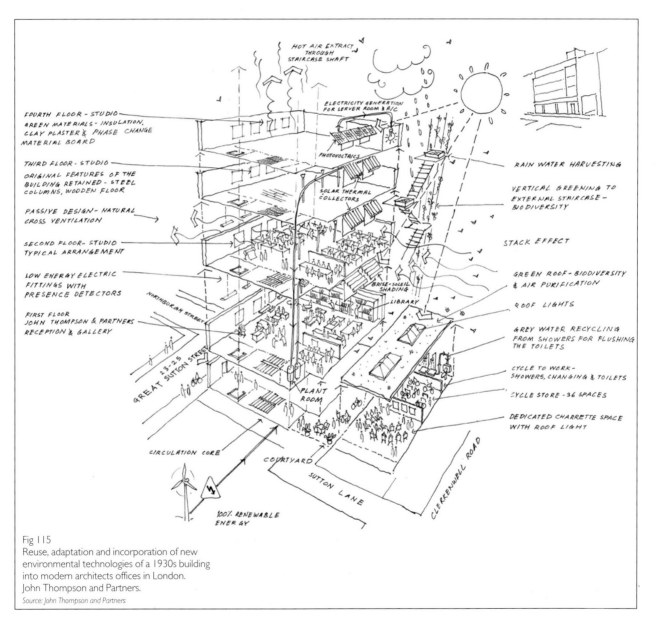

HOT AIR EXTRACT
THROUGH
STAIRCASE SHAFT

ELECTRICITY GENERATION
FOR SERVER ROOM & A/C

FOURTH FLOOR - STUDIO
GREEN MATERIALS - INSULATION,
CLAY PLASTER & PHASE CHANGE
MATERIAL BOARD

PHOTOVOLTAICS

RAIN WATER HARVESTING

THIRD FLOOR - STUDIO
ORIGINAL FEATURES OF THE
BUILDING RETAINED - STEEL
COLUMNS, WOODEN FLOOR

SOLAR THERMAL
COLLECTORS

VERTICAL GREENING TO
EXTERNAL STAIRCASE -
BIODIVERSITY

PASSIVE DESIGN - NATURAL
CROSS VENTILATION

STACK EFFECT

SECOND FLOOR - STUDIO
TYPICAL ARRANGEMENT

GREEN ROOF - BIODIVERSITY
& AIR PURIFICATION

LOW ENERGY ELECTRIC
FITTINGS WITH
PRESENCE DETECTORS

BRISE-SOLEIL
SHADING

LIBRARY

ROOF LIGHTS

GREY WATER RECYCLING
FROM SHOWERS FOR FLUSHING
THE TOILETS

FIRST FLOOR
JOHN THOMPSON & PARTNERS
RECEPTION & GALLERY

NORTHBURGH STREET

CYCLE TO WORK -
SHOWERS, CHANGING & TOILETS

CYCLE STORE - 36 SPACES

GREAT 23-25 SUTTON STREET

DEDICATED CHARRETTE SPACE
WITH ROOF LIGHT

PLANT
ROOM

CIRCULATION CORE

COURTYARD

SUTTON LANE

CLERKENWELL ROAD

100% RENEWABLE
ENERGY

Fig 115
Reuse, adaptation and incorporation of new
environmental technologies of a 1930s building
into modern architects offices in London.
John Thompson and Partners.
Source: John Thompson and Partners

layout and construction. However, in a period of rapid social and technological change, such closely tailored buildings quickly become redundant – either the social or economic expectations on which they were based evaporate or new technology makes them obsolete. Obsolete buildings are normally demolished, adding to future resource stress, disturbance, pollution and waste. The better path is to reuse the building, but it must have been built in a certain way for this to happen. A building is more likely to be reused if:

- it makes good use of natural light and ventilation
- is well served by infrastructure of various kinds (public transport, utilities, etc.)
- does not contain toxic materials
- is well constructed, preferably using 'natural' materials
- has attractive spaces and character
- is culturally valued
- has access to renewable energy resources (solar, wind).

Clearly, some buildings perform better than others, but the task for the designer is to create a structure with the inherent characteristics that make it suitable for reuse. Architects need to realise that their drawing-board decisions often close options for subsequent alternative uses. What is needed is a rebalancing of the form/function contract to allow for possible future functions to shape the initial form. Considering their impact on resources, buildings should be primarily robust intergenerational assets rather than objects with an inflexible singularity of function. This means greater understanding of sustainability at all levels and the benefits of 'loose-fit' functional solutions.

Reuse also entails the rescuing of elements of construction (steel beams, timber, bricks, etc.) for use in other buildings. Not many new buildings are designed or constructed to encourage reuse. Steel members are welded (rather than bolted) and given toxic finishes (oil paints, powder-coated epoxy resins). Bricks, too, are used with cement mortars that are often stronger than the bricks themselves, thus preventing their reuse. The use of a weaker mortar (one containing lime) and the avoidance of plaster finishes greatly enhance the chances of reuse. Since the embodied energy of a brick would drive a car five miles, the consequences are enormous for the millions of bricks created (and wasted) every year. A reused brick saves on: the excavation of clay; the baking of bricks (consuming fossil fuels and causing air pollution); and landfill waste at end of life.

Fig 116
Squatter housing in Tokyo using salvaged
materials and plastic sheeting.

So the reuse philosophy requires a change in how we design our buildings and a corresponding change in how we construct them. Architects could create a major demand for reused components simply by specifying them. This would not only generate a market for reused components but also lead to buildings of greater aesthetic richness and social value.

Some architects have sought to create new buildings out of waste. Their approach is not just to employ construction waste but to search out potential materials from a wider palette of consumer or industrial waste. A typical advocate of this approach is the American architect Michael Reynolds who uses waste drink cans, beer bottles and car tyres in his new buildings such as the Earthship at Taos, New Mexico. Waste materials are recovered, cleaned and recycled as structural or decorative elements where they are combined with organic materials such as mud or clay to form stable walls. By using large areas of glass the thermal capacity of the unusual mixture of car tyres, cans and clay is exploited in the desert context. Such architecture points less towards solutions for the developed world (although it is commendable for the inventive use of waste) than to possibilities in Africa and South America.

Recycle
Recycling is the next step. It involves rescuing the useful parts of a material by extraction and remanufacture. In the case of aluminium, it entails melting

Fig 117
The Earthship community in Arizona, designed
by Michael Reynolds, uses construction
based largely upon waste. Walls are built of:
(a) recycled bottles; or (b) tyres and rammed
earth. The resulting house: (c) and village;
(d) challenges normal measures of architectural
excellence.
Source: Sam Hughes

aluminium scrap and reforming the material into further useful products
(aluminium structural members, clips, etc.). Unlike reuse, recycling requires further
energy in the reforging process but is preferable to the total loss of the material.

Certain construction materials, especially those with high embodied energy, are
commonly recycled: steel, aluminium, lead, copper.

Recycling often involves the extraction of energy from a material and the
separation of other parts for subsequent reuse. Old timber can be incinerated,
perhaps in waste-based power stations, and plasterboard can be reformed. It is
important to consider the recycling potential, the environmental impacts at each
stage, and the full life-cycle costing characteristics of the options of reuse and
recycling.

Recover

Half of the global human population lives in cities, most in conurbations of over
a million. Urban areas are a major source of air pollution and, as a consequence,
pose an increasing risk to human health. In the EU, for example, poor air quality
in cities is now the second major cause of death because it leads to heart attacks,
cancer and bronchitis. Much of this air pollution originates in buildings or as a
consequence of the need to travel to buildings. Any strategy for recovering cities
needs to encompass the contribution building design can make to healthier living.
There are obvious areas that urban design can address, such as: the avoidance of
deep-planned offices, with their high energy loads and pollution costs; the lack
of pedestrian and cycle-friendly spaces; and the poor public transport provision.
Urban air quality is also improved by planting trees, which act as air cleansers,
climate modifiers and shading devices.

Building, landscape and urban design can, in unison, help to recover cities from pollution, chaos and alienation. The city is now home for most people: we spend 80 per cent of our time inside buildings and the remainder mainly in polluted urban areas. The human habitat is now predominately urban, and architects have a key role to play in creating civilised, clean and productive cities. Many modern polluted urban centres (Hong Kong, Tokyo, London) are the result of a lack of regulation and poor design. If the 20th century saw the fashioning of cities as we know them, the 21st will witness unprecedented action to reclaim them from pollution and chaos.

The second major arena for recovery is contaminated land, the so-called brownfield sites. Air pollution is fairly readily dissipated (to become someone else's problem in the form of acid rain or climate change) but land pollution remains static and persists, blighting large areas. It is estimated that 20 per cent of land in most Western cities lies vacant and underused, often because of contamination. Old industrial cities (Detroit, Glasgow, Turin) have extensive tracts of contaminated land. It often forms a ring around the commercial centre (e.g. Manchester) or wedges, which run from the centre to the outskirts along former industrial corridors (e.g. Sheffield). Since the latter are often based on river courses, there are valleys of pollution affecting water, land and air quality.

Action by all agencies (governmental, professional and private) is needed to tackle urban land contamination. In Western cities such areas stand idle and neglected; in Eastern and Southern cities they are often colonised by squatters, who establish townships on the land nobody else will use. Like air pollution, contaminated land is a threat to human health as well as being ecologically degrading. The degree of pollution depends on the chemicals or agents present. There is often arsenic where chemical plants were located, radiation on sites of former factories or hospitals, heavy metals (cadmium, lead, mercury) at steel or large-scale manufacturing plants, and asbestos at former power stations. As industry has moved out of cities it has often left behind sites suffering from a range of unknown and often toxic forms of pollution.

To enable this land to be put into productive use again, it needs to be retrieved from its polluted state. Expertise is required to survey and analyse this land, to deal with the contamination, and to design buildings that reduce exposure to any surviving sources of pollution. Architects are frequently involved in advising on site selection and subsequently in design, and so need to become familiar with the problems associated with contaminated land.

Many brownfield sites contain elements of contamination (land, water or air). If the land is to be recovered, different design strategies are needed depending on the source or type of contamination. The main methods employed fall into four categories:

- removal of toxic material, often soil soaked in chemicals
- capping and sealing the source of pollution including the contaminated soil
- cleansing the land using biological methods
- cleansing the land using chemical methods.

There are advantages and disadvantages with each, and often all four strategies are used on the same site. Removal of toxic material simply takes the pollution to somebody else's backyard (either a private or a local authority waste site). Either way, it sweeps the problem under the carpet rather than solving it. The effectiveness of capping is dependent on proper seals and, given the life of buildings (50–100 years), architects need to feel confident that underground bunkers or tanks are resistant to corrosion or fracture. Biological methods are the most benign and are based on toxin-neutralising plants (alder, willow, poplar, reed) which either naturally break down pollution or absorb it. The planting can then be cut down and the pollution transported to locations where it can be effectively treated by combustion or composting. The method is ecologically safe but requires time. Chemical treatment involves the use of synthetic agents that break down the pollution source or make it more accessible. It can then be treated by other means (such as incineration) or removed. Cost and time are key factors in remedial land treatment but it is vital that environmental factors such as spillage or run-off are not ignored.

NOTES

[1]   Eoin O'Cofaigh and Owen Lewis, 'The Principles and Practice of Sustainable Architectural Design', in *European Directory of Sustainable and Energy-efficient Building*, James & James, 1999, p. 61.

[2]   A. Arasteh, 'The heat is off', *Brick Bulletin*, Spring 2009, pp. 22–3.

[3]   See www.bre/greenguide.com

[4]   *The Architects Journal*, 27 November 2008, pp. 48–9.

Section D
Design for sustainability

Essay – Nature as a Guide to Building Design

WHAT IS DESIGN IN A GREEN AGE?

Design is the practice of visualising, shaping and then making the human environment. It involves modifying nature, yet working within nature's rules; it is concerned with giving meaning to our lives, and generating through space, light, shelter and artefacts a certain pleasure in living. Design goes beyond creating habitats for mere existence – it involves generating happiness.

We spend at least 80 per cent of our lives in buildings, and most of the remainder being out and about in cities. Seventy-five per cent of the European population is now urban, and the year 2000 marked not only the birth of the six billionth human, but also the first time the global human population was predominantly urban rather than rural.

With the growth of city living comes a distancing from the land. We have lost sight of seasonal cycles, of the struggle for food or warmth, and instead we have become interested in culture, sport and media. Architecture under the influence of 'modernism', broke free of its old bonds to locally sourced materials, vernacular traditions, and the union between buildings and the land. Modern mega-cities owe little allegiance to the 'carrying capacity' of the landscape in which they are sited; that is, they draw on food, water, resources and human energy from all corners of the globe believing such resources are infinite.

Successful cities measure their wealth and enterprise against international yardsticks, not local ones. As a consequence, the ecological footprint of London now exceeds the productive rural capacity of all of England. Cities and buildings are increasingly disconnected from the landscape in all but economic terms. Modernism, with its bedrock of function, material and fossil fuel exploitation and new technologies, has been exposed as demanding too much of planet earth.

Globally, 'nature' is used as the guiding light of sustainability in quite distinct ways. Different designers have learnt to employ nature's order in their own fashion, from Edward Cullinan and Thomas Herzog's timber forest buildings, to Ken Yeang's adoption of termite structure principles of natural ventilation in office buildings for hot climates. Nature, however, is not without problems as a design framework: it lacks a technological base and its outputs are rarely cross-species benign. However, by blending technology *and* ecology it is possible to design a fresh generation of buildings that reduces environmental impact in numerous ways. Nature not only recycles, its systems move upwards towards even greater complexity and beauty. As such, nature seems to have an in-built motor of diversity, shunning repetition, cloning and the mindless search for perfect duplication. In this, natural ecology offers a model for designers to employ as they strive to apply prefabrication.

Sustainable architecture: creative tensions		
Sustainable development	*Versus*	**Sustainability**
Energy conservation		Personal health
Global		Local
Holistic		Analytical
Systemic		Linear
'Them'		'Us'
Human time		Ecological time
Incremental change		Radical change
Ecological design		Low-energy design
Natural capital		Cultural capital

Learning from nature entails using ecological principles in quite distinct ways. Nature, however, is not neutral – it has its own laws and methods of working. Darwin helped to discover the keys to the evolution of species and their interdependence within habitats. Others have unravelled the genetic code to life itself. The human race is master of this knowledge but too rarely brings the fundamental laws of nature to bear upon architectural design. The linear thinking of prefabrication and factory perfection is preferred to organic design. Our buildings are increasingly cloned one on another and only 2 per cent of Europe's major rivers are in a natural, non-canalised state. As for the world's mega-cities, these are dying just like the coral reefs – pollution, global warming and waste ultimately destroy all that which is delicate and beautiful. An analogy can be thus be drawn between buildings (species) and cities (habitats).

Nature can be a useful guide to building design in four quite distinctive ways[1]:

- learning from nature
- using nature's models to inform

- making nature explicit
- using nature for ecological accounting.

Learning from nature

'Learning from nature' was Ian McHarg's clarion call in his remarkable book of 1969, *Design with Nature*.[2] Nature employs patterns and orders that can be used in the design of buildings, a point noted much earlier by the eco-geographer Patrick Geddes.

Since the Rio Earth Summit of 1992, ecological concerns have begun to impact on systems rather than resources. Although the agreements at Rio sought to protect endangered habitats, species and the genetic inheritance of all living things (genetic diversity within species), ecological design has taken on a broader remit, and now attempts to put these systems into the linear, functional equations normally employed by architects.

The logical progression of this concept thus takes us to life-cycle assessment (LCA), which treats the building as if it had the characteristics of natural systems, with inputs, outputs and loops, and has at its heart the ecological methodology of cradle-to-grave measurement. LCA has been expanded since the second UK edition of this book (2005), leading to the 'cradle-to-cradle' concept, where the emphasis is on reuse and recycling. Here, the assumption propagated by the American architect William McDonough and German chemist Michael Braungart is that there is no grave in nature, only rebirth. By designing so that every part can be reused and every process breaks down naturally to produce nutrients to support future life, there is no waste, only recycling. The cradle-to-cradle idea is based upon two cycles – biological and technical. People know how the biological system works but have less knowledge of the technical cycles and opportunity for reuse in building design.

Learning from nature encourages an appreciation of the interaction between resource – energy, water and materials going in; and waste, pollution and contamination coming out. In effect, we have an architectural ecosystem with its own potential recycling path and waste chain.

Professional interpretations of nature as design guide[3]	
Lord Foster	'Less is more in ecological terms …'
Lord Rogers	'Nature provides inspiration, information and analogy …'
Ken Yeang	'Our built systems should be mimetic ecosystems …'
Thomas Herzog	'Lessons from nature are efficiency, performance, adaptability, variety and beauty.'
Jan Kaplicky (Future Systems)	'Nature can be used as a model at many different levels – nature's structures have a lightness not found in man-made constructions.'

Using nature's models to inform

Ecological design highlights the paucity of traditional human design thinking. As a rule, nature creates the maximum of richness and complexity with the minimum of resources and the maximum of recycling; whereas humankind creates the minimum of richness and complexity with the maximum of resources and the minimum of recycling. As a consequence, mature systems in nature (rainforests, coral reefs) are beautiful and life enhancing (for all species). Humankind's mature systems (cities) are rarely beautiful or life enhancing. Frequently, they are polluted, alienating and divisive. Ecology provides a useful framework to bring mankind and nature closer together. After all, in nature the ecological cycles seek to purify water, air and soil; they generate richness and diversity; they support health and biological wealth creation; and they grow natural capital.[4] There are lessons here for mankind as it grapples with the challenge of sustainable development.

Ecological structures are thoroughly tested, often in hostile environments. The shapes, compositions, configurations and materials used in nature are enduring and sustainable. Foster's gherkin-shaped Swiss Re tower in London is an obvious example of bio-mimicry. His debating hall for the GLA, which resembles a section through a human lung, is another. In both cases, nature's tried and tested models are adapted to provide a responsive, breathing architecture. Lord Rogers' references to the chameleon as a model for a potential building that can change its 'skin' according to weather and light is another. Others, from Future Systems to Santiago Calatrava, draw upon a repertoire of forms found in nature, and the effect is to produce elegant rather than ugly design.

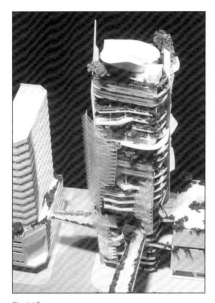

Fig 118
Ken Yeang has set an example of using new sustainable technologies to reinvigorate skyscraper design.
Source: Ken Yeang

Making nature explicit

Architectural design brings nature into the equation – either inside or out, or directly – in the construction materials employed. Nature is a source of tactile, visual and aural pleasure. Welcomed into buildings, nature serves both a practical purpose (to cleanse the air) and a spiritual one (to uplift the spirit and reduce stress). The growth in atria within buildings has been accompanied by a corresponding increase in the practice of bringing nature indoors. Like the Victorian palm house, nature is now a commodity in commercial premises and almost a pet in the home. This has led some to speculate that our buildings are joined to us as another species – a kind of living entity which shares our life as a dynamic organism. Nature gives buildings their 'anima' and, hence, in Jungian terms, they are transcended from inanimate to living things.

On the other hand, there are internal conflicts between low-energy design, ecology and environmental design. The materials employed for energy efficiency, such as glass fibre, polystyrene and foaming agents used in insulation, have a considerable environmental impact. The use of hardwood, often employed as a window product in low-energy design, has ecological consequences. There are also potential conflicts between quarrying (to provide local materials) and ecology. But not all impacts are negative. The extraction of gravel and clay can provide useful wetland habitats to compensate for those lost during 19th-century land drainage. Even quarries can create nesting sites for birds of prey and undisturbed cliff faces provided sites for endangered flora. The important point is to balance the agendas of energy, ecology and environment, rather than to pursue one aspect at the expense of the others. This is the path to a richer, more environmentally responsive, humane architecture than the former obsessive pursuit of energy efficiency.

Fig 119 *(right)*
Light entering the Welsh Assembly Building in Cardiff through an oak chamber, designed by Richard Rogers Partnership.
Source: Torben Dahl

Fig 120 *(far right)*
Project ZED: low-energy office in Toulouse, designed by Future Systems.
Source: Future Systems

Using nature for ecological accounting

All environmental assessment systems have an ecological basis although, because of the pressure of global warming, energy is normally the dominant theme. BREEAM in the UK, Quantum-auditing in The Netherlands, and LEED in the USA employ an auditing system which treats the building as a habitat. Each subject, be it water, materials or energy, is a resource; and the value of that resource can be weighted according to scarcity or damaging impact. The idea of nature-based accounting leads to the identification of 'indicators' that relieve designers of the task of assessing everything. These indicators are guides to good practice – they cast light on the health of the building and as a consequence on the wider environment.

Nature's language	Architects/organisation	Example
Learning from nature	Feilden Clegg Bradley ECD Thomas Herzog Lucien Kroll	BRE Offices, Watford Slimbridge Visitor Centre German Pavilion, Hanover Expo Ecolonia, Aalphen, Holland
Using nature's models to inform design	Norman Foster Future Systems Santiago Calatrava Ken Yeang Chetwood Associates	Swiss Re Building, London Media Centre, Lord's Cricket Ground, London Bilbao Airport Shanghai Armoury Tower, Pudong Sainsburys, Greenwich
Using nature as a tool	Richard Rogers Nicholas Grimshaw Michael Hopkins Ted Cullinan	Madrid Airport Eden Centre Jubilee Campus, Nottingham Hooke Park, Dorset
Using nature for ecological accounting	Novem (The Netherlands) BRE (UK) Kyoto Protocol Green Building Council	Eco-auditing system BREEAM, EcoHomes Carbon trading LEED

NOTES

[1] Adapted from Brian Edwards, 'Design Challenge of Sustainability', *Green Architecture*, AD Monograph, Wiley-Academy, London, 2001, pp. 22–5.

[2] Ian L. McHand, *Design with Nature*, Natural History Press, 1969.

[3] Based on interviews conducted with the author and published in *Green Architecture*, Wiley-Academy, 2001, Vol. 71, No. 4.

[4] William McDonough and Michael Braungart, *Cradle to cradle: Remaking the way we make things*, North Point Press, 2002.

7 Design for a Changing Climate

Buildings designed and engineered today will still be standing when climate change bites. By 2050, it is estimated that global temperatures could have risen by 2°C and by 2100 by perhaps as much as 4°C or even 5°C. Once triggered, the rise is exponential. An increase in global temperatures would change the familiar weather patterns of the UK, leading to more frequent and more violent storms and heavy subtropical rainfall. This in turn will result in pressure on drainage systems, on the building fabric itself, on land settlement patterns and on transportation.

Apart from avoiding further building on flood plains, there are three principles to follow in designing buildings for climate change:

- the building shell, orientation and footprint is fundamental to long-term survival, adaptability and energy efficiency
- build to a higher initial standard (better insulation, higher quality materials)
- provide the means to upgrade building systems, especially in the areas of cooling and in the provision of renewable energy.

Although at present buildings in the UK are not regularly mechanically cooled (except for shops and offices), in future it is likely that there will be pressure, especially in the domestic sector, to cool buildings in the summer. Good design (for example, exploiting thermal capacity, good orientation planning) is essential to avoid the use of clip-on air-conditioning units that are commonplace in hotter climates. Such units are particularly expensive in electrical energy and, being short-lived and rarely recycled, pose further problems of resource consumption and waste disposal.

Buildings that are adaptable are likely to survive. The concept of 'long life, loose fit, low energy' design coined in 1970 by the RIBA president Alex Gordon, remains the mantra for today. Charles Darwin noted that it was not the most intelligent nor the strongest species that survived but those which were most adaptable to a changing world – buildings need to be capable of adaptation.

However, in architecture, adaptability depends upon the demands of different parts of the building ecosystem, and different buildings adapt in different ways and over different time scales and under different pressures. Generally, each upgrading of the building over its 100-year life span provides an opportunity to improve the environmental performance. Typically, refurbishment and improvement occurs at fairly regular intervals and each phase provides the chance to change the energy or ecological profile of the building, including the provision of new energy technologies.

Upgrading	Timeframe	Typical measures	Energy or ecological opportunity
Internal finishes	5–10 years	New surfaces	Improve daylight penetration and reduce indoor air pollution
Services	10–20 years	New heating or ventilation system	Install renewable energy and upgrade insulation
External cladding	20–30 years	Façade remodelling	Install solar and PV panels. Improve insulation
Re-roofing	30–50 years	Re-tiling and felting	Add green living roof and exploit wind energy
Structural remodelling	50 plus years	Upgrade steel or concrete frame	Improve thermal mass
Major extensions	30–75 years	New wing and partial demolition	Rebalance energy demands using solar, wind or geothermal design

GREEN DESIGN – THE 21ST-CENTURY ARCHITECTURAL PARADIGM

Benefits of environmentalism to the construction industry
☐ Cost savings in long run
☐ Ensures legislative compliance today and anticipates future legislation
☐ Reduces environmental risk to consumers
☐ Improves relations with regulators
☐ Improves public image of building
☐ Increases market opportunities for designers
☐ Enhances employee productivity for occupiers of green buildings

In many ways the current economic difficulties, which have led to wholesale redundancies and lack of opportunity for design graduates, are a symptom of society's imbalance. Over the past decade the lack of equilibrium between economic growth and environmental or social safeguards has found expression in recession. High levels of consumerism coupled with inflated property values have conspired to topple the balance advocated by Brundtland (see Essay – A short history of sustainable development) in the triple bottom line of sustainable development – economic, environmental and social sustainability. Now we have to rebuild the economic order around less waste, less energy use and less ignorance.

Politicians have also shifted over the past decade, from a position of narrowly focussed concern for global warming with its associated international agreements

Fig 121
Supermarket which provides natural light.
Sainsbury's Supermarket, designed by
Chetwood Architects.
Source: Chetwood Architects

(Rio, Kyoto, Johannesburg) to a wider concern for the state of cities, the global environment, resource shortages and ecological health. This shift is central to the notion of sustainable development, and it is intellectually more interesting, professionally more challenging and, in design terms, more exacting than any other agenda. Thus sustainable development has emerged as the new cutting edge in science, the basis for innovative technologies and design approaches, the fresh paradigm for social equity, and the lens through which businesses increasingly plot their future. However, what is often ignored in architectural circles is the way 'sustainable development' as a concept bridges the two central agendas of modernism – technological innovation and social provision.

It is time to take stock of where green architecture is going. Early eco-designers emphasised the energy dimension of sustainability. It remains a primary concern due to the accelerating levels of global carbon dioxide emissions. But does low-energy design on its own produce great architecture? There is little evidence to link high aesthetics to energy conservation – in fact the contrary is often the case. It is only when the full picture of ecological design is addressed that a rich, complex and beautiful architecture emerges.[1]

The work of the offices of Grimshaw and Feilden Clegg Bradley in the UK, Piano's in Italy and Ken Yeang's in Malaysia are landmarks to sustainable design, not just low-energy design. Their buildings address human need, both physical and psychological, as well as the demands of energy efficiency.

The search for a responsive environment is driven as much by human appetite for aesthetic uplift as by the need for technological fixes. Social, ecological, cultural and technological sustainability will be the measures employed to judge tomorrow's buildings. However, there are many tensions which need to be resolved, which necessarily lead to variety in the solutions being adopted to solve the environmental problems ahead. Such tensions vary according to building type, to climate and to national traditions. Although environmental care must underpin all design choices, the need for cultural or spiritual sensitivity is greater today if we are to avoid globalising the aesthetic landscape. The standardisation of energy-conscious design stands in contrast to the richness which flows from ecological design approaches.

Fig 122
Models can do much to explain the aesthetic and environmental qualities of architecture. Sverre Fehn exhibition, Oslo.

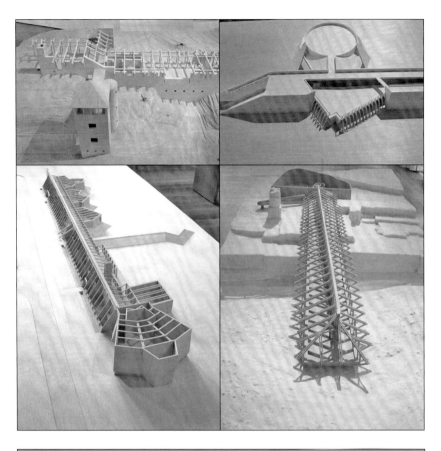

Some professional quotations of sustainable design[2]	
Lord Foster	'Sustainable design means doing the most with the least means.'
Lord Rogers	'The key issues are low energy, loose fit, resource efficiency.'
Ken Yeang	'Sustainable design is design which fits seamlessly with ecological systems …'
Thomas Herzog	'Sustainable design is about the preservation of natural resources – using renewable forms of energy, especially solar …'
Jan Kaplicky (Future Systems)	'Sustainable design is about making buildings as self-sufficient in energy as possible, and using less resources and energy to produce them.'

NEW DESIGN PROCESSES

Design is what architects do, and green design is what architects will do more of in the future.

Many architects will argue that sustainable design is what they have always sought since the treatises of Vitruvius and Alberti influenced building practice. However, as the science and practice of construction evolve, architects develop new skills and apply new technologies. But just because we have new tools, new technologies, and face new problems, that does not mean the design and building professions should throw away well-honed skills. Design for a sustainable future will continue to involve four key processes[3]:

- **Defining the problem**. Establish the criteria needed to solve the specific problem in hand. This will involve searching for appropriate precedents, identifying the knowledge needs, reviewing recent research and distinguishing critical from non-critical factors. Without a strong problem definition with associated key issues, there will be little chance of innovative green design.
- **Sharing the problem**. Collaboration is essential if the solution is to evolve in a sustainable way. Involving the client in the identification the key issues and in the design process itself is often a key to the successful delivery of green buildings. Participation by all stakeholders (users, community groups, consultants, planning officer, building standards officer) throughout the process leads to better design.
- **Innovation**. As society's needs change, as science evolves, and as resources become depleted, the architect increasingly has to innovate to solve the problem. Innovation normally comes in two forms – existing technologies are applied in new ways; or new technologies are developed and applied in the project for the first time. The latter is rare and full of potential hazard for the client, user and reputation of the design team. More commonly, old techniques and construction processes are modified to suit the particular brief and site in hand. Often there is also design innovation, and this too comes in a similar pattern. There may be 10 per cent creativity but 90 per cent of effort is devoted to getting the details right. As Darwin pointed out nearly two hundred years ago, new species evolve from old ones, not from scratch. To search for new solutions the whole time is not how nature works.

- **Ownership**. The client who has collaborated in the design process becomes the owner and is responsible for the life-cycle costings which follow. The client – whether private or public – needs to believe in the building and share the values that it contains. By participation in the design process, the architect can cultivate real ownership and care of the building by the client. After all, most of the environmental impact starts at occupation and ends a hundred years later at demolition. The owners and users of the building are key players in the eventual energy footprint and hence the building's contribution to global warming.

The role of technology

Technology holds the key to architecture's green future. Designers have been busy testing and developing new construction technologies based on solar cells, intelligent façades, breathing walls, thermal mass, turning waste into construction materials and utilising innovative forms of natural ventilation. The new order of sustainability, translated at the macro and micro level, influences every decision. There are four key principles to follow:

- the use of ecology as an accounting system for design
- the broadening of sustainability beyond the issue of energy efficiency
- the interaction between people, space, nature and technology within a sustainability paradigm
- awareness of resource scarcity, the discipline it imposes and the opportunities it raises to reinvent architecture.

All four influence architectural culture in important new ways. They introduce designers to the idea of reuse and recycling, to considering the source as well as the use of materials, to water conservation, and to the health of both construction workers and the occupants of buildings. This new thinking requires new technologies, be they borrowed from other industries, alternative technologies, revivals of old technologies (such as lime mortars – brought back to life by the demands of sustainability) or others that have yet to be developed. All of this gives rise to fresh perspectives. One such is the recognition that healthier buildings are also more productive ones. The human environments that architects create influence health – both physical and psychological (as discussed in chapter 8). Buildings can lead to stress or relieve it; buildings can cause cancer or help prolong life. Productivity, technology and sustainability are being recognised as an important package of interactions, especially in working environments. Green buildings pay, not just in terms of energy conservation but in promoting healthy lifestyles and in helping to achieve social cohesion.

The recent history of green design has been based on the principle that the three Es (energy, ecology and environment) lead to three Rs – reduce, respect and repair (discussed in chapter 6). However, this approach does not automatically generate good architecture. In fact in the wrong hands the single goal of low-energy design can produce low level aesthetics. On the other hand 'green' or 'ecological' design produces a richness and beauty because of the way it mimics nature's systems. Design innovation that puts ecological thinking before construction systems, CO_2 accounting and tick-box assessments can generate a socially acceptable architecture. Eco-design is a path to new cultural paradigms.

Eco-innovation and its impact on the design of buildings – the 4 Es	
Eco-innovation (design approach)	Resulting building
Less energy	Efficient
Fewer materials	Elegant
Greater recyclability	Equitable
Design with nature	Ecological

The technologies that designers employ impose a practical discipline and make a cultural statement. Building construction is not value free – it is influenced by many factors, such as cost, buildability, sustainability and aesthetics. Green design embraces all technologies – the large-scale (such as sustainable transport) through medium-scale technologies (such as photovoltaics) to the micro-scale technologies such as surface glass treatments. The choice of every component and every element of construction or material is now subject to green examination.

But 'eco-architecture' runs the risk of becoming 'eco-tech', with a reliance on super-technology alone. However, true sustainability resides in a balance of high and low technologies and in the integration of natural materials and synthetic ones. This mixing of hard and soft technologies applied in a typical building means that advanced materials are used to moderate climatic extremes with natural means employed for the bulk of operation. Sustainable design changes everything – the space plan, the sectional profile, the choice of technologies, materials and how they are put together in construction. At times it is risky; sustainability is not an easy path, it runs the risk of technological failure, cost over-runs and litigation.

Old professional practices	New green practices
Functional design problem solving	Sustainable design problem solving
Linear thinking	Lateral thinking
Symmetrical and value-free	Asymmetrical and value-rich
Solutions lie in present thinking	Solutions lie in future thinking
Adapted from: Martin Torke, RDAFA, 2008	

If this new drive for sustainability does not change the pattern of spaces in buildings, the configuration of external densities and hence city form, it will have failed to become mainstream. Technology is the key to sustainable construction just as urban design is the key to sustainable cities. Only when green thinking changes the politics of city form, when social sustainability and new green technologies are fully integrated, will we finally have reclaimed architecture and urbanism from 20th-century excesses.

The interaction between programme and technology is the single most important generator of sustainable design. The architect's role is critical – bearing in mind that 80 per cent of environmental impact over a building's life span is determined at the design stage. Building science and functionality have been the two dominant strands of form generation for at least a century. Since function in a world of rapid social and economic change becomes quickly obsolete, space has become more elastic and less specific. Buildings are increasingly big volumes without specific long-term uses (e.g. Olympic or UK Millennium structures). At a fundamental level, technology allows us to convert resources into useful artefacts (from cities at one end of the scale, to mobile phones at the other). Technology is the blend of science, ingenuity and design which added to the human dimension imparted by creative thinkers, allow us to imagine and make the future. Architects impart cultural value – their role is to fashion technology, to make it appropriate for the task in hand. Some add artistic value, others high tech but the new challenge is to make this process more ecologically conscious, to see buildings as a marriage not only of use and technology but also of biology and fashion.

Lessons from vernacular architecture

The traditional architecture of the world represents a resource that has considerable potential for helping us to understand the principles of sustainable design and construction. Vernacular buildings are made of locally available materials, employ local, mainly renewable, sources of energy, and adopt construction practices that favour recycling and respect for nature. These characteristics are to be found in rural housing as well as in urban buildings, and in Africa and Asia as well as in pre-industrial Europe. The lessons from vernacular architecture concern both the individual building and the urban layout, and also the relationship between villages, farms and natural resources, and how buildings have been adapted over time.

Putting aside the historical interest of old towns and rural buildings (whether ancient or vernacular), the principles or lessons that can be identified from them are as follows.

Energy

Most of the energy required to heat, light or ventilate vernacular buildings is locally sourced. It comes in a variety of forms, including carbon-based fuels, such as wood, coal, methane and straw-based fuel (e.g. dried animal dung), and renewable energy in the form of sun and wind. These various sources are combined in

Fig 123
This adaptation of a Scottish stone house by Brian Edwards combines modern energy efficiency with traditional heavyweight construction.

Fig 124
Modern approach to solar screening in
Cape Town.

ingenious ways, with local variations to suit different climatic requirements. Hence
in the cold north the hearth and chimney will be used for heating, while nearer to
the equator the chimney's primary role is be that of ventilation. Likewise, in the
north the courtyard plan may be employed for shelter from cold winds, while in
the hot south the same plan, though with subtle variation, is likely to be the result
of the need to provide shelter from the sun's heat.

The position of the building within a plot, its orientation and plan, and the location
of windows, doors and fireplaces are also all likely to be determined by energy
considerations. The regional variations reflect different energy sources and
different energy strategies. By learning about these variations it is possible to gain
perspectives on future energy design.

Construction materials

Vernacular buildings normally employ locally sourced construction materials.
These may be gained directly from the ground or forests (stone and timber)
or may be modified through baking (bricks and tiles). Traditional construction
normally consists of a combination of virgin materials and those that have been
modified. For example, a vernacular house may have brick walls and a timber
roof covered in thatch. Alternatively, it may be a timber-framed house with a
brick fireplace and chimney, or a bamboo house with a hand-moulded clay stove.
Vernacular construction contains a high percentage of indigenous materials which,
over time, assume cultural meaning in parallel with their practical purpose.

Since transport costs in the past were high, vernacular buildings are normally
constructed of locally sourced materials that could be carried by hand, by cart or

Fig 125
The Hawkes eco-house in Kent, UK, uses
local clay construction materials and adopts
traditional building methods to produce a
distinctive energy-efficient house: (a) view;
(b) plan; (c) section.
Source: Richard Hawkes

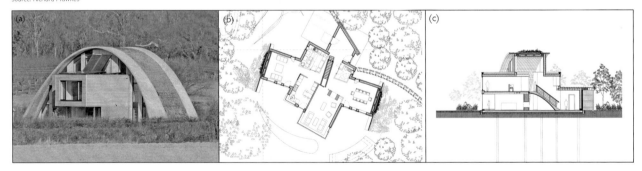

over water. Water was often the key to the location of settlements (for transport and power), for food supplies and sanitation. As a general rule, the weight of construction materials not only determined how far they were carried but also influenced the shape and size of construction elements. Hence, heavy materials were produced in units that could be readily transported. Clay was formed into bricks, while timber was split into planks that could be floated on rafts or carried through the forest. The length, size and shape of construction materials were directly related to the means and capacity of the transport system.

Where materials were very heavy, it was common practice to build near the source rather than to transport the material to a distant site. Hence, where stone was the predominant building material houses, farms and towns were built near quarries (or quarries were opened up to serve them). Similarly, in marshy areas buildings were constructed on stilts to take advantage of the reeds and bamboo on the doorstep.

Settlements that used construction materials with a short life span tended to move in response to the availability of the resources, both for construction and for energy or food. With intermittent settlement went a light touch in terms of environmental impact, which in turn gave time for the ecosystem to recover.

Local crafts

Distinctive patterns of building grew up in response to locally available construction materials and different regional climatic conditions. The result was a flourishing industry of building crafts, which was equipped to extract the maximum potential from available resources – energy, water and materials. Since the crafts had their own practices and bodies of knowledge, the skills were intergenerational and, in time, the products of labour became cultural as well as material assets. Innovation was slow since materials and climate did not change. As a consequence, building failure was rare and architecture was respected as embodying wider social and cultural values. Examples today can be seen in the courtyard houses of the Middle East, the sun-baked earth buildings of Central Africa, the timber farm buildings of southern Russia, and the bamboo dwellings of the Philippines.

The crafts have both a construction role and a symbolic one. Traditions grew up which gave identity to the vernacular buildings of the world. Details of construction, decorative elements and distinctive forms help define regional variations in vernacular architecture. These are invariably the result of functional or practical considerations as well as artistic ones. However, the distribution of built forms and their supporting crafts reflect human and material resources in a way that illustrates sustainable practice. Since there is wide regional variation in vernacular building, the geography of vernacular architecture challenges the universality of modern global architecture with its imported materials, energy and labour.

Reuse

The reuse of construction materials is a feature of vernacular architecture. New buildings often incorporate parts of older buildings, whether in the form of structural members (such as timber beams), cladding material (such as stone slates) or built-in fittings (such as store cupboards). Recycling was encouraged through local scarcity and made possible by the use of reversible fixing techniques. For example, timber was pegged rather than nailed together, bricks and stone were cemented using lime mortar, and doors and windows were held in place using wedges. A culture of recycling existed until modern times and often consisted of the reuse of materials from outside domestic architecture; timber from ships was used in houses, and when corn mills were upgraded the millstones were employed as doorsteps. Materials from rich houses also found their way into poor ones as the former were rebuilt, and from modest houses to farm buildings.

This approach to construction survives today in many parts of the world. Perhaps as many as one building in eight in the world is made from recycled or waste materials. Plastic, cheap sheet metal, timber packing cases and cardboard boxes are frequently modified to form the basic structure and enclosure of houses built in the expanding squatter villages of Africa, Asia and Latin America. Resourceful people with little income build shelters from waste as a stepping stone from a life of rural hardship to one of urban possibility. Their towns, usually built without planning permission or sanitation, in time become settlements that are adopted by the local authority, which then provides water, roads, electricity and schools for populations that can be counted in millions. These are towns that are truly vernacular in spirit and which owe their origin to the creative exploitation of urban waste as a physical resource.

Condensation

Traditional architecture had well-developed techniques for dealing with the build up of condensation. Roofs were generally well ventilated with air spaces deliberately created in the gable; walls were allowed to breathe using lime mortar or clay as finishes (rather than cement or oil-based paint); and windows featured a combination of external and internal shutters as well as glazing and insect screens. As a result buildings were well-aired and condensation was not a problem. Today the striving for air-tightness which stems from energy efficiency measures can lead to condensation due to lack of air movement. In this sense building regulations can undermine centuries of building tradition and importing models such as PassivHaus (described in chapter 9) into the damp UK has limitations.

Humidity can, however, be used positively by exploiting the cooling effect of evaporation. In hot countries techniques were developed to take moisture out of the building and evaporate it using the heat of the sun, thereby producing cooling air currents. On hard cold surfaces moisture would gather overnight which, when heated by the sun, lowered the temperature of the building during the daytime. In the courtyard houses of the Middle East, the technique was amplified through the employment of pools and water channels. Here chimneys were built into walls to draw the cool air through the habitable rooms which surrounded the central open court. Such lessons from history have only recently been revived in new construction. Using condensation as a positive cooling force (as many mammals do) offers many benefits for architecture as it faces rising global temperatures.

Traditional architecture was also a long history of using of curtains and blinds. The climate was moderated by occupiers who made adjustments to suit external conditions and internal needs. Curtains are a form of active insulation which were employed to both control temperature and condensation. Curtains came in different types (heavy for the winter and light for the summer) and formed another climatic layer between inside and out. Today curtains are unfashionable and building laws would rather we designed small triple glazed windows than large double glazed windows with curtains. In the pursuit of heat conservation we run the risk of condensation and daylight problems which older practices avoided by the use of simple means — the curtain.

SUSTAINABILITY AS A KEY QUALITY INDICATOR

Sustainability is not a stand-alone feature of design but one of several characteristics to which an architect should aspire. Since design quality is dependent upon available resources, sustainable design is about generating better value over a longer timescale with the resources available.[4] Design Quality Indicators (DQIs) bring together the linked attributes of function, building quality and impact in such a way as to allow for the rational measurement of sustainability. After all, a design is not economically sustainable if it does not effectively serve a function; is not environmentally sustainable if it lacks robustness in construction; and is not socially sustainable if it is not enjoyed by users. The Vitruvian triangle of firmness, utility and delight shares similarities with the modern-day triangulation of sustainable development: social, economic and environmental sustainability.

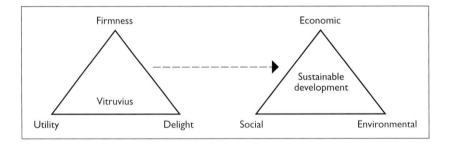

Fig 126
The Vitruvian triangle shares similarities with the triangulation of sustainable development.

It is important that performance measurement tools take account of present-day resource impacts and possible future scarcity. Fitness for purpose may well vary in the future as different resources come under strain and as the climatic environment changes. A material or energy system that is selected today may not be the best choice in the future. Therefore, predictive tools such as BREEAM and LEED (see chapter 3) need to recognise life-cycle issues in an unstable and unpredictable world. Whatever tools are employed, there is an urgent need to make buildings more resource efficient and flexible while also contributing to human satisfaction and to business performance.[5]

The UK government has sought to link design quality with sustainable development in its Planning Policy Statement 1: Delivering Sustainable

Fig 127
Bamboo-clad eco-housing in Madrid, designed by Foreign Office Architects (FOA). Residents can adjust levels of sunlight filtered through folding bamboo screens.

Development (PPS1), which states that 'high standards of building design help achieve sustainable development'.[6] The emphasis on design is a welcome change – until recently a succession of British governments failed to acknowledge the social, economic and environmental advantages of good design. PPS1 requires architects and planners to cooperate more to help promote economic development, social inclusion and environmental protection.

The importance of stakeholders

Environmental assessment of projects at the design stage has highlighted the need to involve all stakeholders in striving for sustainable development. Although a huge lifetime impact is imparted at sketch design, the starting point for green thinking is the brief. Hence the person who draws up the brief for a new building can influence its performance over many decades. Unless environmentalism is imprinted into the aspirations for the building right at the start, it is unlikely that sustainability will follow.

The brief determines the sustainable options, which in turn influence the design strategies, the detailed design, the construction process, and finally the completed building. For the system to work well there needs to be synergy and understanding between the players – those who commission, design, build and occupy the building. A lack of understanding or trust between the stakeholders can seriously undermine the performance of the building environmentally.

Thus the key to a green building lies in shared values across lengthy timeframes. They involve communication and empowerment between:

- **clients** – who prepare the brief and discuss needs (particularly energy and health) with future users
- **designers and engineers** – who use best practice, innovate using new sustainable technologies, and learn from earlier projects (their own and others)
- **builders** – who instil the culture of sustainability amongst the workforce and are committed to high environmental standards as a company
- **users** – who are kept informed of the working of the building, who engage in monitoring its environmental performance, share in its culture, and invest in upgrading over time.

A BLUEPRINT FOR GREEN DESIGN

The dual imperatives of climate change and fossil fuel depletion place a responsibility upon architects and engineers to design more elegant, fitter, ecologically resourceful and adaptable buildings. Existing buildings are inevitably more difficult to change than are those on the drawing board. As a general rule, the older the building the more difficult it is to adapt. Given that the life of a building at present is typically 100 years (as against the design for life of 50 years) anything built today or tomorrow will be around during a period of climate and resource stress. Thus my rules for constructing a generation of fitter, more adaptable buildings are listed as follows:

- **Apply green principles from the outset**: Green principles must be put into the brief at the very beginning to ensure that costs will not be increased. If sustainable technologies are bolted on later, building costs will rise.
- **Avoid functional specificity**: Although function is the basis of form (and building character) it is also relatively short-lived compared with the structural life of buildings. Over-specific buildings are inherently inflexible.
- **Maximise access to daylight and natural ventilation**: Green buildings are those that are not too deep in plan, too high or too irregular in shape. Buildings should be no deeper than 12–15 m and generally no higher than 4–6 storeys. A combination of narrow floor plate construction and atria can enhance access to daylight and reduce energy use through stack-effect ventilation.
- **Design for simplicity of operation**: Over-complicated buildings are not fit in the long term (although they may be for short periods). The means of servicing

and the degree of user control of the interior environment are i
considerations. Simplicity of service and constructional systems allows for
periodic upgrading and permits building users to understand the building,
generating respect over its life span.

- **Design for long life**: Since buildings last at least as long as people, they
obviously affect future generations. Low-quality construction can become a
burden on subsequent generations. Long-lived, low-maintenance buildings may
entail higher costs at the outset, but over their life they are a wiser investment.
Long-lived buildings save on energy and waste.
- **Maximise use of renewable energy**: Although solar energy generation may not
be exploited in the first decade in the life of a building, it is likely to be added
over subsequent decades. It is imperative that maximum access is provided
for renewable energy (sun, wind and possibly geothermal). Wind and sun
are both readily available in the UK, and when one is not accessible the other
generally is. Buildings have the potential to be not only self-sufficient in energy
but also exporters of energy (through the generation of electricity supplied
to the National Grid). To maximise renewable energy exploitation, buildings
should be correctly orientated (south on a major façade), angled appropriately

Fig 128
Low-energy college in Chur, Switzerland,
designed by Bearth & Deplazes: (a) author's
interpretative section; and (b) author's sketch
of façade.

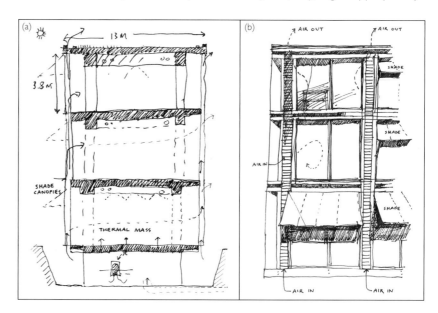

in section and spaced to give access to the sun (especially winter sun at about 18°). In terms of wind energy, it is necessary to avoid obstruction to air flow, such as by tall buildings or trees, and roofs should be designed to support wind generators.

■ **Design for replaceability**: Since buildings always eventually fail, in part or whole, it must be possible to upgrade or replace a component or system. The materials of construction must allow for simple replacement. Flexible, demountable construction is more easily renewed than monolithic construction. Obstacles to replaceability include rigid adhesives, welded (as against bolted) connections, the use of over-strong cement mortars (rather than lime-based ones) and specially tooled proprietary details. At the design stage, allow for separate structural, component and servicing life cycles.

NOTES

[1]   Michael Pawley, 'Biomimicry and Architecture'. Lecture given to Danish Architecture Centre, 9 March 2009.

[2]   Based on interviews conducted with the author and published in *Green Architecture*, Wiley-Academy, 2001, Vol. 71, No. 4.

[3]   This list is adapted from lecture by Rogier van der Heide of ARUP given at the Royal Danish Academy of Fine Arts, School of Architecture, 22 January 2009.

[4]   Sunand Prasad, 'Inclusive Maps', in Sebastian Macmillan (ed.), *Designing Better Buildings*, Spon Press, London, 2004, p. 179.

[5]   Bill Bordass, 'Cost and value: fact or fiction', *Building Research and Information*, Vol. 28, No. 5/6, pp. 338–52.

[6]   Planning Policy Statement 1: Delivering Sustainable Development, available at www.communities.gov.uk/ planningandbuilding

8 Sustainable Buildings are Healthy Buildings

Health is defined by the World Health Organization (WHO) as a state of complete physical, mental and social well-being.[1] Buildings contribute to this state and it follows, therefore, that they have a profound impact on quality of life. Any design which subjects users to health risks is both unethical and exposes the architect or engineer to potential litigation. Such a broad definition of health poses certain dilemmas but, at the same time, opens up fresh avenues of architectural development.

Health is emerging as a new catalyst in building design. The environmentalists' former emphasis on global warming, pollution and resource depletion placed personal health well behind that of planetary well-being. Buildings were to be energy efficient in spite of the use of potentially toxic insulation, of reduced levels of ventilation and reduced window area. Now, however, a new philosophy is emerging from the ecological movement, one which balances energy efficiency with both global and human health. The new emphasis is not on energy efficiency at any price but on more holistic solutions that bring natural (and hence healthy) systems into the equation.[2]

Health is dependent on adequate comfort levels, but comfort alone does not promote healthy living or working environments. The three key components of healthy building environments are:

- comfort
- pollution free
- responsive and stimulating to human needs.

Each of these components has its own principles, science base and practice in construction, but they cannot be considered in isolation.

COMFORT

This concept is central to the creation of healthy human environments. Comfort embraces thermal comfort, humidity, ventilation and lighting. We need to feel comfortable, to be able to see without glare or dimness, and have the right balance of humidity and ventilation. Healthy environments are normally those based on natural sources of light, ventilation and materials.

Fig 129
Limestone is a healthy, recyclable and robust building material. Its use also keeps alive traditional crafts, which helps to maintain cultural continuity.

Comfort can be achieved by other means (in much of the world, air-conditioning is currently used to maintain comfort levels) but, wherever possible, natural systems and technologies are preferable to mechanical ones. For example, comfort can be enhanced by improved levels of insulation; by adopting 'breathing wall' principles whereby the building acts like a lung in response to fluctuating external conditions; by eliminating unwanted air movement (draughts); and by maintaining stable temperatures.

The lack of comfortable conditions can promote mould and bacteria growth. High levels of moisture, insufficient ventilation and the presence of bacteria lead to mould colonisation. In its wake come dust mites, which eat the mould and excrete tiny droppings. These are then inhaled by occupants, leading to respiratory problems and other forms of ill health caused by bacteriological contamination. The root of this problem, which manifests itself in sickness or allergy, is poor design and construction.

There are four main types of comfort which interact with each other in the typical building:

- thermal comfort, which is primarily a question of heating and cooling
- acoustic comfort, which is concerned with noise levels and audibility
- health or hygienic comfort, which is addressed through ventilation and sanitation
- aesthetic comfort which is concerned with visual and to a degree spiritual matters.

All four are influenced by wider issues surrounding sustainability and the choices architects make throughout the design process. However, the interaction between climate and comfort is one of the key drivers of 'green design' as society adjusts to a low carbon economy.[3]

The role of glass in comfort

Glass is an important material in maintaining interaction between the interior and exterior worlds and in providing shelter and hence comfort levels. Glass too allows sunlight to be captured for space heating using a combination of glazing types, areas, thickness and finishes to suit conditions. Tinting of glass reduces glare and unwanted solar gain; and using double or triple glazing improves insulation

Fig 130
Central skylights are an increasingly common feature of low-energy houses in an attempt to reduce electric consumption in lighting and cooling.

levels, particularly when cavities are gas-filled. However, glazing reduces daylight penetration and hence window size and glazing design need to be carefully considered. Triple glazing can reduce interior light levels by nearly 40 per cent and even more in polluted urban areas.

Light loss with multiple glazing	
Number of sheets of glass	Light loss (%)
nil	nil
1	15
2	28
3	39

There have been various strategies over the past 50 years for establishing the right balance between comfort, light levels, energy efficiency and window area. Although the rule of thumb which said that windows should be about 20 per cent of floor area has been modified in recent years to 25 per cent (because of the energy costs of electric lighting) there has also been a marked shift in attitudes to lighting levels, driven partly by changes in building law. Some studies suggest that windows in northern climates should be 40 per cent of the façade area with a 2-to-1 bias towards southern orientation. Such windows should be double glazed to the south and triple glazed to north. Since the trend is to reduce window area for heat conservation (50 per cent of building heat loss is normally through windows), the risk is that buildings will be too dark leading to more electricity for lighting and poorer architectural qualities of interior space.

New energy standards have led to new glazing technologies and new design approaches. The post-war period also saw a marked change from natural systems of climate control (opening windows and natural light) to artificial ones driven mainly by electricity (fans, artificial lighting, air-conditioning). The effect on comfort, both physical and psychological, and on energy use has been large. For example, in UK housing heating demand has fallen by about 40 per cent since 1970 due to improved construction while electricity consumption has risen by 25 per cent. With global warming the trend is towards less energy for heating and more for cooling, and since most of the cooling energy is delivered electrically, the consequences for CO_2 reduction and future supplies are worrying. The problem facing architects is how to cool by natural means and how to adjust window area and type to meet changing expectations for comfort. The trend towards less permeability between inside and outside environments (driven by rising energy regulations) runs the risk of sealing the human habitat and distancing mankind from the natural world.

Changes in glazing design: 1960–2009	
1960s	Large, often single glazed window areas
1970s	Small to medium double glazed windows
1980s	Medium- to large-size smart-glazing windows
1990s	Atria, conservatories and roof glazing
2000 onwards	Sun-pipes, hybrid PV and smart glazing

The expectations for comfort vary across cultures and age ranges. Elderly people expect more space, better light and warmer conditions than most. This is because they spend more time at home, have failing eyesight and feel the cold or excessive heat more than others. By 2020 it is expected that half of Europeans will be over 50 years old. This presents a challenge for architects, particularly in the field of climate and comfort. The elderly need bigger spaces (perhaps some for wheelchairs), controls which are easily understood and readily operated, and more natural light. They often need exterior, sunlit sitting spaces adjacent to the building which are reached without steps.

BEING POLLUTION-FREE

If buildings are polluted they are not healthy, even though they may be energy efficient. Pollution comes in many guises: toxicity (poor air quality), noise pollution and, to a degree, space pollution (the psychologically stressful effect of overcrowding). All three are legitimate design concerns, especially taking the WHO definition of health into account.

Air pollution occurs indoors by:

- the entry of external air pollution

- contamination of air which is the result of planned combustion (boilers, cooking, etc.)
- contamination resulting from unplanned combustion (smoking)
- off-gassing of chemicals used in construction or furnishings
- radon entering the building through the ground.

Although each is important and can affect human health, it is the cocktail of chemicals which probably poses the greatest risk.

Airborne water vapour enhances the absorption of the chemicals into our bodies through breathing. Volatile organic compounds (VOCs) are commonly ten times the level inside buildings than outside, leading to allergies and sick building syndrome. VOCs occur as a by-product of manufacture and are slowly released into the atmosphere during the lifetime of the building. Their release is accelerated by wear and tear, cutting or drilling, and stresses caused by temperature variations.

What is good for the building is good for the occupant. To put it another way, if there are mould attacks, outbreaks of timber rot, or fabric cracking due to an excessively hot or dry indoor climate, it is bad news for the building and bad news for those who use it, too.

Since many construction materials have not been in existence for more than a few years and many new ones are introduced onto the market each year, it is wise to exercise caution or scepticism in their use. If there is doubt, err on the side of caution: do not expose people to unknown risk. But the guiding principle should be, where ever possible, 'naturalness'. Materials taken directly from nature (timber) or those from organic or inert sources (bricks and clay tiles) are inherently safer than synthetic materials (plastics).

Buildings last a long time and the pollution placed in their fabric at the start (i.e. in construction) can blight the building throughout its life. Glass fibre quilt insulation, for example, desirable as an energy-efficiency measure, poses a greater health risk than insulation based on organic materials (cellulose fibre, sheep's wool). However, poor detailing in the use of organic materials can lead to decay, which threatens both the building and its occupants. So, with natural materials, particular attention must be paid to moisture levels, ventilation and rodent control. As with all construction detail, detailing and site supervision are essential to avoid health risks. Research suggests that many of the problems occur as a result of poor site operations or lack of understanding by users or janitors of the working of the building.

Radon is a problem in parts of Europe. This radioactive gas occurs naturally in the UK counties of Cornwall, Devon and Derbyshire, as well as in large areas of Wales and the Highlands of Scotland. It is odourless and is a major source of lung cancer, especially for those who also smoke. It enters the building through the ground. Poorly ventilated underfloor cavities can result in a build-up of radon, which then permeates the building through cracks in floorboards or through service runs.

Chlorofluorocarbons (CFCs) are commonly found in buildings, even though the Montreal Protocol of 1989 banned their manufacture.[4] CFCs and the material used as a substitute, hydrochlorofluorocarbon (HCFC), are highly damaging to global and personal health. These chemicals have 20,000 times the global warming impact of the same volume of CO_2 and are responsible in addition for the thinning of the ozone layer (see chapter 1). The ozone layer protects us from ultraviolet light, and as the ozone layer is depleted and as more of this waveband of light reaches the surface of the Earth, there is an increase in skin cancer and eye cataracts. Skin cancer is now the UK's second most common cancer and, though it is not a big killer, it leads to considerable disfigurement. An extra 60,000 cases of skin cancer in the UK per year are attributed to ozone thinning. Half of all CFC use was related to buildings – either as a chemical used in cooling or as a foaming agent employed in the manufacture of insulation products.

Although CFCs are no longer specified, they remain in many buildings, especially those with air-conditioning. CFCs can be retrieved safely at demolition to prevent release into the atmosphere, and many local authorities offer a free CFC recovery service. Unfortunately, there is a black market in CFCs and they are still used in less regulated parts of the world.

As for asbestos, we only became aware of the health problems late in the day: it confirms the importance of exercising caution when new products are brought onto the market.

Fig 131
Art Lover's House, Glasgow, designed by
Charles Rennie Mackintosh – a study in healthy,
stimulating design.

RESPONSIVE AND STIMULATING ENVIRONMENTS

Since health has a psychological dimension it becomes incumbent upon designers to create environments that reduce stress and which respond positively to user need. Occupational stress can be the result of overwork, of environments that are difficult to moderate, or of the loss of contact with natural cycles (daylight, sunlight, night-time). Sensory stimulation can provide a natural counterbalance to our frequent reliance on artificial stimulants (alcohol, caffeine), which contribute to stress.

Natural stimulation comes from the play of sunlight on walls, from well-ventilated rooms bathed in daylight, from the presence of plants inside and contact with trees and shrubs outside. Quantitative indicators of healthy environments need to be matched with qualitative ones.[5] It is the subtle play of space and light which comes closest to natural conditions and which is at the root of forging stress-free buildings.

The interaction between mind and body is as important as that between body and building. Inevitably, these connections are not fully understood but it is essential that the architect creates spaces that reduce stress. This can be achieved by employing technologies that are under the control of building users. Research suggests that in office buildings those closest to windows suffer less stress and are, as a consequence, more healthy and productive than those further away from windows. Similar research from hospitals establishes a parallel correlation between the personal control of light and ventilation by patients and the rate of stress, antisocial behaviour and recovery.[6] In the home, where the bulk of life is conducted, it is important to avoid systems, materials, products and processes that frustrate or damage health.

Responsiveness is partly achieved by user-friendliness of technologies. Over-complex controls lead to stress and alienate people from their environment. As a result, instead of turning down heater controls, people open windows and, instead of setting timers, they leave systems running when they are not needed. A responsive environment is not only a natural one (i.e. natural light and ventilation in the day rather than artificial light and mechanical ventilation) but also a simple one.

Fig 132
Interior of Barclaycard office, Northampton, UK, designed by Fitzroy Robinson.

A balance is needed between simplicity and stimulation: an overly simple interior may be soporific. Light (particularly sunlight), space (particularly vertical space) and interior planting (especially exotic species) can provide a stimulating well-tempered environment. Add to this the sound of leaves rustling or the smell of aromatic plants and the responsive feel of the space is complete. A visual and audible interaction between the interior and exterior world is also important, although not if the exterior environment is hostile, in which case it should be excluded.

Noise is also an aspect of sustainability. Noisy environments are not environmental friendly and although they may be energy efficient, consumers will reject places with excessive aural assault. Road and rail traffic are major sources of noise in cities; likewise planes and motorways in the outer suburbs.

Good acoustics is central to sustainable design, yet often energy considerations lead to subjecting people to noisy living or working environments. Architects should ensure that reducing the carbon footprint does not add to problems elsewhere. For example, wind generators produce noise, particularly those attached to buildings such as micro-generators. City noise thus restricts the opportunity for passive solar design, cross-ventilation and windcatchers.

PROMOTING HEALTH THROUGH DESIGN

The market for natural materials in the UK is relatively depressed compared with much of Europe. In Germany, in 2000, the use of water-based paints was 20 times that in England and, in Denmark, natural insulation products accounted for 10 per cent of the market while in the UK they make up only 1 per cent at the time.[7] Although Britain has moved forward since then, British construction remains less motivated by the organic argument than its European counterparts. It is not sufficient, however, to simply specify green products: new construction techniques are also required. The design of the building needs to recognise the potential health problems posed by everyday construction detailing. As concern over health begins to drive the sustainability agenda beyond that of low-energy issues, it carries a fresh generation of construction materials, details, technologies and site techniques in its wake.

Fig 133
Green office in Glasgow, designed by McEwan
Smith: (a) atrium; (b) exterior; and (c) section.
Source: McEwan Smith

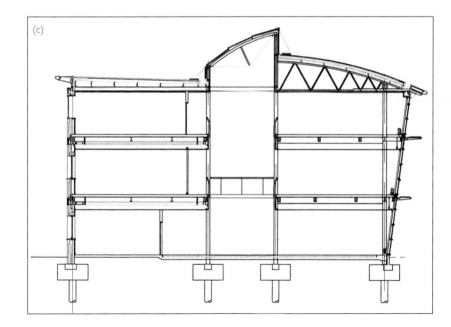

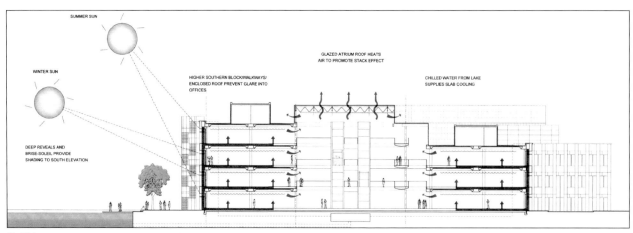

Fig 134
Environmental strategy at the British Energy
Office, designed by Fitzroy Robinson and Partners.
Source: Fitzroy Robinson and Partners

Fig 135
New materials and new technologies open up
fresh possibilities for creating a more sustainable
architecture.

Healthy materials

As a general rule, natural building materials are also healthy ones. The problem
is that the lack of technical performance from organic materials often results in
architects selecting manufactured products. However, traditional materials, some
neglected because of fashion or poor performance, are being revived as a result
of their undoubted healthiness. As they are revived, new techniques are being
developed to use them in new ways.[8]

Earth products
These range from earth blocks, sun-baked bricks and clay mortars to
earth-based plasters. They have been used for centuries in Europe and are
low-embodied-energy materials with zero toxicity and, with careful detailing,
long life. There is interest at present in exploring unfired bricks as an alternative to
kiln-baked bricks in UK construction.

Stone
Stone walling and structural members have long been employed in construction.
They are the basis of many ancient buildings and have stood the ravages of time
and human use well. Few have given rise to health problems. Because it occurs
naturally, stone is healthy, enduring and attractive. Health problems can occur
during quarrying and site cutting (especially the inhalation of dust) but generally

Fig 136
Detail of cob wall (sand, clay and straw) at
house near Worcester, UK, designed by
Associated Architects.
Source: Associated Architects

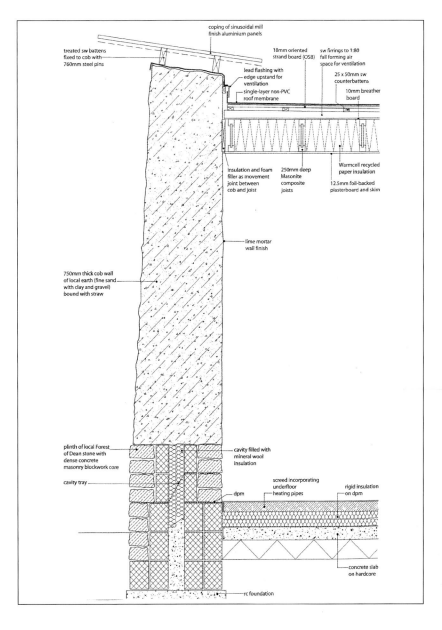

coping of sinusoidal mill
finish aluminium panels

treated sw battens
fixed to cob with
760mm steel pins

18mm oriented
strand board (OSB)

sw firrings to 1:80
fall forming air
space for ventilation

lead flashing with
edge upstand for
ventilation

25 x 50mm sw
counterbattens

single-layer non-PVC
roof membrane

10mm breather
board

insulation and foam
filler as movement
joint between
cob and joist

250mm deep
Masonite
composite
joists

Warmcell recycled
paper insulation

12.5mm foil-backed
plasterboard and skim

lime mortar
wall finish

750mm thick cob wall
of local earth (fine sand
with clay and gravel)
bound with straw

plinth of local Forest
of Dean stone with
dense concrete
masonry blockwork core

cavity filled with
mineral wool
insulation

cavity tray

screed incorporating
underfloor
heating pipes

rigid insulation
on dpm

dpm

concrete slab
on hardcore

rc foundation

stone poses little pollution risk. Quarrying is, however, visually and ecologically damaging, and there are large transportation energy costs involved. There are long-term sources of limestone and sandstone in the UK and, provided quarries are local, stone is an obvious choice of material to use in construction. Stone is also readily recycled, and its high thermal capacity, combined with its endurance, makes it an attractive choice for many reasons.

Timber

Wood-based products and timber structural members form the basis of much vernacular and modern construction (not just in the domestic realm). Timber is a sustainable, self-renewing product and, as living wood, helps in the conversion of CO_2 back into oxygen (thereby reducing global warming). Timber, however, needs to be sourced from a reputable supplier to prevent habitat loss, especially distant rainforests. Locally grown hardwoods are increasingly used in UK construction, especially green oak, which has benefits of ease of workmanship and pliability if used before fully seasoned. Softwoods are more generally employed but may need chemical treatment, which raises health and pollution problems.

Lime mortars

These have long been used in buildings and, until the introduction of cement in the late 19th century, were the major bonding element for stone and masonry. Lime is also used as a plaster and external wall finish. Lime (as putty, hydraulic lime or lime mortar) has many applications and, if used as brickwork or blockwork mortar, allows the bricks and blocks to be recovered and reused. However, lime is a caustic material and appropriate precautions must be taken by the site workers using it.

Organic insulation

Natural products can be turned into building insulation for use in roofs and walls. Various materials form the basis of organic insulation – e.g. cellulose fibre, vegetable fibre, sheep's wool. Unlike manufactured insulation (such as expanded polystyrene), natural insulation materials are low in embodied energy, are not toxic, and do not release ozone-depleting chemicals.

Water-based paints

Paints and varnishes that are not oil-based are now widely available. Being water-based, they pose little threat to the health of construction workers or

Fig 137
Façade of the Scottish Parliament Building in
Edinburgh, designed by Enric Miralles / RMJM,
using locally sourced building materials which
make reference to the Scottish landscape.

building occupants. Oil-based paints are particularly toxic: professional painters have a 40 per cent higher incidence of lung cancer than other workers.[9] An alternative is to use natural resin oil or water-based equivalents as a paint primer.

Ethylene tetrafluoroethylene
Although not a natural material, Ethylene tetrafluoroethylene (ETFE) performs many of the function of glass and often does so with greater material efficiency. ETFE has only 2 per cent of the embodied energy of glass, less than 1 per cent of its weight, is more flexible in terms of geometrics, and can be patched and easily repaired. Being lightweight it allows for less steel on site, has much lower transport energy costs, and allows for more sunlight penetration than glass. Used as a pillow with an air cushion it offers good insulation (particularly when a double skin is used) and provides an attractive alternative to glass. Its use on prestige projects, such as the Eden Centre in Cornwall, UK, and the Beijing Olympics Aquatic Centre, has increased the profile of this relatively green material.

Healthy technologies

Windcatchers
By maximising the use of wind and sun, windcatchers make a major contribution to sustainable design. Through the skilful utilisation of renewable resources, windcatchers provide natural ventilation in modern buildings where air-conditioning or mechanical systems normally predominate. Windcatchers have an ancient pedigree, being employed from about the second century BC in parts of the Middle East, and are still common in the region. They work by catching the wind at high level and drawing ventilation through the building at low level because of the different air pressure. Windcatchers are primarily wind driven but also utilise temperature gradients, and can be solar-assisted as well as wind driven.

Windcatchers break the mould of window or vent-based, low-level, cross-ventilation. They use instead controlled ventilation at high level, taking advantage of the wind pressure which is invariably present. As a consequence of their shape and position, windcatchers can normally utilise wind from any direction and, via the use of dampers, of any speed.

Windcatchers can be a more effective means of ventilating large, deep-plan buildings than side window vents. The rate of ventilation can also be more readily

Fig 138
Traditional windcatcher used for ventilating courtyard housing in the Middle East.

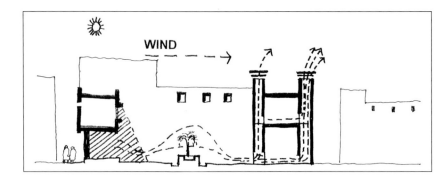

controlled and integrated with other ventilation strategies such as the stack effect. Hence, wind and sun can be jointly employed to reduce the demand made on mechanical ventilation systems. In this regard, windcatchers have become popular with green architects, and their presence on the roof of a building (as at Portcullis House, London by Michael Hopkins & Partners) is a sure sign of a natural ventilation strategy.

As a general rule, the catchment area of a windcatcher is the same as that which would have been provided by wall openings (i.e. windows and vents). Since the roof-mounted windcatchers are unobstructed (unlike windows), manufacturers claim that there is a constant flow of fresh air irrespective of wind direction. However, the combination of windcatchers and traditional windows means that in the summertime windcatchers act as exhaust vents for the warmed air using the stack effect. It is this combination which is increasingly attractive as temperatures rise under the influence of global warming.

Windcatchers are normally internally divided into two chambers – one for incoming air, the other for exhaust air. The external wind movement creates a negative pressure or suction zone to one side while pressurising the other. As a consequence, air is driven into the building and controlled via dampers at ceiling level. The volume control dampers determine the amount of air flow and can be adjusted mechanically or via a computer programme, depending on internal and external temperature levels. Windcatchers can be integrated with suncatchers, a system which brings natural light into the building via a silvered sun pipe placed in the centre of the windcatcher unit. This has the advantage of conveying natural light and natural ventilation simultaneously – very useful for deep-plan buildings,

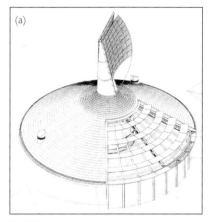

Fig 139
Wind cowl used: (a) to ventilate ICI visitor centre in Runcom designed by Amec Design; and (b) at the Brighton Library by Bennett Associates.
Source: Amec Design and Bennetts Associates

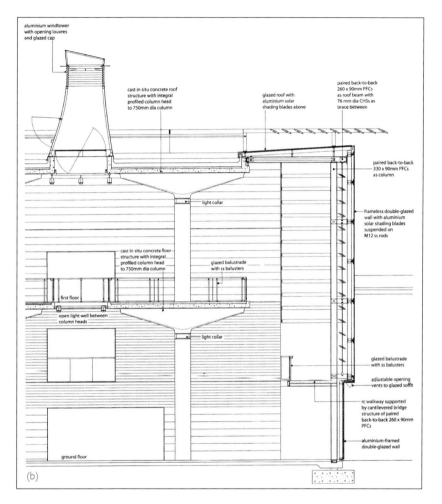

particularly where noise or ground-level air pollution restrict the use of window vents.

Specialist design advice should be sought when considering the use of windcatchers. The number, size and position of units is important, and how they interact with solar-assisted stack effect strategies via atria should be the

Fig 140
Detail of wind cowls and PV panels at Jubilee Campus, Nottingham, UK, designed by Michael Hopkins and Partners.
Source: Michael Hopkins and Partners

subject of computer modelling. One particular problem is that of excessive night-time cooling with cold air entering the building via the units. Dampers and windjammers are required to ensure that the desirable effect of night-time cooling does not become an excessive energy demand on the building in terms of daytime heating.

It is unusual to employ windcatchers on their own. More normally they form part of a mixed economy of ventilation techniques (windows, atria, mechanical backup). It has been claimed that the use of windcatchers can reduce the energy load of ventilation by 40 per cent with initial capital costs 15 per cent lower than conventional solutions. There is also less space required for plant rooms and, due to the simplicity of windcatcher technology, maintenance costs are significantly lower.[10]

Sunpipes
Sunpipes (sometimes called lightpipes) are roof-mounted chambers (normally tubes) which bring light into the building from the sky above. They can be combined with windcatchers – providing both natural light and ventilation. Sunpipes are usually silvered mirror-finished aluminium tubes, 400–600 mm in diameter, which direct daylight and sunlight into the building. Most have a polycarbonate capping at the top (with ultra-violet protection) and a prismatic diffuser at the bottom to ensure even light distribution.

Sunpipes have emerged as a useful technology to improve daylight levels in deep-plan buildings and, as such, reduce demand for electric lighting. They are effective in both sunny and overcast conditions, offer low-maintenance access to renewable energy, provide long-term cost savings and CO_2 reductions. They are particularly useful in single-storey buildings that require deep plans such as schools, factories and shops, and in areas where privacy is important such as health clinics and doctors' surgeries. They also offer greater security than traditional windows, because the narrow pipe diameter does not allow human penetration.

Window design
As discussed earlier in the context of comfort, the design of windows is a great deal more complex than simply satisfying U-value requirements. The U-value standard of 1.8 for windows required under Part L of the UK Building Regulations (2006) ignores the site-specific interrelationships between heat loss, solar gain,

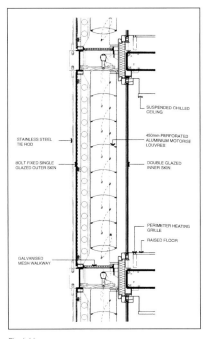

Fig 141
Window detail at Helicon Building, London,
designed by Sheppard Robson.
Source: Sheppard Robson

daylight penetration and air infiltration. Windows are complex design problems requiring attention to size, shape, location and position as well as the angle of splays, position of blinds (internal and external) and the size of openings. Added to this, the type of glass and its coatings (low-emissivity such as Pilkington K Glass, for example) have a significant impact on energy performance, daylight levels and aesthetic factors.

Under ideal conditions, windows provide effective cross-ventilation and daylight penetration. However, for ventilation they do not work effectively on still hot days or under very windy conditions. Also, users are reluctant to open windows when the outside temperature is low, particularly if they are responsible for the energy bills. Opening and closing windows has ramifications for energy efficiency, ventilation levels and the acoustic environment. This is why stack effect ventilation is often preferred, why there are pressures (particularly with climate change) to increase the level of use of air-conditioning, to develop new technologies (often based on old ones) of windcatchers and sunpipes, and why window design is subject to close attention.

The tightening of standards for windows to match those elsewhere in Europe under amendments to the Building Regulations in 2006, and the application of the new regulations to refurbishment as well as new construction, have resulted in considerable carbon savings. However, the energy efficiency of windows is better assessed using the European Window Energy Rating Scheme. This evaluates the energy performance of windows on the basis of their thermal insulation, useful solar gain and air infiltration as a total package in a specific location. The resulting assessment provides a rating number which is site-related rather than universal. Hence, orientation, exposure and other factors are taken into account.

High-performance windows are rated against three criteria – air-tightness, frame thermal conductivity and glazing performance (known as Ug value). Normally the PassivHaus standard (see chapter 9) requires triple glazing with argon or krypton filling, low-emissivity coatings and spaced using polymer or extruded foam rather than aluminium members. As with all construction, the provenance of the materials, life-cycle performance and ease of installation are important considerations. Super-high-tech windows in low performance walls makes little sense, neither is it ethical to specify timber windows without confirming the origin of the hardwoods.

NOTES

[1] Source: www.who.int/en
[2] Neil May, 'Energy-efficiency and Ecology in the Renovation of Vernacular Buildings', *Building for a Future*, Spring 2000, p. 63.
[3] Torben Dahl and Winnie Friis Möller, *Klimat og Arkitectur*, RDAFA, 2008, pp. 6–12.
[4] The Montreal Protocol Foreign Office Command Paper, Treaty Series No. 19, HMSO, 1990.
[5] Fionn Stevenson and Nick Williams, *Sustainable Housing Design Guide for Scotland*, HMSO, 2000, pp. 70–1.
[6] C. Gates, 'Design speeds recovery', *Building Design*, 25 April 2003, p. 6, see also 'Assessing benefits in the health sector', in Sebastian Macmillan (ed.) *Designing Better Buildings*, Spon Press, London, 2004, pp. 100–6.
[7] Quoted by Neil May at the *Green Buildings Pay* seminar, Aylesbury, Buckinghamshire, 18 October 2000.
[8] The author here is indebted to the Natural Buildings Technologies Company for the list and summary.
[9] Op. cit., Stevenson and Williams, p. 68.
[10] 'Passivent' brochure C1/SFB (57), March 2001, p. 3.

9 Sustainable Design in Practice

A 'green' building will usually involve a combination of innovative technologies, connection in some way with UK or EU government policy (including any financial incentives that may be available), and a client who recognises the health and social benefits of low-energy design. It is this combination, for instance, which is behind the Hampshire green schools, green office projects such as the Barclaycard Building in Northampton designed by Fitzroy Robinson and Partners, and green housing schemes such as BedZed and RuralZed designed by Bill Dunster. Government policy on its own will not achieve the necessary

Fig 142 (*above and right*)
Compact low-energy social housing at Beddington (BedZed), London, designed by Bill Dunster.
Source: BedZed, Bill Dunster

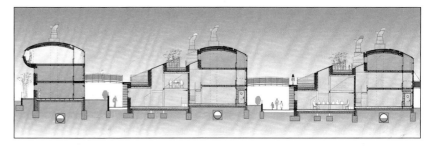

changes – innovations in technology, construction and design are also required. Added to this, clients need to feel that there is a business case for sustainable design, which shows real benefits in the balance sheet. Hence it is important to integrate the three factors that lead to energy-efficient and sustainable design – technology push; policy pull; enlightened self interest.

THE IMPORTANCE OF 'TECHNOLOGY PUSH' TO THE ARCHITECT

For the architect, energy technologies can usefully be divided into two types – new forms of energy and better use of existing energy. The former include renewable energy, new hydrogen-based fuels and biofuels. The latter includes greater efficiency in the use of existing energy (whether fossil fuel based or renewable) by better design, from optimum orientation to super-insulation, and improved management of buildings from boilers to room controls. In the past, the architect and building services engineer were occupied mainly with improving the efficiency with which energy supplies were utilised, but today they are increasingly concerned with alternative forms of energy generation at the building itself (e.g. solar or wind

Fig 143
RuralZed designed by Bill Dunster, a low-energy house designed to achieve Level 6 of the Code for Sustainable Homes (CSH).
Source: ZEDfactory

power). The improved technology of generation of electricity from photovoltaic panels and micro-wind generators means that buildings will have an important role to play in meeting national energy needs over the next century.

Broadly speaking, energy conservation and the associated problem of global warming will be addressed by five main mechanisms:

- move from fossil fuels to renewable energy sources
- improve existing energy technologies
- change attitudes and consumer behaviour
- use price mechanisms and international laws to regulate consumption
- better design of infrastructure, including buildings.

Architects and engineers have an important role to play, so too do clients who commission buildings and politicians who establish the framework for action. Attitudinal change can be achieved by using green buildings and green transport to set an example. Unfortunately, most people in the developed world lead consumer-led, energy-intensive and resource-wasteful lives, whether in the buildings they choose to live or work in, in their choice of mobility or in the products they consume.[1]

Because of its visibility – in actuality and on the TV screen – architecture is an important vehicle in raising awareness of sustainability. It can show that a green future is as rich, beautiful and healthy as older patterns of lifestyle. Green futures are essentially about the application of new technologies, particularly in the design of cities and their buildings. Here, the architect has an important role in shaping the future of the planet.

The following sections describe differing approaches to the design of sustainable buildings in three key sectors: offices, schools and housing. The final section reviews how these individual buildings might come together in sustainable communities.

OFFICES

Sustainability has probably altered the design of offices more than any other building type. There are two reasons for this: first, the relative inefficiency of

Typical energy consumption related to office buildings in the UK
☐ Travel to work – 50 per cent
☐ In-use energy – 39 per cent
☐ Fmbodied energy – 11 per cent

Typical annual investment associated with office buildings in UK
☐ Salaries – 60–80 per cent
☐ Buildings – 7 per cent
☐ In-use energy – 4 per cent
☐ Equipment, etc. – 9 per cent

earlier typologies, with their dependence on air-conditioning, electric lighting and mechanical ventilation; and second, the new awareness of the beneficial effects of more natural methods of lighting and ventilation upon psychological stress levels and, as a consequence, upon worker productivity.

General characteristics of green office design	
☐ Shallow floor plates (12–15 m) for maximum daylight and ease of cross-ventilation.	☐ Solar control by means of external screens and internal blinds.
☐ Use of atria or glazed malls to promote solar-assisted ventilation.	☐ Use of thermal capacity to moderate temperatures.
☐ Height to promote stack-effect ventilation.	☐ Air-conditioning restricted to 'hot spots'.
☐ Orientation on east–west axis to give long north and south elevations.	

The general characteristics of a green office are supplemented by a range of specific constructional strategies which can be modified to suit different types of office, level of occupation and extent of IT use. They can be categorised according to four sustainable design themes – energy, water, materials and health. Not all of the general or specific features can be incorporated into a single project, but as a rule of thumb it should be possible to achieve 75 per cent compliance with the options shown in the table opposite.

Since the bulk of energy used in a typical office is derived from electricity (lighting, fans, computers), it is here that particular efforts to reduce energy consumption should be directed. The easiest economies are to optimise the use of daylight and to use low-energy light fittings.

Daylight penetration can be enhanced by the use of daylight shelves outside, by improving the design of window soffits and reveals, and by profiling the ceiling. Daylight cannot be projected beyond a distance of 7 m (depending upon level of external illumination), thereby restricting the depth of an office to around 14 m (assuming windows on both sides). However, the use of high ceilings can enhance light penetration.

Normally, offices deeper than 14 m are subdivided by glazed courts or atria. These provide a source not only of daylight but also of sunlight, the heat from which can be employed to provide natural ventilation via the stack effect. It is also important to utilise the roof for daylight.

Specific characteristics of green office design	
Energy	Natural or displacement ventilation Optimum use of daylight High thermal mass, preferably exposed Solar shading and light shelves Waste heat recovery High levels of insulation
Water	Dual-flush toilets Spray taps Urinal sensors Rainwater collection
Materials	Use of recycled/reused/renewable materials Local sourcing of materials Construction for disassembly High-tech materials for energy engineering
Health	Limited automation of environmental control Low-toxicity materials Natural environment/materials Social space as well as work space Nature visible inside and out

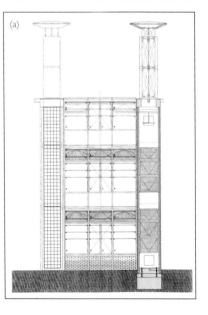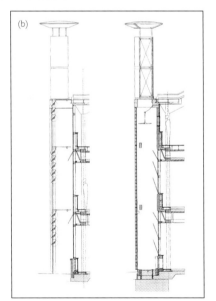

Fig 144
BRE office, Watford, designed by Feilden Clegg
Bradley: (a) façade detail; (b) façade section;
(c) view; (d) floor section.
Source: Feilden Clegg Bradley

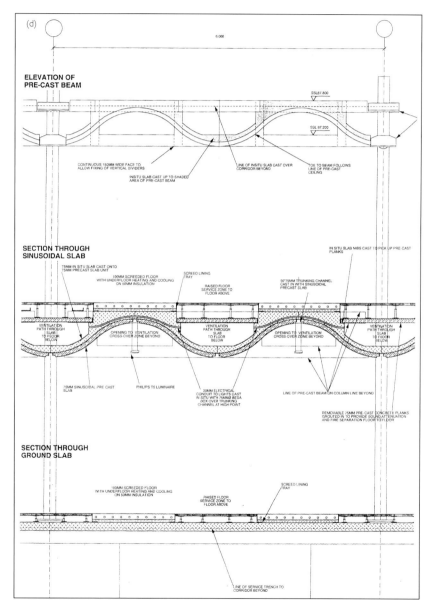

Research suggests that office workers placed near to windows suffer less stress than those further away. Being close to windows increases access to natural light (including sunlight), natural ventilation and views – all properties which promote physical health and a sense of psychological well-being. Research also confirms the importance of lighting, humidity and ventilation switches being under the control of the office worker. In modern offices such controls are often automated and adjusted by a building management system triggered by sensors. Although this may help reduce energy use, it can frustrate workers, who like to feel they can alter their workspace to suit their own needs. The 'feel good' factor of green design – where control is put back into the hands of the building's users – has only recently begun to influence workspace design.

The correct orientation of an office building is also important. Difficulties such as excessive solar gain, glare and light reflection on computer screens can occur when the sun is at a low angle. Ideally, offices should be aligned to an east–west axis so that there is one long south elevation and a long north elevation. The south façade can then be protected by solar screens, vented at the top through

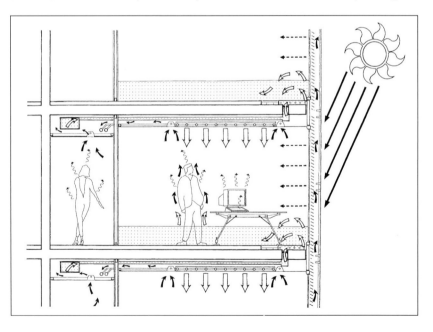

Fig 145
Attention to the quality of the working environment as well as energy efficiency leads to productivity benefits.
Source: Foster and Partners

a deep double or triple wall, with light levels adjusted by mechanically controlled louvres or blinds. Conversely, the north façade can be clear glazed without fear of provoking any of the complications associated with sunlight. The east and west façades, being narrow, can contain accommodation such as photocopy rooms or toilets. Their special needs can be matched by a façade that is more solid in character.

Office buildings that are glazed on all façades, often in order to maximise daylight penetration and external views, can experience difficulties. Several strategies can be employed to achieve relatively high levels of energy efficiency, such as double skins that incorporate different types of glass according to orientation, translucent insulation and self-venting façades. Increasingly, the office envelope consists of intelligent façade technology controlled by a computerised management system. As already described, such systems give the benefit of better energy efficiency but have the disadvantage of being indifferent to the variety of human needs.

Office buildings also commonly employ a system of external louvres which provide three functions in one device – solar protection, daylight shelves and walkways for building maintenance. This approach has the advantage of simplicity, and being fixed in nature, these appendages do not suffer from the high cost of maintaining moving parts (which is a problem with mechanical louvres, for instance). Another benefit of this combined system is the uniformity it can give to façade design, thereby aiding prefabrication and cost reduction. A permanent walkway constructed to project beyond the glazing line in the proportion of 1 m width for every 3 m ceiling height helps to keep windows clean and shaded from the midday sun. Many urban offices suffer from a loss of energy efficiency (approaching 15 per cent) as a combined result of dirty glass and the cooling load needed to deal with solar heat gain.

Planting is often used to moderate the environment. External tree planting can provide useful solar shade in the summer, but when the leaves drop in the autumn the same trees offer little obstruction to the penetration of winter daylight and desirable solar gains. Trees planted in atria and shrubs positioned in office areas have the benefit of purifying the air and of reducing stress levels associated with sterile working environments. Internal planting also encourages social exchange, which can enhance the sense of community within commercial buildings.

Fig 146
This low-energy office for Aardman in Bristol, designed by Alex French Architects, features many sustainable practices.

Fig 147
Attention to quality of daylight penetration
at Wessex Water HQ, UK, designed by
Bennetts Associates: (a) exterior sunscreen;
(b) façade section.
Source: Bennetts Associates

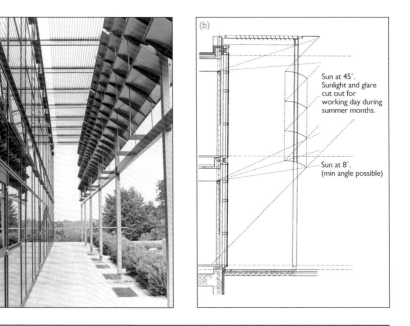

Sun at 45°.
Sunlight and glare
cut out for
working day during
summer months.

Sun at 8°.
(min angle possible)

Advantages of concrete office buildings

☐ Stable indoor environment due to high
  thermal capacity.
☐ Attractive and healthy indoor environment.
☐ Ability to exploit natural light through
  pale-coloured concrete soffits shaped as light
  scoops.
☐ Ability to incorporate water-filled cooling
  pipes or air ducts within concrete structures
  to reduce cooling load.

☐ Ability to design out suspended ceilings
  and air-conditioning (reducing costs by
  5–7 per cent).
☐ Potential to improve staff productivity by
  better levels of natural light and enhanced air
  quality (improvement of 6 per cent claimed)

Source: Eco concrete, British Cement Association, 2001, p. 6

Comparison of benefits of natural cooling systems over air-conditioning

☐ 50 per cent reduction in carbon dioxide
  emissions
☐ 20 per cent reduction in building services
  component of construction costs

☐ 5–7 per cent reduction in building
  maintenance costs
☐ Potential staff productivity benefits

Source: Eco concrete, British Cement Association, 2001, p. 6

Natural cooling systems in office buildings[2]	
Technique	Energy benefit (W/m² of floor area)
Exposed soffits of floor slabs, coffered to maximise heat exchange area	25
Air ducting through concrete slabs (e.g. Termodeck system)	40
Water cooling through concrete slabs (embedded pipes)	64

Clearly, there are many strategies available to achieve the green office. The depth of floor plates is important; so is access to daylight, sunlight (in atria spaces) and natural ventilation. Orientation is also important, especially in suburban development, and planting can aid energy efficiency. The use of alternate office floors and glazed atria begins to recall the pattern of streets and malls found in cities. The dynamics of large offices are, after all, like those of small cities in the way that the number of people employed leads to a sense of community, which design can consolidate. Atria, important as they are for low-energy design, are equally valued as social spaces by the people who work in buildings that have them. At the Barclaycard Building in Northampton, which accommodates over

Fig 148
This low-energy office for the Ministry of Defence near Bristol, designed by Percy Thomas Architects, sets a good example of enlightened procurement.
Source: Percy Thomas Architects

2000 employees, for example, the internal galleria successfully provides a variety of environmental and social functions.[3]

Economic benefits of green offices

It is now increasingly recognised that green office buildings – which give staff some perceptual contact with the outside world of wind, rain and sun as well as with sunlit internal spaces – lead to enhanced levels of staff satisfaction and performance. This in turn leads to lower turnover of staff through greater job satisfaction. Research suggests that the naturally lit and ventilated office generates less absenteeism through sickness or poor morale than air-conditioned offices.[4] In other words, green buildings not only conserve energy, they also help reduce company staff costs by stimulating better staff motivation. In fact, the 2–4 per cent increase in worker productivity recorded by studies of green offices nearly pays for all the annual energy costs of a typical large company building.

Studies in the USA of office buildings accredited by LEED (see chapter 3) suggest that, over a 20-year period, the productivity benefits of green design outweigh the energy benefits by a factor of six.[5] In life-cycle costing terms, although sustainable approaches may add 1–3 per cent to building costs, the financial benefits are accrued in 5–8 years, mainly as a result of improved productivity.

Thus, for many companies procuring a green building is as much a question of investment in people as it is an exercise in saving energy. In this sense, the current UK government's emphasis on energy efficiency is too narrow a focus for the business sector. For many companies the motive for sustainable design stems from a genuine concern to invest in people – to give the workforce an environment which promotes health, commitment and productivity.

The main benefits of investing in environmentally smart office buildings are:

- reduced investment risk through changes to environmental legislation and rising fuel prices
- improved rental income through better image for the building
- increased lettable area through a reduction in the volume of building services
- improved building flexibility through structural simplicity
- lower construction and maintenance costs by avoiding air-conditioning

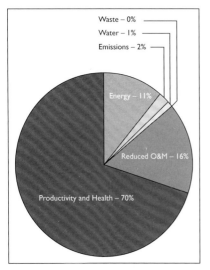

Fig 149
The financial benefits of green offices in the USA over a 20-year period, according to research undertaken by Capital-E.

Source: Capital-E Analysis, www.cap-e.com

- enhanced company profile
- better productivity of the workforce through improved working environment.

Against these benefits, however, are a number of concerns, such as:

- noise problems as a result of open plan and atrium configurations
- overheating problems as a result of reliance on natural cooling and ventilation, a problem exacerbated by climate change
- lack of occupant control over working conditions due to computerised building management systems
- lack of thermal mass due to the drive towards prefabrication and the speed offered by steel construction.

As a general rule the greater the 'naturalness' of the working environment, especially with regard to natural light and ventilation, the greater the economic benefits through enhanced productivity.[6] Studies indicate that a well-designed green office needs an intelligent system of controls to achieve overall energy efficiency, but that a means of overriding it should be provided for the person

Fig 150
Design for a green office of the future by ECD Architects.
Source: ECD Architects

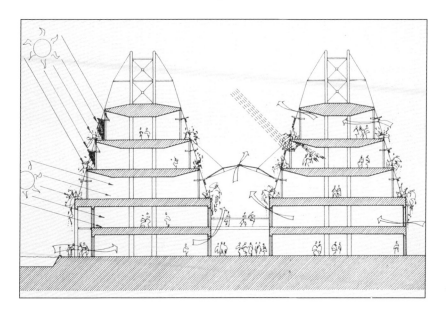

Fig 151
This data centre in Kuala Lumpur, designed by Hamzah & Yeang, integrates façade planting, green interior spaces and PV roofscape to produce a distinctive ecological office building.
Source: Hamzah & Yeang

who works in that particular space.[7] Another issue is the relationship between energy conservation and noise disturbance. The trend in green offices is towards more open plan working, and the use of atria and malls inside buildings to maximise daylight penetration and promote solar-assisted ventilation. There is also the growing intensification of the use of space (especially in call centres) and the concept of 'hot-desking'. Added to this, the speed and flexibility afforded by prefabricated construction have reduced the acoustic and thermal mass of modern buildings, adding to potential noise levels and temperature fluctuations in the workplace. As a consequence, noise and comfort toleration is a growing problem in green buildings. So whereas the natural conditions in green offices are favoured by workers, adding to productivity and reduced absenteeism, there is a risk of high levels of ambient noise and temperature peaks, which can have a detrimental impact on the very people sustainable design is seeking to benefit.[8] Noise is not only a limiting factor in green offices – it has also proved to be a problem with green schools, hospitals and libraries.[9]

Procurement of green offices

The procurement of innovative sustainable buildings can be a precarious business undertaking, despite the productivity advantages that result from higher morale, less staff illness and lower levels of staff turnover. For companies that build for their own staff, there is clearly an incentive to invest in green design, but where developers build speculatively there is little motivation to care for an unknown workforce.[10] In the latter case, the arguments in favour of green design lead to developers addressing energy and other utility costs rather than the performance of occupants or the image of tenants. It remains a sobering reflection upon the UK construction industry that 20 per cent of all energy used in buildings is wasted by poor design and inadequate understanding of those who manage the buildings.[11] Guidance from government has moved in the past ten years from design and technology solutions to management and procurement ones.[12]

Analysis of buildings such as the MOD office at Abbey Wood, the Bristol and West plc headquarters and the BP office at Sunbury confirms the business advantages of green offices.[13] However, there is also evidence that there are many formerly invisible benefits of good environmental design which purely technical performance indicators failed to identify.[14] As a result, a new set of

Benefits and costs of green office design to different stakeholders		
Stakeholder		Benefit
Public	Government	Lower healthcare costs Improved performance of the national economy Greater energy efficiency and lower fossil fuel dependency
	Regulatory bodies	Helps achieve national and international environmental obligations Improves regional image
Private	Developer	Enhanced business efficiency Reduced long-term costs Greater competitiveness through enhanced staff productivity Improved company image
	Designer	Enhanced reputation Better relationship with regulators Improved profile through publications Development of 'future' skills Ethical compliance
	User	Enhanced levels of productivity Improvement in personnel health Stimulating working environment and less stress More sociable working life

Design Quality Indicators (DQIs) and Key Performance Indicators (KPIs) have been developed through a joint initiative of CABE (Commission for Architecture and the Built Environment), the RIBA and RICS which put sustainability into the procurement process.[15]

PROBE Studies

In parallel with the studies mentioned above, a group of researchers undertook an initiative known as PROBE (Post-occupancy Review of Buildings and their Engineering).[16] PROBE (and the more recent work undertaken in the USA by G. H. Kats[17]) was keen to compare the energy performance of green buildings in use with the predictions made at the design stage, and to correlate these findings with user and management consequences. What was discovered was that green buildings often failed to achieve energy-saving expectations, not through design shortcomings but as a result of poor construction or building operation.[18] From these studies, it appears that the weak link is the user – and specifically how occupants sought to modify the internal working environment to meet their own personal needs, often at the expense of the performance of the building as a whole. The main conclusions were that:

- buildings are not as air-tight as expected, resulting in draughts, poor energy performance and user modification
- window blinds do not work as planned (especially at corners of buildings)
- users complain of the lack of control over their working environment
- noise is a problem, especially in open plan buildings
- management can be slow to adjust environmental systems
- maintenance of building plant is difficult, and the energy systems are not always understood by managers.

In drawing attention to the interrelationships between design, construction, occupant comfort and management issues, the PROBE studies have provided useful insights into green buildings.

Users prefer:

- shallow building plans which provide an interface between inside and outside
- high thermal mass for stable temperatures
- windows that they can open and blinds they can control
- clearly defined occupancy zones (cellular offices rather than open plan) with social as well as functional spaces
- personal interface between PC keyboard and control of the working environment
- building management which responds quickly to internal environmental problems
- natural materials and planting in the workplace.

The list highlights not only the necessary overlap between design and management but also the importance of placing the needs of the user to the fore at the briefing stage. PROBE also highlighted the gap that often exists between concept and execution, with poor workmanship (rather than design) being responsible for the bulk of energy problems. The studies also showed that management was often indifferent or under-informed about the technical operation of the building, a problem which increases with time.

The more innovative the office building, the greater the need for shared environmental values between client, designer, building manager and user. As PROBE notes, good performance normally stems from 'relatively simple, thoughtful solutions, implemented … with attention to detail'.[19] However, unless the user is taken on board and management acts as an effective bridge between concept and reality, the benefits of sustainable design can be undermined by a revengeful workforce. Two main conclusions can be drawn. First, sustainable design principles should be in the brief, and understood by all. Second, the benefit to users of a healthy and stimulating working environment should be recognised in economic and cultural terms.

GREEN SCHOOLS[20]

Numerous guides are available to help architects and engineers develop school designs that are both effective as learning environments and help achieve sustainable solutions. Many architects aspire to create stimulating, light, spacious and airy schools which exploit solar energy for heat gain and ventilation. The most useful guides for the UK are the former Department for Education and Skills' (DfES) Building Bulletin 87: Guidelines for Environmental Design in Schools (second edition 2003) which is now largely superseded by BREEAM for Schools, and the earlier but nevertheless useful Building Research Energy Conservation Support Unit's (BRECSU) Good Practice Guide 173: Energy Efficient Design of New Buildings and Extensions – For Schools and Colleges. These provide valuable guidance on topics such as orientation, materials, finishes, daylight, ventilation, acoustics and thermal performance. Guidance is also provided on plan type and to a degree on the sectional profile of school buildings in order to support low-energy solutions. As a consequence, school design in the UK is relatively well-prescribed, leading to recognisable layouts for different types of school (rural or urban) and schools at different levels (primary or secondary).

Since 2004 the UK government has been testing new approaches to school design via the Exemplar Schools, Classroom of the Future and Building Schools for the Future (BSF) programmes. These, and investment in inner city academy schools, have focussed on the classroom as the prime learning space in the school and hence the area where environmental conditions most impact upon learning.

Five main plan typologies[21] are commonly adopted for schools:

- compact urban plan
- courtyard plan
- radial plan
- linear plan
- organic plan.

The most commonly used roof profiles are:

- flat roof with central atria, glazed mall and classroom roof-lights
- pitched roof with glazed perimeter buffer or solar spaces, sometimes with central mall
- wave or stepped roof to provide cross-ventilation at different levels, often solar assisted.

These plan and sectional typologies are used in simple or hybrid form according to site characteristics, design brief, sustainability aspiration and orientation. Passive solar design schools are usually single or two storey with extensive south-facing classroom glazing, conservatories and high-level ventilation on the north side. Some green schools adopt a more pluralistic approach and employ central wind-tower ventilation systems (based on windcatcher technology), while others use woodchip heating systems and occasionally PV panels for electricity production. Some of the Exemplar Schools designs have organic shapes dictated by ecological factors or site features.

Many schools employ central glazed malls to provide central solar-heated buffer zones, which in turn provide exhibition-cum-social space. In all configurations, the objective is to meet the educational needs at reduced energy and resource costs. In the process, the school can be employed to help reinforce the message of environmentalism through the interaction between pedagogy and design. In this sense the school becomes part of the curriculum in the manner promoted by the Eco-Schools movement.[22]

Whatever plan form is adopted it is crucial that there is ample and well-distributed daylight and sufficient ventilation to exhaust internal pollutants, particularly carbon dioxide. It is also very important to consider the acoustic needs of learners and teachers in the classroom, since with open plan solar schools there can be excess noise transmission from one classroom to another. Here, the use of carpet finishes employed for comfort and sound insulation may run counter to the need for exposed thermal mass (to moderate peaks in temperature, especially with passive solar schools) and the reflectivity of floor finishes (essential for daylight penetration into deep classrooms). Since electricity has a high CO_2 rating per unit of power, there needs to be particular attention paid to both artificial lighting and fan-assisted mechanical ventilation. By exploiting wind and sun as a source of energy in the school it may be possible to generate electricity (using PV panels or wind generators), thereby driving down running costs and preparing pupils for a life without cheap fossil fuels.

Atria, glazed malls and attached conservatories are a common feature of school design. They provide a valuable unheated amenity-cum-classroom space. Glazed malls bisecting deep school buildings, as employed for example at Swanlea School in Whitechapel in London, provide a chance for pupils to socialise under teacher surveillance during school breaks. Unlike playgrounds, where socialising is often

Fig 152 *(right)*
Inner-city London: Swanlea School, Whitechapel, with glazed mall.
Source: Percy Thomas Architects

Fig 153 *(far right)*
Environmental control at the edge of a classroom.
Source: ECD Architects

unsupervised (and hence where bullying tends to occur), these amenity spaces which are justified on low-energy grounds also provide useful support for the life and welfare of the school. However, such spaces can prove so attractive that teachers are tempted to heat them using mobile fan heaters. This tends to undermine the energy strategy for the school as a whole, disrupting the balance between solar heating and natural ventilation established at the design stage. Also, because such spaces are uninsulated, heating adds considerably to energy costs (and CO_2). As with office buildings, the ethos of the school and the environmental strategies need to be understood by teachers, janitors and pupils alike.

Usually, the glazed malls and atria that divide blocks of classrooms are separated from the teaching areas by walls which have opening windows or large double doors. These openings can act as flexible links between classrooms and sun-spaces. The flow of warmed air should be encouraged from the sun-space on sunny days and discouraged on overcast days. The obvious benefit of glazed malls is that of modification of the internal climate of the school by allowing the interior and exterior worlds to be connected climatically. It also allows the exterior environment of the school to perceptually enter the classroom, to the benefit of pupil well-being. As a teaching aid, the temperature gradients can be mapped, encouraging the pupils to understand the laws of physics without resorting to textbooks.

To achieve maximum benefit from low-energy design in the classroom there needs to be:

- adequate window and door control between teaching and sun-spaces
- adequate acoustic protection of the classroom from both interior ambient noise and external disturbance
- recognition that sun-spaces reduce the daylight and ventilation of the teaching areas to which they are attached
- a responsive system of blinds and solar shading to prevent overheating in the summer and heat loss in winter
- finishes which maximise daylight penetration
- ventilation which is solar or wind assisted via low-level and high-level windows, perhaps supported by sloping classroom ceilings
- an understanding by teachers and janitors of the energy design strategy.

Advantages of different plan types[23]

The compact plan is commonly adopted in school design especially in urban areas. In brief, it consists of a square with classrooms on two or three sides and the school hall, offices and library on another. It is sometimes left open on one side to allow for solar penetration or external views, and frequently has a partial or full atrium in the centre. The compact plan is relatively energy efficient as long as the classrooms face mainly to the south and advantage is taken of using the roof for lighting and ventilation. The plan works well in single-storey or multi-storey form, although the angle of roofs should be kept low (but not flat) to allow for solar penetration. Two good examples are the Bridge Academy in London designed by BDP and Ørestad High School in Copenhagen designed by 3XN.

In the compact plan, particular attention needs to be paid to lighting the classrooms. Ideally, daylight should be available from opposite sides (often via an atrium) which gives an even distribution of daylight and facilitates natural cross-ventilation. The disadvantage is that high levels of computer use add to incidental heat gains, which in turn may necessitate mechanical cooling – increasing background noise levels; a considerable problem, since the spoken word must be heard clearly in all corners of the classroom.

The courtyard plan shares similarities with the compact plan except that there is an open and unroofed square in the centre. Normally, the entrance, library

Fig 154
The low-energy Ørestad High School, Copenhagen, designed by 3XN, features flexible vertical solar shading: (a) plan; (b) section; and (c) view.
3XN Architects and Brian Edwards

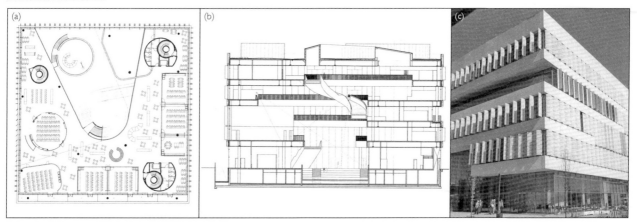

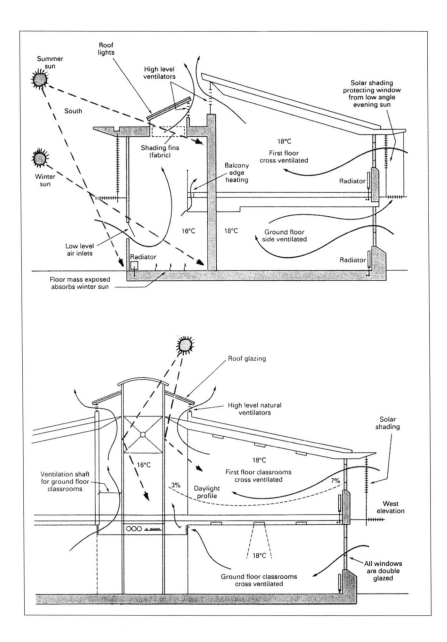

Fig 155
Sections through classrooms at John Cabot
School, Bristol, designed by Feilden Clegg
Bradley, showing the ventilation strategy at
difference seasons.
Source: Feilden Clegg Bradley

and school hall are placed to the north and the classrooms wrap around on the other sides. Since the number of classrooms does not normally fill three sides of the courtyard it is more common for the classrooms to occupy two wings (orientated south–east and south–west) with offices, library, etc., placed on the third side. This allows the school to address both the internal and external worlds.

With the courtyard plan the sectional profile of classrooms is similar to that in compact layouts (southerly roof overhangs and high-level north-facing windows). One advantage of the courtyard plan is that the central corridor provides views into both the courtyard and the classrooms – providing good surveillance for teachers and a welcoming atmosphere for visitors. But a disadvantage is the high ratio between perimeter wall area and internal volume, which can add to construction costs. However, the courtyard form readily adapts to rectangular shaped sites, providing a formal architecture which suits the character of many urban locations. Like the traditional courtyard house, the courtyard school plan provides a high level of security, good environmental performance and the potential benefit of standardised units of construction.

The radiant plan is arranged so that the classrooms occupy linear projections from a central communal area. The plan allows the wings to radiate out to take advantage of climatic and environmental features. As in other layouts, it is important that the classrooms face generally to the south, but the detailed design needs to overcome summertime overheating by employing external sunshades, internal blinds or special glass. With this configuration there is also the need to ensure that classroom spacing allows for adequate daylight penetration in the winter. Ideally, south-east to south orientation should be sought for classrooms rather than west since winter solar gain can be beneficial in reducing heating loads. In this layout, larger specialist spaces in the school (such as a hall and a library) can benefit from the northern light. Another advantage of the layout is the way that wings can be aligned to protect the school from adverse climatic conditions, creating sheltered spaces in the gaps between classrooms.

As a general rule in schools, southern glazing should be around 60 per cent of the wall area and northern glazing about 30 per cent. This allows for an optimum balance to be struck between winter solar gain and daylight penetration while also avoiding fabric heat loss and summer overheating. However, overshadowing by

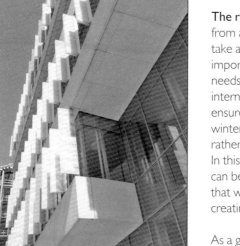

Fig 156
Solar shading used artistically by 3XN at Ørestad High School.

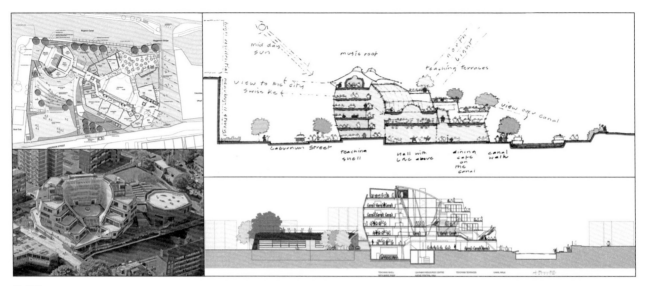

Fig 157
Plan, sketch, view and section of Bridge
Academy, London, designed by BDP.
Source: BDP and Commission Air

adjacent buildings and trees may affect these ratios, and local variations in climate must also to be accommodated. Hence an ideal solution for a school in northern Scotland will be quite different to one for a school in southern England.

The linear plan is arguably the most common plan type for schools in the UK and is much adopted in the Building Schools for the Future (BSF) programme. This plan offers many organisational, social and environmental benefits. The classrooms usually face south with the other accommodation to the north, separated by a spine corridor or glazed street. The building section is arranged so that the classrooms take advantage of high-level windows facing north, alongside the spine corridor. The accommodation to the north also benefits from roof-lights facing south, sometimes looking into the glazed street. The section not only allows daylight to penetrate deep into the plan but also facilitates cross-ventilation without mechanical backup. Of all the plan types, this one gives greatest access to renewable energy.

However, the linear form requires particular attention to be paid to the shapes and angles of roofs and the heights of walls. Daylight, sunlight and ventilation are encouraged by employing wave-shaped roofs and different heights of

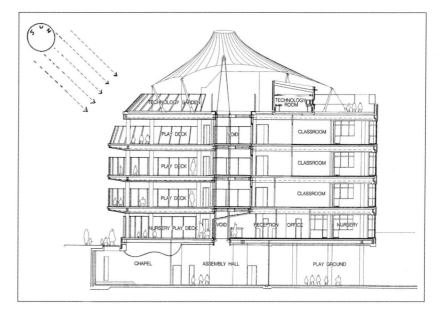

rooms. As with other green school plan types, the area of glazing needs to be adjusted according to orientation, local climate and the balance between fossil fuel and renewable energy use at the school. The linear plan is best suited to a site which offers a long east–west axis (i.e. with a long south-facing aspect). If it is employed at right angles to this axis there can be serious problems in the classroom with glare when the sun angle is low, as well as considerable energy inefficiency.

The organic plan is often employed as a hybridisation of the other plans and has the advantage that the layout can respond directly to the natural features of the site. Also, where vernacular methods of building are employed (in order to maintain regional building traditions), the resulting design tends to reflect ecological principles rather than low-energy ones. As a result, the school is likely to have randomly oriented classrooms, a footprint which is readily absorbed into the local scene, and materials of construction which are local in origin (such as timber) rather than machine made (such as concrete block). The organic plan generally results in organic elevations since the same principles that shape the

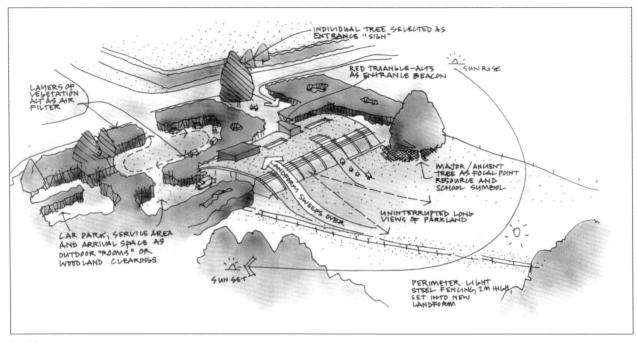

INDIVIDUAL TREE SELECTED AS
ENTRANCE "SIGN"

RED TRIANGLE-ACTS
AS ENTRANCE BEACON

SUNRISE

LAYERS OF
VEGETATION
ACT AS AIR
FILTER

LANDFORM SWEEPS OVER

MAJOR / ANCIENT
TREE AS FOCAL POINT
RESOURCE AND
SCHOOL SYMBOL

UNINTERRUPTED LONG
VIEWS OF PARKLAND

CAR PARK, SERVICE AREA
AND ARRIVAL SPACE AS
OUTDOOR "ROOMS" OR
WOODLAND CLEARINGS

SUNSET

PERIMETER LIGHT
STEEL FENCING, 2M HIGH,
SET INTO NEW
LANDFORM

Fig 159
Design for sustainable school in Sevenoaks, UK,
by Architects Design Partnership.
Source: Architects Design Partnership

plan find expression in the section and construction details (e.g. Stoke Park Infants
School at Bishopstoke in Hampshire).

Selecting the plan type
The first four plan configurations are remarkably similar in terms of potential
energy efficiency. The organic form is unlikely to be as energy efficient; however,
it does bring other environmental benefits, and if local construction materials
are employed the embodied energy levels will be lower. The organic plan offers
a quasi-vernacular solution which may suit semi-rural locations or the use of
traditional forms of construction.

The choice of plan type is likely to be the result of site characteristics and the
preferences of the local education authority rather than the search for sustainable
design per se. However, if more clients were to prioritise green aspirations in
the brief there would be greater motivation to apply innovative eco-thinking by

designers. The plan analysis also suggests that ecological design tends to favour indigenous, organic layouts, inspired perhaps by vernacular practices, while for energy efficiency and economy of construction more rational plan types are preferable (e.g. the compact, courtyard or linear plan).

The choice of layout needs also to address aspects of social sustainability and the interactions between teacher, pupil, parent and community. The school is an important place for the social development of children, and different plan types offer quite distinctive spaces for socialising. The courtyard form, for instance, provides an inner world which is easily supervised, while the linear form offers a long central space whose characteristics are not unlike a shopping mall. The radiant plan provides spaces which address the external world of playgrounds and sports fields. Different plan types also take advantage of different degrees of solar access and different levels of climatic exposure. The linear form is well suited to an open southerly aspect, the courtyard form to where shelter is required (from wind and noise), the compact form to where land is at a premium, and the organic to where harmony between buildings and nature is required. Whichever plan arrangement is used it is important that the architect understands that the school must be a learning environment as well as a low-energy one.

The French philosopher Roland Barthes described the classroom as 'four walls around a future'. Architects have the difficult task of designing those walls and deciding whether walls are needed at all. At Bexley Academy in London, Foster and Partners created a school which, through its flexible almost wall-less classrooms and high levels of IT learning, questioned the fundamental assumptions behind the design of the classroom.

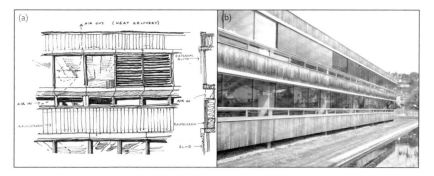

Fig 160
PassivHaus school at Klaus, Austria, designed by Untertrifaller Architects: (a) author's sketch; and (b) view.

SUSTAINABLE HOUSING

Sustainable housing is often presented purely as an exercise in low-energy design, although it is as much a question of creating sustainable communities. Social welfare, cultural inclusion and energy efficiency come together most closely in the arena of housing. The efficient use of resources, especially energy, should concur with the spatial dimensions and social parameters needed to create robust communities. Too often, a concentration on technological innovation, high-rise utopianism and low cost have led to housing which has performed badly in terms of social cohesion and sustainable development. Often models from other climates and cultures are used to solve problems leading to misfit in performance and expectation.

Sustainable housing may be defined as 'housing that creates sustainable communities in a resource-efficient manner'. Here, of course, the resources referred to are energy, water, land, materials and human labour. Sustainable housing projects need to be:

- energy efficient and able to plug-in new technologies over time
- efficient in the use of other resources, especially water
- designed to create robust, self-sustaining mixed-use communities
- designed for long life
- designed for flexibility in lifestyle and tenure
- designed to maximise recycling
- healthy
- designed to embrace ecological principles.

Sustainable housing is more than an exercise in physical attributes. It will be judged a success only if it leads to economic prosperity, stimulates social cohesion, provides security, supports social welfare and is designed to enhance personal, community and global health. Sustainable housing brings together physical, social and cultural factors into a single agenda. Dealing with the complexity of architecture and of the complexity of sustainability with the limited budgets available for most housing projects taxes most accomplished designers.

One issue to address is that of life-cycle flexibility. A great many of resources are wasted in do-it-yourself and costly adaptations of existing houses. One idea that is emerging is that of providing only the basic framework of a house, allowing tenants or new owners to adapt the building to suit their own needs. This approach provides flexibility and offers potential change to suit different family sizes, lifestyles and energy priorities. Hence the architect designs only the basic structure and perimeter enclosure, leaving fit-out to others. What is implied here is the provision of only 90 per cent of the completed house. New owners can upgrade within a more loose fitting armature to suit their needs including that of new energy technologies such as photovoltaic panels.

Housing and CO_2 emissions

Housing is responsible for more than a quarter of the UK's production of CO_2 through the burning of fossil fuels, either in the home or indirectly through the use of electricity. Sixty per cent of domestic CO_2 is produced by heating and 25 per cent by lighting; the other significant (and growing) culprit being domestic equipment – computers, televisions, cookers, refrigerators, etc.

Taking all the fossil fuel energy impacts together (building and domestic activities), housing is responsible for between a quarter and a third of total carbon emissions in the UK, and if transport to homes is included then housing design and associated urban layout accounts for 40 per cent of national carbon emissions.

There is a clear correlation between housing density and energy use. Generally speaking, the more compact the housing, the greater the energy efficiency. This

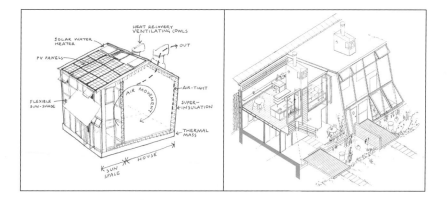

Fig 161
(*right*) Author's interpretation of a house at RuralZed, designed by Bill Dunster Architects; and (*far right*) isometric of solar house, Denmark, by Vandkunsten Architects.
Source: Brian Edwards and Vandkunsten

greater efficiency comes from a number of sources – domestic heating, transport, and communal energy initiatives such as combined heat and power (CHP) and heat recovery. The main constraints on density are access to daylight and sunlight, and social acceptability.

The advantage of compact buildings is that heat loss from one dwelling becomes the heat gain for another. If housing is mixed with offices, shops or small workshops, the heat loss from these during the day can make a useful contribution to the heating of the neighbouring housing units during the evening and overnight (when they are most occupied). As density increases so does the opportunity to employ heat recovery from air and waste water. Hence, a dense mixed-use neighbourhood consumes significantly less primary energy than a dispersed, low-density one. Also, only medium-to-high density development can sustain public transport, with all the energy and community benefits this entails. A relatively high density of about 200 units per hectare, achieved with four-storey buildings, consumes less than a third of the fossil fuel energy that suburban housing constructed at 20 units per hectare consumes. Taking into account transport to shops, schools and work, the energy differential (and hence carbon emission ratio) further benefits compact forms.

So, from an energy efficiency point of view, suburban development is undesirable. Unfortunately, it is the standard 21st-century solution for much of the world – promoted inadvertently on TV series such as Neighbours and The Simpsons.

On the other hand, as density rises, so do other problems, such as crime, lack of personal security, alienation and loss of community.

Factors that have significant impact on energy consumption in housing
☐ Built form: the benefits of compact development. ☐ Building construction: the use of thermal capacity to absorb solar radiation and delay the night-time temperature falls coupled with high levels of insulation. ☐ Orientation: layout to maximise exposure to sun and minimise exposure to prevailing winds.	☐ Microclimate: use building layout to create shelter, working with planting design. ☐ Transport: locate buildings to reduce vehicular movement and increase density at transport nodes and along public transport routes.

Template for sustainable urban housing

☐ Plan depth limited to 10–12 m.
☐ Solar orientation best between south-east and south-west.
☐ Avoid obstruction angle above 30°.
☐ Theoretical design density is 200 dwellings per hectare or 1000 rooms per hectare.

☐ Three- and four-storey buildings preferable.
☐ Every percentage point increase in obstruction over 30° results in the same percentage point increase in energy use.

Adapted from Koen Steemers, The Architects' Journal, 2 November 2000, p. 42

Fig 162
Low-energy community-based housing in Leeds, UK, designed by Levitt Bernstein.
Source: Levitt Bernstein

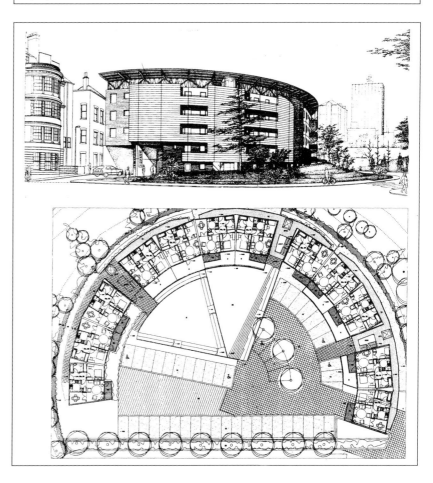

Fig 163
Low-energy community-based housing in
London, designed by Cartwright Pickard.
Source: Cartwright Pickard

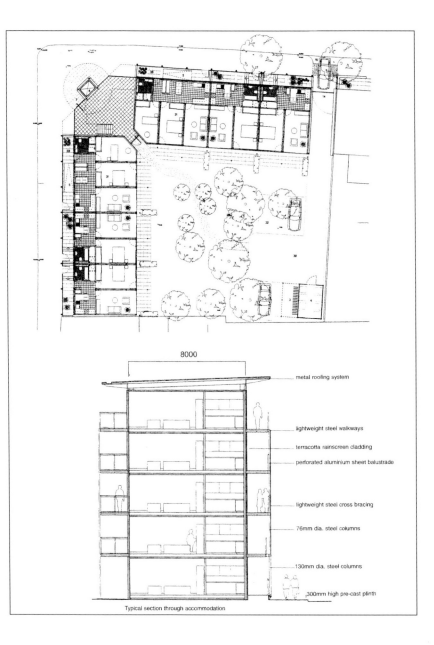

8000

metal roofing system

lightweight steel walkways

terracotta rainscreen cladding

perforated aluminium sheet balustrade

lightweight steel cross bracing

76mm dia. steel columns

130mm dia. steel columns

300mm high pre-cast plinth

Typical section through accommodation

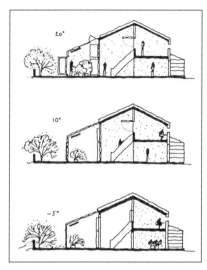

Fig 164
Zoning the use of a house according to season. Notice how the solar room to the south (left) improves living conditions for much of the year without fossil fuel energy input. Design by Peter Sørensen.
Source: Peter Sørensen

A balance is needed between defensible space and sustainability, producing streets that are neither alienating nor energy inefficient. Beyond 80 dwellings per hectare, overshadowing makes it difficult to take advantage of passive solar gain. Solar gain can provide 20 per cent of the primary energy needs of a typical house and, with the enlargement of windows to the south, the use of conservatories and solar water heaters, the total energy savings can approach 40 per cent in southern Britain and 35 per cent in Scotland. These advantages decrease as density increases. However, for dwellings on upper floors these advantages persist.

To take advantage of passive solar gain, buildings need to be orientated to the south, with roofs which do not overshadow neighbours. As a result, with anything other than linear forms (e.g. courtyard forms) it is difficult to achieve similar levels of energy efficiency. Here lies another dilemma for sustainable housing: the creation of communities entails shared values, shared space and physical enclosure, whereas the physics of solar gain leads to long antisocial spaces, parallel buildings and private gardens (to protect southern solar apertures). It is a dilemma which is likely to increase as pressure mounts to erect PV panels on roofs and to create sun-spaces for passive solar heating.

Different strategies for the design of housing exist for different house types. However, as a general rule:

- maximise solar radiation and minimise shading
- ensure that 60–75 per cent of window area faces south but provide solar-shading and other control mechanisms

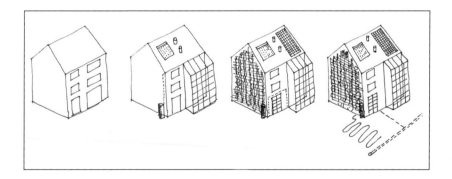

Fig 165
Re-fitting the English house with new environmental technologies every ten years.

- use triple glazing on all non-south-facing windows but do not jeopardise daylight (this simply shifts the energy problem from heating to lighting)
- use thermal capacity coupled with night-time cooling
- ensure envelop is highly insulated on all surfaces, including ground
- provide maximum opportunity for renewable energy use and provide plug-in facilities for changing energy technologies over time.
- use mechanical ventilation with heat recovery
- ensure air-tightness but control potential condensation
- conserve, reuse and trap rainwater
- use sustainable urban drainage systems.

New models for housing

Different models are emerging for energy-efficient housing in different regions of the world. In the UK the south-facing terraced house is often cited as the most energy-efficient form and has been adopted by RuralZed designed by Bill Dunster

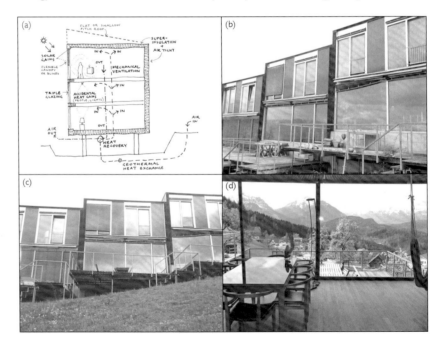

Fig 166
(a) Author's sketch of main generic features of PassivHaus design; (b) and (c) PassivHaus development in Batschuns, Austria, designed by Walter Unterrainer; and (d) a view from one of the houses.

Architects. In Germany the detached house and apartment block based on 'PassivHaus' principles is increasingly popular. However, the characteristics of different climates and building traditions limits the application of universal solutions. In their key qualities of super-insulation, high air-tightness, solar gain and mechanical ventilation with heat recovery These two housing models are leading to an emerging a consensus on construction. This is evident in, for instance, the Kingspan Lighthouse and Barratt Green House built recently in the UK and in Active House built in Denmark as well as examples of PassivHaus built in Germany. What is important is to adapt best practice into mutations adapted to specific climates and culture.

The Lighthouse, designed by Sheppard Robson and built by Kingspan in collaboration with the BRE (the UK's major building research centre), is a demonstration house built to Code for Sustainable Homes (CSH) Level 6 (i.e. 'zero carbon'). Glazing is restricted to 18 per cent of the external wall, which is about half normal practice, but it has a central skylight and ventilation chimney, over 4 m^2 of photovoltaics, uses a biomass boiler, heat recovery, solar water heating and grey water recycling. It also places bedrooms beneath the living rooms, inverting normal practice to avoid over-hot conditions in sleeping areas. The house in thin, tall and has a curved steeply pitched roof. At the time of writing it is the lowest energy consuming house in UK and approaches carbon neutral.

The Barratt Green House, also a CSH Level 6 house, constructed in 2008 is more conventional than the Lighthouse but again uses heat pumps, super-insulation, triple glazing, solar water heating and PV technology. Like the Lighthouse, rainwater is harvested for use in toilets but the Barratt House uses concrete construction for floors and walls in order to maximise thermal capacity. The walls are particularly thick, with 180 mm of insulation placed outside 200 mm thick perimeter planks. A key feature of this house is the high-performance windows (U-value 0.7 W/m^2 K) and automatic shutters operated by a BMS which control the amount of solar gain.

An alternative approach is the 'Active House' principle, with an example known as 'Home for Life' built recently near Aarhus in Denmark. It is the first of eight prototype low-energy houses currently being developed by VKR Holding, the parent company of Velux and Velfac. Like the Barratt Green House and BRE Kingspan Lighthouse built at the BRE Innovation Park near Watford in the UK,

Fig 167
BRE Kingspan House, designed by Sheppard Robson at BRE Innovation Park and Osborne Homes' low-energy demonstration house.

Lessons from PassivHaus

The PassivHaus standard is widely applied in Germany, Austria and Switzerland in the design of homes and non-residential buildings. The standard is high in UK and Danish terms, and sets a criteria of 15 kWh/m²/yr for heating with U-values for walls, roofs and floors of 0.15 W/m²K or above, and for windows of 0.8 W/m²K. Added to this, air-tightness must be at least 1 m³/hr/m² at 50 pascals and mechanical ventilation which achieves 75 per cent recovery of heat exhausted needs to be specified.[24]

PassivHaus is based on super-insulated building envelopes (all external surfaces), high-performance openings (particularly windows), use of solar or geothermal energy where available and mechanical whole-house ventilation with heat recovery. It suits locations where winters are cold and dry, solar energy is available, and a high proportion of the electricity comes from renewable energy sources. Moreover, the emphasis on technology (rather than construction) means that site standards are high, suggesting that PassivHaus may not become widely adopted in Britain in spite of current interest.

A significant problem with the wider application of PassivHaus to the UK is the need for basements to house plant rooms. Also Britain has a milder and damper climate than central Europe where the standard evolved, and since a great deal of electrical energy (as against space heating) is consumed to run the ventilation system, the reduction in heating CO_2 can be at the expense of consumption elsewhere.

Experience in Europe suggests that raising the energy regulations has standardised building design, leading to almost universal use of rain screen cladding, thick external insulation, triple glazed windows and shallow pitched or flat roofs. Just as nearly everybody in Germany drives a BMW, so too the aspiration is to live in a PassivHaus.

Active House is the result of research and design development aimed at securing a foothold in volume house construction in an anticipated low-carbon future. Designed by Aart architects and engineered by Esbensen Consulting, Active House builds upon the principles of PassivHaus but adapts them for the conditions of northern Europe, where the lack of solar gain in the grey north and resulting higher humidity levels limit PassivHaus technology.

Fig 168
'Home for Life', an Active House developed by VKR and Aart Architects at Aarhus, Denmark. It shares similarities with PassivHaus but is adapted for the Scandinavian climate.
Source: VKR/Aart Architects

Whereas PassivHaus relies on passive solar and accidental heat gains from lighting and equipment to provide satisfactory winter conditions, Active House uses an active system of underfloor heating, which is supplied from the heatpump in combination with solar heating and solar cells, in order to guarantee acceptable midwinter temperatures. Both Active House and PassivHaus use whole-house mechanical ventilation with heat recovery and are heavily dependent upon super-insulation and high air-tightness.

In terms of space heating, Active House is planned to operate at around 15 kWh/m^2/yr, compared to typically 12 kWh/m^2/yr for PassivHaus, 19 kWh/m^2/yr for Kingspan Lighthouse (using the PHPP calculation tool) and just over 15 kWh/m^2/yr for the new Barratt Green House (using the SAP method). However, as these figures are based on different methodologies, direct comparisons can be unreliable.

In energy terms, Active House is close to the UK Code for Sustainable Homes Level 6. It is designed to test the Danish building regulations of 2015 which under Class One set a target of 15 kWh/m^2/yr, with an anticipated reduction to 12 kWh/m^2/yr by 2020. However, space heating is only part of the picture.

Where Active House departs from general practice is the amount of daylight provided (with consequent heating disadvantages). By maximising daylight, the designers of Active House believe they will reduce demand for electricity in the form of lighting while also helping to combat the Scandinavian ailment of 'winter depression' – which is believed to be related to daylight deprivation. In fact, Active House has a window area of 40 per cent of the floor area with windows facing in all four directions.

In order to solve the dilemma implicit in the daylight–heat loss relationship, Velux and Velfac have developed a new generation of energy-efficient windows and façade systems for this and other projects. Using integral solar collectors, heat pumps, solar cells (50 m^2 of poly-crystalline cells are on south-facing roofs), the building is able to generate over 60 kWh/m^2/yr of heat and power. This supplements imported energy and gives legitimacy to the claim that over the lifetime of the building, the full life-cycle carbon equation is neutral (allowing for construction and use over a 40-year period).

ENERGY CONCEPT

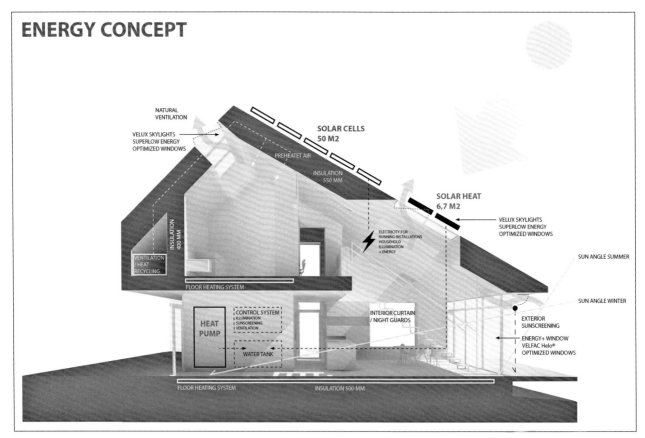

Fig 169
Energy strategy for Active House near Aarhus,
Denmark, designed by Aart Architects.
Source: Aart Architects/VKR Holding

The construction is relatively traditional with timber framing (laminated and softwood) above a concrete raft. The lack of thermal and acoustic capacity is offset by the flexibility provided by the timber stud walls. U-values are 0.10 in walls and 0.07 in floor and roof. The building is clad externally in slate fixed to timber battens, floor tiles are mosaic made from recycled glass, and windows incorporate new energy-saving glass technology and thermal breaks at frame. Ventilation, which is seen as key to consumer satisfaction, is computer operated (with manual over-ride) using Velux's 'Windowmaster' and incorporated into an active façade system from Velfac known as 'Helo'. The heat recover system operates with 85 per cent efficiency and incorporates sensors to adjust to external relative humidity levels.

Sustainability assessment methods for housing

Various assessment tools which were discussed in chapter 3, guide the designer with regard to the design of new housing and how best to the upgrading of existing buildings. Two are commonly used in the UK: BREDEM[25] and the Standard Assessment Procedure for Energy Rating of Dwellings (SAP)[26] and Code for Sustainable Homes (CSH).

BREDEM can be used for:

- estimating energy requirements in different dwelling types
- estimating heating running costs in a property
- ensuring that the most appropriate measures are taken when upgrading property
- estimating the savings arising from different energy measures
- estimating internal temperature and comfort conditions.

In other words, BREDEM is an energy modelling tool. Its weakness is that it does not consider other factors (such as water use) or related matters (such as life-cycle costing of different energy upgrading solutions) which are now covered by the Code for Sustainable Homes (CSH). It remains, however, a useful measure of the interaction between physical characteristics, heating, insulation, orientation and level of occupancy. Subsequent testing confirms that the BREDEM model is reasonably accurate, its predictions normally being within 10 per cent of actual

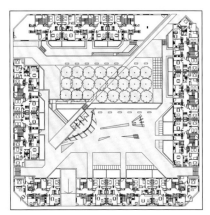

Fig 170 (*above, below and below right*)
Social housing project in Madrid designed by Feilden Clegg Bradley: site plan; section; perspective.
Source: Feilden Clegg Bradley

Fig 171
Three examples of housing design for energy efficiency: (a) House of the Future, designed by Jestico and Whiles; (b) MacRae House, Bristol, designed by Michael MacRae; (c) Apartment Building, Greenwich, designed by Andrew Wright.

Source: Jestico and Whiles, Michael McRae, Andrew Wright

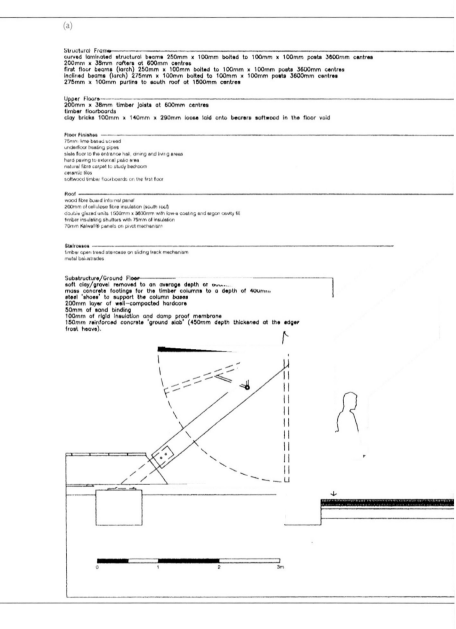

(a)

Structural Frame
curved laminated structural beams 250mm x 100mm bolted to 100mm x 100mm posts 3600mm centres
200mm x 38mm rafters at 600mm centres
first floor beams (larch) 250mm x 100mm bolted to 100mm x 100mm posts 3600mm centres
inclined beams (larch) 275mm x 100mm bolted to 100mm x 100mm posts 3600mm centres
275mm x 100mm purlins to south roof at 1500mm centres

Upper Floors
200mm x 38mm timber joists at 600mm centres
timber floorboards
clay bricks 100mm x 140mm x 290mm loose laid onto bearers softwood in the floor void

Floor Finishes
75mm lime-based screed
underfloor heating pipes
slate floor to the entrance hall, dining and living areas
hard paving to external patio area
natural fibre carpet to study bedroom
ceramic tiles
softwood timber floorboards on the first floor

Roof
wood fibre board internal panel
200mm of cellulose fibre insulation (south roof)
double glazed units 1500mm x 3600mm with low-e coating and argon cavity fill
timber insulating shutters with 75mm of insulation
70mm Kalwall® panels on pivot mechanism

Staircases
timber open tread staircase on sliding track mechanism
metal balustrades

Substructure/Ground Floor
soft clay/gravel removed to an average depth of 600mm
mass concrete footings for the timber columns to a depth of 400mm
steel 'shoes' to support the column bases
200mm layer of well-compacted hardcore
50mm of sand binding
100mm of rigid insulation and damp proof membrane
150mm reinforced concrete 'ground slab' (450mm depth thickened at the edges frost heave).

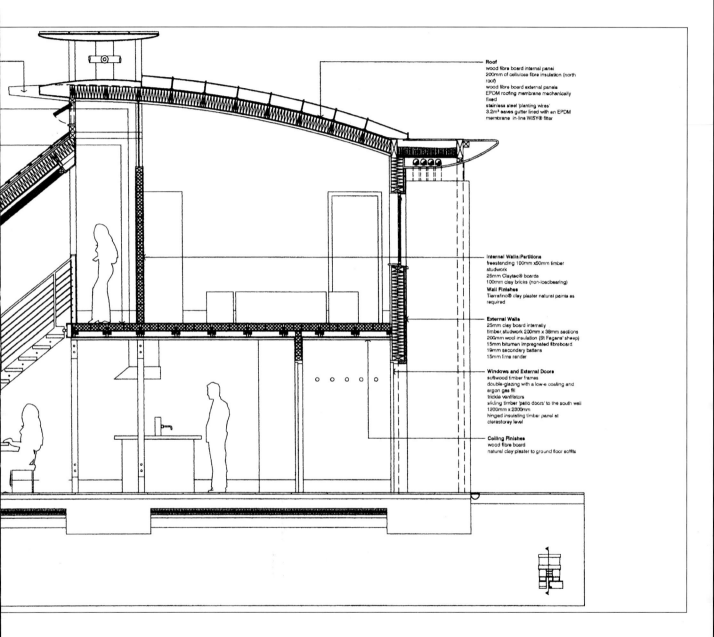

Roof
wood fibre board internal panel
200mm of cellulose fibre insulation (north roof)
wood fibre board external panels
EPDM roofing membrane mechanically fixed
stainless steel 'planting wires'
3.2m³ eaves gutter lined with an EPDM membrane in-line WISY® filter

Internal Walls/Partitions
freestanding 100mm x50mm timber studwork
25mm Claytec® boards
100mm clay bricks (non-loadbearing)
Wall Finishes
Tierrafino® clay plaster natural paints as required

External Walls
25mm clay board internally
timber studwork 200mm x 38mm sections
200mm wool insulation (St Fagans' sheep)
15mm bitumen impregnated fibreboard
19mm secondary battens
15mm lime render

Windows and External Doors
softwood timber frames
double-glazing with a low-e coating and argon gas fill
trickle ventilators
sliding timber 'patio doors' to the south wall
1200mm x 2300mm
hinged insulating timber panel at clerestorey level

Ceiling Finishes
wood fibre board
natural clay plaster to ground floor soffits

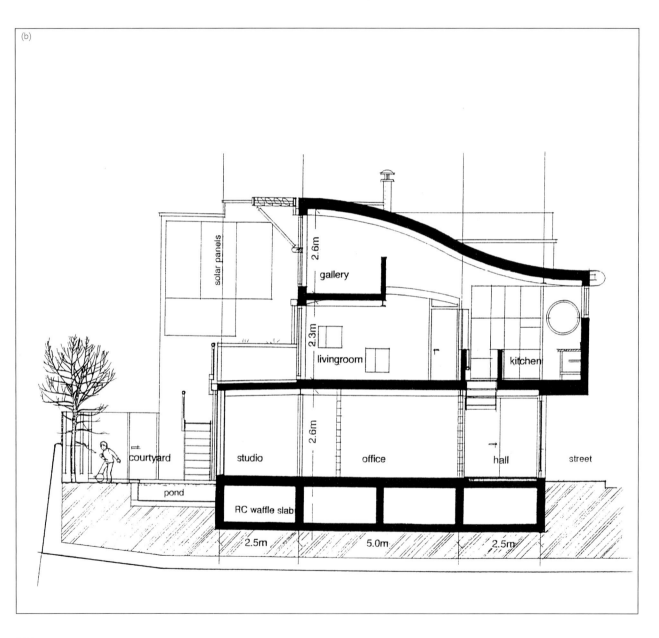

(b)

solar panels

2.6m

gallery

2.3m

livingroom

kitchen

2.6m

courtyard

studio

office

hall

street

pond

RC waffle slab

2.5m   5.0m   2.5m

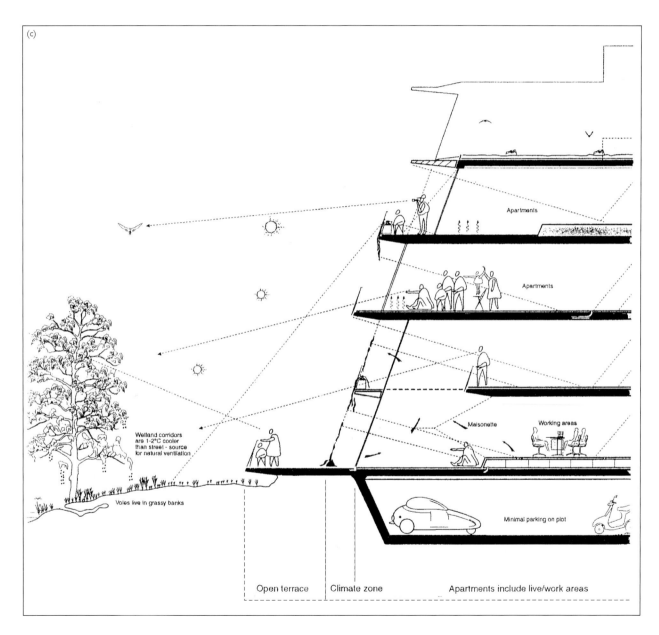

(c)

Apartments

Apartments

Maisonette

Working areas

Wetland corridors
are 1-2°C cooler
than street - source
for natural ventilation

Voles live in grassy banks

Minimal parking on plot

Open terrace | Climate zone | Apartments include live/work areas

energy use. There is also EcoHomes, the homes version of BREEAM, sponsored by the NHBC, which helps address environmental performance under seven headings: energy, water, pollution, materials transport, ecology and land use, and health and well-being.

A more simple measure is SAP, which provides energy ratings for dwellings without taking account of occupancy differences. SAP assumes a standard occupancy pattern and consistent heating regimes between regions, building types and floor areas. The SAP rating is a score out of 100 – the higher the score the better the energy performance. Like BREDEM, the SAP rating is based on physical design characteristics (solar gain, ventilation rates, insulation levels, etc.) and also on the efficiency of and ability to control the heating and hot-water systems. SAP is a useful guide not only to the efficiency of different heating strategies but also to the likely energy bills for a given type of fuel. As such, it is a welcome addition to our knowledge of wider environmental issues (such as CO_2 emissions) and of the relationship between fuel poverty and multiple deprivation (especially of council housing estates). SAP is now incorporated in CSH.

Evidence suggests that poorly insulated properties with inefficient boilers and old fashioned windows aggravate deprivation, which contributes to social exclusion.[27] This is one reason why all new housing built in the UK has to have an EPC at the point of sale or letting. The Code for Sustainable Homes (CSH) which is now part of UK building law and PassivHaus standards (discussed in chapters 3 and 9, respectively) are increasingly taking over as pressure increases to tackle global warming.

Measures to improve energy efficiency in the existing housing stock

Existing buildings are central to any strategy for carbon-emission reduction, since we add to our housing stock at a rate of only 1–2 per cent per year. A study for the Energy Saving Trust (EST), published in 2000, found that 79 per cent of British people claim they have an 'environmental conscience'; however, only 8 per cent consider energy efficiency when they buy a home or an appliance.[28]

The UK government's ambitious target of achieving an 80 per cent reduction in CO_2 emissions by 2050 can only be met by having a better educated public and better informed and motivated construction industry. The EST advocates the following relatively easy measures for people to take with regard to their homes:

- **Lighting**: Use energy-efficient light bulbs. They consume only 25 per cent of the electricity of conventional ones and last up to ten times longer. If all the UK moved to them, the energy saving would pay for all of the country's street lighting.
- **Heating**: Replacing old boilers with modern condensing boilers can save 45 per cent of energy use. Simply maintaining old boilers properly can save 10–15 per cent.
- **Insulation**: Cavity fill insulation to existing buildings can reduce energy loads by 60 per cent. Increasing loft insulation to 50 mm can save 20 per cent on heating bills. Taking all the insulation measures together – cavity fill, loft super-insulation, double glazing using low-emissivity glass and draught proofing – can avoid the need for conventional heating boilers altogether.
- **Controls**: Adding modern controls to old central heating systems can be highly cost (and energy) efficient. The new controls need to be at both the radiator and the boiler to be most effective.

Energy use per person has grown nearly fourfold over the past 100 years. As a global average, each person in 2005 used energy at a rate of 2.5 kW, compared with 0.6 kW in 1900.[29] Much of this increase is the result of energy used in existing homes, and so this is where much current architectural effort is concentrated. Also, since 86 per cent of global energy use in derived from fossil fuels, housing represents a major challenge for designers both in evolving more energy-efficient solutions and in upgrading the existing building stock.

COMMUNITIES AND CITIES

The sustainability of individual dwellings is inextricably linked to the sustainability of communities and, at the macro level, to cities.

Quality of housing affects quality of life – arguably more so than other forms of built development. It impacts on several areas of government policy –

employment, education, transport, health and, most importantly, community well-being. As such, there is a great deal of guidance provided by the UK government on the density and layout of towns in documents such as Planning Policy Statement 1: Delivering Sustainable Development (PPS1) and Planning Policy Guidance 3: Housing (PPG3).

Housing is a fixed long-term capital asset or, depending on how you look at it, liability. The physical building is both a financial investment and a cultural statement. Sustainable housing, therefore, addresses three important areas in parallel:

- energy conservation, waste minimisation and resource efficiency, etc.
- community well-being and social welfare
- economic prosperity, especially employment, education and training.

The environmental dimension is necessarily balanced by social, cultural and economic factors. Residential design is primarily concerned with creating coherent, high-quality, socially responsive, low-energy neighbourhoods.[30] The performance of existing areas can be assessed using simple measures, such as property values, public-health statistics, energy consumption per square metre (deduced from utility accounts) and turnover.

Neighbourhood sustainability, which underpins building sustainability, depends on many factors, not all of which are within the province of architecture and planning. However, both are valuable in creating or nurturing environments that foster social interaction and economic prosperity.

Neighbourhood or settlement design has, at a macro level, a big impact on energy efficiency (especially in transportation) and, at the medium scale, can be addressed through climate-responsive urban design.

Energy efficiency should be the overriding discipline behind questions of layout, density and extent of non-residential land uses. CO_2 reduction provides the basis for housing layout in broad physical terms, but social integration across wealth and tenure barriers should inform the detailed design considerations. Community and social harmony are essential if the building resources are to be successful long-term assets.

Fig 172
Solar and earth-sheltered housing at Hockerton,
Nottinghamshire, UK, designed by Robert and
Brenda Vale.
Source: Hockerton Energy Village Trust

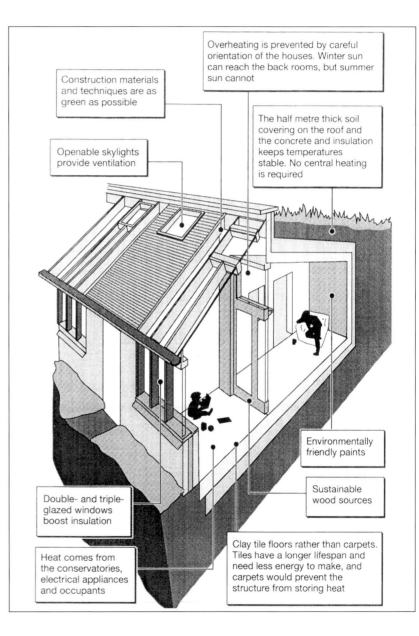

Overheating is prevented by careful orientation of the houses. Winter sun can reach the back rooms, but summer sun cannot

Construction materials and techniques are as green as possible

The half metre thick soil covering on the roof and the concrete and insulation keeps temperatures stable. No central heating is required

Openable skylights provide ventilation

Environmentally friendly paints

Sustainable wood sources

Double- and triple-glazed windows boost insulation

Heat comes from the conservatories, electrical appliances and occupants

Clay tile floors rather than carpets. Tiles have a longer lifespan and need less energy to make, and carpets would prevent the structure from storing heat

Policies for sustainable housing	
☐ Ensure social integration through mixed tenure housing types	☐ Limit car parking by setting maximum, not minimum, parking standards
☐ Integrate residential and non-residential land uses	☐ Place garages and tall buildings to the north of developments
☐ Use energy efficiency to dictate settlement density and layout	☐ Exploit existing infrastructure to the full
☐ Maintain density to support public transport	☐ Reuse urban land and buildings
☐ Use urban design to modify climate	☐ Create car-free developments
☐ Ensure access for all	☐ Exploit renewable energy sources
	☐ Source materials and labour locally

Sustainable transportation

The greater the density of housing and the greater the diversity of land uses, the more viable becomes public transport. Above about 200 persons per hectare and two land uses per hectare (e.g. housing and shopping) it becomes viable to provide a bus service. Above 250 persons per hectare and three land uses (housing, shopping, offices) within a ten minute walking distance (600 m) of the transport corridor it is possible to run a viable metro or tram service.[31] With 300–500 persons per hectare and a further land use (say, college) within a 10–15 minute walking corridor (900 m), the case can be made for suburban rail services. However, much depends on car constraint or fuel pricing policy and also upon the nature of the community. Where there is social and employment diversity there is more likely to be public transport. Hence the design of the neighbourhood (and not just in terms of densities) has a bearing on the viability of public transport.

Distance from railway station	Ideal development type	Medium of connection
Up to 200 m	Civic functions with some commercial	Pedestrian and cycle routes
Up to 400 m	Commercial functions with some civic and high-density housing	As above but with limited car access
Up to 600 m	High-density housing with limited commercial	Balance of car, cycle and pedestrian routes
Over 600 m	Medium- and low-density housing	Car, bus and cycle routes with 'park and ride'

Density and the benefits of mixed-use neighbourhoods

Only by achieving housing densities above 200 persons per hectare can a diversified pattern of public transport be sustained. According to the Urban Task Force Report, increasing density is important because it progressively reduces the need to use private cars. Above 200 persons or 80 housing units per hectare, development readily supports local shops, employment, schools, etc., and encourages walking, riding bicycles and taking longer journeys by bus, tram or train. Density is crucial to reducing CO_2 reduction and other transport-related pollution, and leads to an urban layout that creates sheltered streets and convivial spaces. As housing density increases, yet further potential is unleashed, such as community-power initiatives and the economic viability of facilities such as art centres and branch libraries, which often bring redundant buildings back into use. So density is the key to sustainable housing.

High density should, however, be accompanied by a clear strategy for open space, landscape and urban design, and the promotion of mixed-use residential neighbourhoods. Mixed use also improves personal security and security of premises and engenders a feeling of respect and safety which elderly people, in particular, value. Mixed-use neighbourhoods are more likely to offer employment locally and encourage links between colleges and workplace, enhancing training opportunities. High-density, mixed-use neighbourhoods give back the sense of place that 20th-century planning policies undermined.

Architects, in parallel with developers, should seek to reuse 'brownfield' sites for new housing. These are normally well serviced by infrastructure of various kinds (electricity, water, sewerage, public transport, etc.), although they may be contaminated or suffer from pollution from roads or industry. Not only does redevelopment of brownfield sites reduce pressure on green-belt land, it also provides the opportunity to create new integrated communities close to work, leisure and education. Significantly, it also provides sites that require a designer solution rather than a developer one, enabling architects to innovate in environmental issues as they relate to building design. Brownfield site redevelopments, such as those at Salford in Manchester and the Gorbals in Glasgow, can do much to regenerate city pride, providing a platform to rebrand the city, an increasingly important aspect of post-industrial reconstruction.

Fig 173 (*both above*)
Attention to microclimate and biodiversity
at Accordia housing project, Cambridge, UK.
Many existing trees were retained to provide
ecological continuity.
Source: Tim Cocker and Feilden Clegg Bradley Studios

Brownfield site use is central to UK government policy on housing. Sixty per cent of the new homes required to accommodate an expected 4.1 million new households by 2016 are to be built on existing urban land.[32] As the Urban Task Force, under the guidance of Richard Rogers (Lord Rogers of Riverside), stated[33] reusing inner city land assists in social and economic regeneration as well as enhancing the appearance of towns. However, density is critical not just to effective land utilisation but also to the support of public services on which quality of life increasingly depends. Without schools, health centres, libraries and public transport, many people, especially the elderly and poor, are disadvantaged despite being centrally located.

Microclimate design

As density and the complexity of land uses and tenure increase, so too does the need for integrated measures across the frontiers of urban, landscape, transport and building design. In the past, urban design was neglected and overtaken by mechanistic measures of performance (leading to high-rise and monotonous system-built blocks). Without a structure of urban patterns based on climatic design principles, the benefits of high density are negated. Urban design for housing needs to respond to five imperatives:

- the forging of social space
- the enhancement of the urban microclimate
- the inclusion of nature in urban layouts
- the creation of place not placelessness
- the provision of solar penetration without windy conditions.

Urban design can engineer social space by developing a clear framework of enclosed volumes (small and large) and by the provision of various forms of linkage (streets, alleys and footpaths). Human interaction often takes place in sheltered, sunny, overlooked spaces, often near to the thresholds of dwellings. Plants, seats and attractive paved finishes give such areas their quality and their sense of purpose. Nature provides richness and tranquillity in urban areas and also creates wildlife corridors essential for future species migration as climate changes.

Comfortable microclimates are created by forming protected external volumes adjacent to south-facing (or at least sunny) dwellings. Groups of houses, either terraced or, more appropriately, built as apartments, should be placed to break down large areas into sheltered parcels. Planting around the edge can deflect or reduce wind speeds and, in the centre, can provide local shelter and summer shade. Surface roughness, achieved through a combination of dense planting and buildings, helps provide an urban texture which enhances the microclimate, especially when sensitively orientated.

Sense of place is an elusive concept: it is formed partly by attitude, partly by use and partly by physical attributes. Whereas space is abstract and measurable, a 'sense of place' is shaped by social perception. Good urban design can help build a sense of place by providing lively areas and focal points and by articulating the public realm through exciting architectural design for key buildings (such as a school or doctors' surgery), public art, the use of water and perhaps a small amphitheatre for community use. Most of all, place requires a critical mass of people, landscape and activity.

City form for the 21st century

Increasing the density of development in urban areas brings the following advantages:

- supports public transport better
- creates the opportunity to form cohesive neighbourhoods with well-defined public spaces
- enhances the urban microclimate
- improves the energy efficiency of buildings.

As density rises, so does physical compaction, which allows heat loss from one building to become the heat gain for another. Greater physical proximity also encourages walking, cycling and the use of public transport.

Fig 174
Relationship between high-density urban nodes
and railway system in Tokyo.

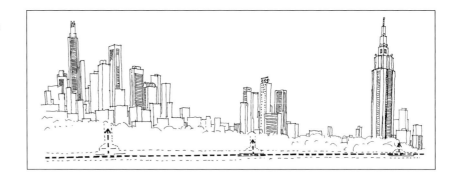

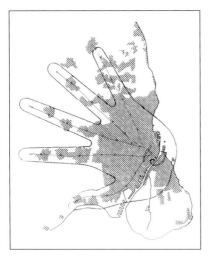

Fig 175
Copenhagen Finger Plan of 1947 with railway
stations added. The dense corridors provide
easy contact with nature in the gaps.

Looking at human development there are, broadly, four patterns of urbanism which constitute models for the future. They are varied in form, carry quite different cultural connotations, are adapted to different climates and functions, and represent different possibilities for the future: the rural model, the suburban model, the European urban model, and the Pacific urban model.

Rural model

This is the legacy of the hunter gatherer, farming tradition which was universal up to the Industrial Revolution. It survives today in remoter parts of the world and is a pattern of living which appeals to the rich (in USA and Australia for example) and is a necessity for the poor in large areas of Africa and South America. It is sustainable in the way local resources of energy (firewood etc.) and food (locally grown or hunted) are utilised. In the rich world much use is made of solar energy for water heating, electricity generation and cooking (using solar ovens) and water is often harvested from roofs. In poor regions animal dung and local timber is employed for cooking. A feature of this lifestyle is the dependency upon renewable and usually local resources not just for sustenance but for construction. There are two main drawbacks: first, the carrying capacity of the environment is low and this limits population; second, the spatial dispersal makes infrastructure (schools etc.) costly and fossil fuel dependency for transport is high. As a result there is little social interaction and no culture. However, as a pattern of development, the rural model can be quite sustainable (as Michael Reynolds' projects in New Mexico testify) particularly when renewable energy is exploited to the full, or when natural capital is high.

Suburban model

The suburbs, which are largely a 20th-century phenomenon, also offer certain green advantages. There is contact with nature, food can be grown locally (in allotments or gardens), there is usually good access to renewable energy sources, and buildings can be orientated to take advantage of favourable climatic conditions (e.g. solar gain). The main disadvantages are in infrastructure provision and public transport. Densities are normally too low to support mass transit systems and, although buses make a compromise, often they run infrequently and need public subsidy.

Suburbs grew up in an age of cheap oil, and the challenge today is to restructure them to make them viable in the post-petroleum age. This entails increasing density, insinuating new metro systems into old development patterns, constructing economic and community nodes around new railway stations, and intensifying land uses in section and plan. Ideally the suburbs will be transformed from single low-density land uses to medium to dense mixed-use ones arranged as 1km wide corridors along transport routes. Linkage between the old suburbs and the new corridors will be by bike and walking, rather than cars.

European urban model

The dense medium-rise mixed-use city common across Europe (and also other regions of the world under European influence) offers many advantages in the search for sustainable urban models.

There is usually sufficient population density to support mass transit (normally a mixture of metro and bus); the bulk of journeys can be on foot or bicycle; mixed use means that heat transfer between buildings is high at the times of the day when it is most beneficial; and land-use integration results in close grained urban textures. The main disadvantages are urban pollution, lack of access to renewable energy (except at rooftops) and disconnection from nature. However, semi-natural areas occur in the form of parks and gardens, in the latter case often in the form of community gardens surrounded by housing blocks. The European model is frequently the urban perimeter block formed as a five- or six-storey-high enclosure of housing built above shops and workplaces which follow gridded street patterns. Such urban blocks are mini-cities within bigger conurbations and effectively integrate social, economic and environmental sustainability. Overall energy consumption per person is around half that of a comparable lifestyle in the suburbs (based on heat loss per dwelling and transport energy consumption).

Pacific urban model

This is the high-rise mixed-use model common to Asia which places in towers many of the characteristics of the European perimeter block. It forms the basis for much of the recent urban development in China and can be seen in more mature form in Hong Kong or Vancouver. The tower block of this type (unlike tower blocks in Europe) normally contains shopping, laundry, restaurant and office accommodation on the lower floors, perhaps a gymnasium on the roof and often an atrium through the centre. Being mixed-use many facilities are contained in the building, making external journeys unnecessary. Such towers are exposed to the elements on many surfaces providing good access to renewable energy. The façade and roof is normally littered with solar panels and satellite disks, and sadly also air-conditioning boxes. Innovative remodelling of the form (by Ken Yeang for example) has developed clever strategies for internal ventilation using spirally placed atria which rise through the full height of the tower. As with the perimeter block, such buildings are mini-cities and operate with their own energy ecologies. Towers provide the basis for high urban densities which in turn sustain efficient public transport and well-maintained public parks. The main drawbacks are the level of pollution which flow from centralised power plants and vehicle emissions.

Since energy consumption is about 40 per cent that of more dispersed forms of development the high-rise mixed-use tower is increasingly seen as a universal model, particularly when it exploits renewable energy (wind and solar) and is integrated with public transport provision.

Towards sustainable urbanism

The compact, mixed-use city remains the preferred sustainable urban model for Europe and much of the USA. It is also the basis for the ambitious Masdar eco-city designed by Foster and Partners in Abu Dhabi where, in a taxing desert region, the masterplan is based on a traditional dense walled town with narrow shaded streets for pedestrians rather than cars. Energy is provided by a detached photovoltaic farm and waste-based combined heat and power (CHP) plant. The plan arranges all the buildings within 200 m walking distance of public transport stops where the major civic functions are also grouped. Masdar seeks to be a model of the zero carbon and zero waste city of the future, with a $22-billion budget available to construct the world's first major post-petroleum conurbation.

However, in many places there are limits to how dense cities of the future will become. For example, commercial buildings need space for cooling and ventilation – over-compaction can lead to an increase in energy use, especially with global warming, and not the reduction that we see in residential neighbourhoods. As densities increase there is a corresponding reduction in access to renewable energy – sun and wind. Too much physical closeness can reduce daylight in buildings and limit access to solar energy. Over-compact cities also suffer from air pollution, which has the effect of damaging the health of people and reducing the energy performance of buildings through pollution. Urban air pollution reduces the opportunities for natural ventilation and dirty glass reduces internal daylight levels as well as undermining the performance of PV panels. So, although there are benefits to increased density, these benefits are limited and vary according to climate, land-use type, culture and latitude.

From a sustainable development perspective, the ideal city is compact, with well-defined edges and medium-rise buildings that are neither too high nor too low. This is because tall buildings require energy for lifts, they are expensive and difficult to maintain, they cast shadows over the surrounding cityscape, they generate damaging microclimates at their bases, and they puncture the 'heat island bubble'. Many city planners argue that the best configuration is a high-density, mixed-use, medium-rise urbanism based upon development six to ten storeys high. Taller buildings are best centred on the railway stations and other transport nodes where commercial, retail and community activities will be concentrated. A recent toolkit from BRE known as Greenprint provides guidance on creating sustainable urban communities.

Variety is one of the keys to the green city of tomorrow. Although masterplans are needed to establish the overall energy policies, density and spatial patterns, social diversity and functional variety is also needed. This gives pleasing contrasts between buildings, allows for culturally rich communities to grow up and provides for energy exchange between individual buildings. A good example is the regeneration of the harbour area in Malmo in Sweden which mixes housing of different types with offices, shops and schools in a dense pattern, all based on 100 per cent renewable energy (from sun, wind and biogas).

Fig 176
Masterplan for the regeneration of the Granton area of Edinburgh, by Llewelyn Davies. Notice how the urban blocks open to the south for solar aperture.
Source: Llewelyn Davies

247

Of course, the ideal city will also contain leafy squares and tree-lined streets to bring nature into the heart of the city, purifying the air and uplifting the spirit. The different districts will have their own parks or other green spaces, which will help to stitch together the urban fabric, civilising neighbourhoods. This type of urbanism, once common across Europe from Copenhagen to Barcelona, is the opposite of the typical Western city of the 20th century, where buildings were massive and often competitive in form and spirit, and existed in an ill-defined landscape of car parks and low-rise burger bars.

The sustainability movement questions the validity of this 20th-century dispersed city form with its consequent neglected and dangerous urban spaces. In spite of the efforts of new urbanists like Rem Koolhaas to civilise the inevitable forms of mass consumption and mega-economics, there is a central dilemma between sustainability and big deep-plan buildings.

Given that the sustainable city of the future is based on public transport, planning for density of occupation and complexity of movement types will be prerequisites for future urban development. People will need to be able to move through the city day and night for purposes as diverse as shopping, leisure, commuting to work and education. The future city will also need inter-modal transport connections – stations which provide smooth access to buses, light railways, taxis and bicycles and which cater for all pedestrians (including disabled people). Such stations would become the new urban nodes, and would act as powerful magnets for commerce, recreation, education and culture, all supported by nearby or connected residential areas, giving shape and legibility to the area. In the urban planning field feet must come before wheels in shaping the future.

Thus urban form in the 21st century will probably consist of a number of such urban nodes dispersed throughout the city. There will be a single main centre, but sub-centres will exist and compete with it for investment and attention. London is already growing into this form, with Docklands, Hammersmith, Croydon and other areas challenging the centre. Other UK cities are developing in similar form – Manchester has powerful sub-centres in places such as Salford Quays, and in Edinburgh, Haymarket is a growth point just outside the traditional commercial core.

Outside the UK there is La Defence in Paris and Orestad in Copenhagen – both new centres which are helping to diversify the city while maintaining the

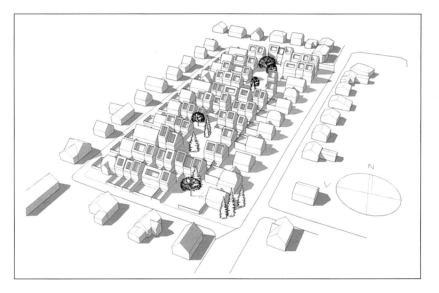

Fig 177
Christian Utzon's plan of solar housing
re-densification in suburb of Copenhagen.
Source: Christian Utzon

Fig 178
Orderly relationship of landscape and city block
in San Francisco.

traditional compaction of older urban areas. Sustainability is also about ensuring that brownfield sites are reused and existing buildings recycled. Historic buildings and structures can help enhance a neighbourhood's identity, and where large industrial structures exist, they should be converted to commercial, cultural or residential use.

A city of sub-centres requires a web of connecting tissue. As well as public transport links, there also needs to be linking streets of special quality (not merely roads). These provide both physical connection and psychological linkage; they are the means by which social exchange takes place, and as such they should be seen as exercises in urban design (not traffic engineering), with the major neighbourhood buildings positioned along their length. These memorable streets (such as The Headrow in Leeds, Buchanan Street in Glasgow or Slottsgatan in Malmo) link together neighbourhoods of commerce and people.

UK government policies for urban design to create conditions for sustainable living	
☐ Improve the 'liveability' of urban areas	☐ Improve access for pedestrians and cyclists
☐ Promote urban regeneration	☐ Concentrate development around public
☐ Promote mixed-use, compact development	transport nodes

The cities of the UK and the USA are in urgent need of repair (mainland Europe has nurtured its towns better). Urban repair follows naturally from a philosophy of sustainable development because it integrates environmental concerns with social and economic ones. Energy is clearly the overriding environmental concern, especially for building designers and urban planners, but concern for the human and natural ecology of the city is also important. Rivers, canals, parks, gardens and planted roofs all offer the opportunity to bring nature back into our cities.

As brownfield sites are developed, the city will again achieve its former vibrancy. The trend in places such as Liverpool and the east end of Glasgow has been to suburbanise older residential areas. Semi-detached houses have replaced compact terraces or multi-storey tenements, reducing density from 400 habitable rooms per hectare (HR/H) to about 150. The sustainable ideal is for densities of 500 HR/H, with up to 1000 HR/H around railway stations or in city centres.

Fig 179
Author's vision for Glasgow in 2040: (1) wind farms; (2) solar power; (3) hydro-power; (4) ecological drainage systems; (5) urban fringe bio-mass planting; (6) tram system; (7) mixed-use dense urban centre; (8) urban fringe farming and allotments; and (9) CHP.

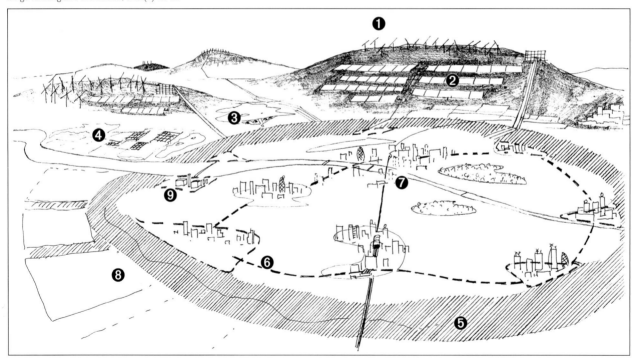

Fig 180
Natural light and natural materials used at the Barajas Airport, Madrid, designed by the Richard Rogers Partnership. The building is the first airport terminal to fully apply the principles of sustainable design and construction.

These central buildings will need to rise to 6–10 storeys before the compact, self-sustaining (in terms of jobs, healthcare, education, leisure and living) city can emerge.

As densities rise, the concept of a 'collage city', proposed by theorists such as Colin Rowe and Fred Koetter,[34] will become a reality. Rowe and Koetter argue that the complex layering of different compact urban forms over centuries creates not disorder but satisfying convivial cities. Changing aspirations give texture and identity to towns, providing those things which civilisation requires in terms of the art and culture of cities. Sustainable development, with its requirement of density, mixed land use and compaction, could implant another layer to older cities such as Rome, Paris or London. For new cities such as Milton Keynes in the UK, it is the basis if not for the founding layer, at least for the structures which colonise it. The imperatives of sustainable design can provide a rich new layer even to new towns that were designed on the assumption of endless supplies of cheap energy. What Rowe and Koetter argue in their influential book *Collage City*, and which Richard Rogers also acknowledges in *Cities for a Small Planet*, is the role that urban typologies play in providing the raw material for civilised and sustainable cities. The street, terrace, square, park, monument and so on are each reinterpreted by successive generations. What makes the concept of sustainable development different is the way climatic

Sustainable development design principles

At city level
☐ Compaction
☐ Streets reclaimed from traffic
☐ Increased density in suburban areas
☐ Intensification of use where areas are well-serviced by public transport (nodes and sub-nodes)
☐ Four-storey housing
☐ Legibility

At neighbourhood level
☐ Diverse pattern of land uses
☐ Safe and friendly streets
☐ Keep historic buildings
☐ Cycle routes
☐ Tram routes/corridors
☐ Use local energy sources

At local level
☐ Design with nature (parks, streets, etc.), biodiversity
☐ Use derelict land/buildings first
☐ Strengthen green belts and green corridors

At building level
☐ Design for low environmental impact (locally, regionally, globally)
☐ Design for durability
☐ Design for reuse
☐ Maximise renewable energy use
☐ Self-sheltering layouts
☐ Energy management under users' control
☐ Design with climate
☐ Design for health
☐ Learn from vernacular practices

design and energy conservation will refashion the urban building blocks of the future.

This can be achieved only by recognising that existing buildings are a valuable resource. The key to a more sustainable future lies in transplanting new low-energy systems into existing structures, and designing new buildings and cities with environmental and ecological imperatives to the fore. We need to transfer design approaches from the new eco-cities and innovative green offices, schools and houses discussed earlier into the mainstream of practice. We also need to pay more attention as a profession to the inefficient buildings inherited from the past. Architects should be at the forefront of the drive for eco-retrofitting schools, houses, hospitals and workplaces. It is not the most glamorous spectrum of professional practice but in terms of sustainability such work represents good environmental value for money and for many community-based architects provides an ethical basis for their work. Without attention being paid to the energy performance of the existing building stock, the new urbanism promulgated by Rogers and others will fail to bring about an urban renaissance.

Buildings need to talk the green message in ways which encourage users to listen. Architectural design is a powerful tool to use in bringing about culture change. Sustainability exists in texts (such as this book) and in buildings themselves – they are the carriers of ideas to society. People are increasingly demanding both energy efficient and healthy environments – the role of architects is to provide them in a manner which does not alienate users by over-complex technologies, bewildering controls and off-putting aesthetics. Good design and good climatic design should be the same thing. This was, after all, Buckminster Fuller's thesis fifty years ago.

Fig 181
The vision of city-wide climate protection, as advocated by Buckminster Fuller, has had a lasting influence on today's architects.

NOTES

[1] Paul Jowitt, 'Engineering civilisation from the shadows', Civil Engineering, Vol. 161, November 2008, pp. 162–8.

[2] BCA, Eco concrete, British Cement Association, 2000, p. 6.

[3] Brian Edwards, Green Buildings Pay, 2nd edn, Spon Press, London, 2003, pp. 114–21.

[4] Brian Edwards, 'Institutional Barriers and advantages of designing office buildings

to sustainable principles', in Environmental Policies: Towards Sustainability, ERP, 1998, pp. 44–8; see also Edwards, Sustainable Development (13) 2005, p. 30.

[5] G. H. Kats, Green Buildings: Costs and Financial Benefits, Massachusetts Technology Collaborative, 2003, pp. 5–6.

[6] G. J. Raw and M. S. Roys, 'Sick Building Syndrome, Productivity and Control',

Property Journal, August 1993, pp. 17–19. See also 'Healthy Buildings and Their Impact on Productivity', Indoor Air '93, Vol. 6, 1993, pp. 41–6, and G. H. Kats, Green Buildings: Costs and Financial Benefits, Massachusetts Technology Collaborative, 2003, pp. 5–6.

[7] Op. cit., Edwards, Green Buildings Pay, 2nd edn, p. 205.

[8]   Bill Bordass and Adrian Leaman, 'Building
      Services in Use; Some Lessons for
      Briefing, Design and Management',
      BIFM Annual Conference, London,
      17 September 1997.
[9]   Op. cit., Edwards, *Green Buildings Pay*,
      2nd edn, pp. 122–57. See also the NHS
      Estates' Achieving Excellence: Design
      Evaluation Toolkit, Department of Health,
      London, 2001.
[10] Brian Edwards 'Benefits of Green Offices
      in the UK: Analysis from examples built in
      the 1990s', *Sustainable Development* (13),
      2005, p. 29.
[11] Paul Ruyssevelt, 'Design for occupant
      interaction', Sustainable Architecture
      Conference, De Montfort University,
      Leicester, 3 May 2001.
[12] See also British Council for Offices,
      BCO Guide to the Specification of Offices,
      London, 2009.
[13] Sebastian Macmillan (ed.), *Designing Better
      Buildings*, Spon Press, London, 2004,
      pp. 72–85.
[14] Brian Edwards, *Green Buildings Pay*,
      1st edn, Spon Press, London, 1998,
      pp. 2–23.
[15] See www.cic.org.uk/dqi and www.
      architecture.com/dqi/schools

[16] Adapted from op. cit., Edwards, *Green
      Buildings Pay*, 2nd edn, pp. 204–8.
[17] G. H. Kats, *Green Buildings: Costs
      and Financial Benefits*, Massachusetts
      Technology Collaborative, 2003, and
      www.cap-e.com
[18] Bill Bordass, 'Lessons from post-occupancy
      surveys', *EcoTech*, Issue 1, March 2000,
      p. 30.
[19] Ibid. p. 31.
[20] Adapted from op. cit., Edwards, *Green
      Buildings Pay*, 2nd edn, pp. 149–57.
[21] Sebastian Macmillan, Nick Baker
      and Michael Buckley, 'Educational
      Environments', *The Architects' Journal*, 26
      February 1998, p. 53. The author has
      adapted and expanded the list.
[22] See www.eco-schools.org.uk
[23] The author is indebted to Macmillan,
      Baker and Buckley (op. cit.) for the analysis
      of plan types.
[24] See www.passivhaus.org.uk
[25] General Information Leaflet 31,
      Department of the Environment, 1999.
[26] *Standard Assessment Procedure for Energy
      Rating of Dwellings Practice Note*, DETR,
      1998.
[27] Hilary Armstrong, 'Sustainability and
      Housing: The Government View', in

      Brian Edwards and David Turrent,
      Sustainable Housing, E&FN Spon, London,
      2000, pp. 1–3.
[28] Helen Jones, 'Money for Nothing', *The
      Guardian*, 26 October 2000, p. 14.
[29] Figures from the Royal Commission on
      Environmental Pollution, quoted in *The
      Architects' Journal*, 16 November 2000,
      p.16, and www.bp.com/sustainability
[30] Fionn Stevenson and Nick Williams,
      *Sustainable Housing Design Guide for
      Scotland*, HMSO, 2000, pp. 9–15. See
      also for the government view *Sustainable
      Communities – Delivering Through Planning*,
      ODPM, 2002.
[31] H. Barton, G. Davis and R. Guise,
      *Sustainable Settlements: a Guide for
      Planners, Designers and Developers*,
      Local Government Management Board,
      1995.
[32] *Planning for Sustainable Development:
      Towards Better Practice*, HMSO, 1998. See
      also Planning Policy Statement 1 (PPS1)
      and Planning Policy Guidelines (PPG) 3, 6
      and 13.
[33] *Towards an Urban Renaissance: Report of
      the Urban Task Force*, E&FN Spon, 1999.
[34] Colin Rowe and Fred Koetter, *Collage City*,
      MIT Press, 1978.

Essay – Architectural Education for a Sustainable Future

Although the city is our oldest work of art it is also our common living room: the place where we engage socially and culturally.[1] The city has been given to us by our ancestors and we, briefly, are its custodians. The concept of sustainable development has been coined to ensure that we hand it over to our children and grandchildren in a healthy state. A great deal of attention has been paid to shaping the principles of sustainable development but little to how the concept can be bedded into society's values. The key is education from primary school to post-graduate degree level and, once we are in work, to keep our skills base up to date. The professions have a key role to play through the course accreditation process, but so too do local education authorities, national curriculum bodies and, of course, schools of architecture.

TEACHING SUSTAINABLE DEVELOPMENT IN SCHOOLS

Education is compulsory, so it is in a unique position to provide the mechanism to foster sustainable development alongside other values. Education is the primary tool for raising awareness of environmental issues, reinforced later by professional training – the whole system being underpinned by exemplar buildings and projects which visibly demonstrate green principles. The starting point for awareness change is the chilling warning from the United Nations Educational, Scientific and Cultural Organisation (UNESCO) that if we want this Earth to provide for the needs of inhabitants of the future, human society must undergo a fundamental transformation.[2] Education is a powerful instrument of change, and environmental education in particular can introduce schoolchildren to the interdisciplinary nature of sustainability. This is achieved by a combination of lessons in school, trips to sites outside school and the use of the school itself as a physical resource of learning. The latter is promoted by the UK Eco Schools initiative[3] which seeks specifically to introduce children to concepts of energy efficiency, recycling and biodiversity through the design of school buildings and use of their grounds.

The United Nations (UN), which was active in helping to coin the concept of sustainable development in the 1980s, is now concerned more with promoting its dissemination. A key report by UNESCO, *Action Plan for the Human Environment*[4], has sought to influence governments by establishing an international programme in environmental education, encompassing all levels and all major stakeholders including the professions. The plan is based on the following key principles:

- sustainable development should be an integrated part of the development process
- the needs of future generations must be respected
- human beings are at the centre of concerns for sustainable development
- the creativity, ideals and courage of youth should be forged in a global sustainable development partnership.

Key factors in achieving sustainable development
☐ Education
☐ Legislation
☐ Taxation
☐ Practice and business application

The plan recognises that, while education is critical, both formal and non-formal means are needed to fully promote the concept of sustainable development. The plan also recognises that, although sustainable development has evolved in the West, it is a global concern which cuts across political, ethnic and cultural divides. It also promotes the idea that sustainable development is basically multi-disciplinary, and should, as a consequence, occur as a theme in a number of subject areas.

The linkage of ideas, concepts, approaches and values in education for sustainable development results in learning which is often project-based. Whether in primary school or at university level, education for sustainable development cuts across old subject boundaries. It also promotes creativity and independence in learning, and respect for other disciplines, methods and procedures. Hence the call for placing the concept of sustainable development into primary and secondary education has potential benefits beyond that of environmental understanding. The life-long and transferable skills of project-based education benefits individuals beyond the acquisition of new knowledge.

Advisory panels on education for sustainable development

In 2000, the UK government established three bodies in order to offer advice and raise awareness of sustainable development:

- The Government Panel on Sustainable Development, to bring together representation of the main sectors and education groups

- Citizens' Environment Initiative, to carry the message at grass roots level
- Sustainable Development Education Panel, to influence all levels of education.

These bodies seek to increase awareness of the part that personal choices play in delivering sustainable solutions. After all, decisions taken by people today on the design of buildings may have an impact on the environment a century later.

The now-defunct Sustainable Development Education Panel[5] was charged with raising awareness, especially in the important area of education and training, of three key principles:

- sustainable development is the responsibility of everyone
- education for sustainable development needs to influence every aspect of life
- the UK's prosperity depends on our capacity to learn about sustainable development.

As a priority, the Panel advised that sustainable development needed to be in the National Curriculum and made a subject in the UK's national education inspection framework (implemented through on-site visits by the non-departmental government body, Ofsted).

Although UK schools are now required to specifically teach sustainable development (under the UN Decade of Education for Sustainable Development), some have gone further and made the school itself a vehicle for relaying the message of sustainable development (see chapter 9). After all, while children represent just 20–30 per cent of the population, they are 100 per cent of our future, and the school is the first public building they encounter.

ARCHITECTURAL EDUCATION FOR SUSTAINABILITY IN THE UK[6]

Environmental design became a coherent theme of architectural education only in the 1970s. Inevitably, at that time, education in schools of architecture was preoccupied with energy rather than the broader concerns of sustainable development. Conceptually, however, the environmental tradition existed in texts which are the very bedrock of architecture. In Vitruvius, for instance, comfort and climate are integrated into the tri-partite model of 'utility, beauty and commodity' – sometimes interpreted as 'durability, beauty and usefulness'. Vitruvius declared that the site of cities, the layout of streets and the orientation of buildings should be determined by environmental factors.[7] He suggested as early as the first century BC that the very act of building design was the primary agent in the mediation between internal comfort and the external climate. For Vitruvius, architecture had a part to play in affording shelter which exploited the resources of nature (sun and wind) rather than excluding them. He was the first to articulate a theory of climatic design, one where form does not just follow function but is shaped by climate.

The Vitruvian model is still promulgated in the curricular division between design, technology and social studies which occurs in many schools of architecture. It is also to be found in the dialogue between science and art, which underpins much of the studio culture in schools of architecture. The idea of sustainability, therefore, draws upon a foundation which is deeply embedded in Classical and Renaissance thought. However, the concept of bioclimatic design is more recent and owes much to visionaries from the 1960s such as Buckminster Fuller and Reyner Banham. Fuller took the Vitruvian challenge of the environmental design of cities to the limit by suggesting enclosing urban activities in a huge glass envelope. Beneath a sheltering glazed embrace, food would be grown, waste recycled as compost, energy demands reduced and social interactions enhanced. His utopianism has left a mark on today's practitioners in the form of the Great Court at the British Museum by Lord Foster or the Eden Centre in Cornwall by Sir Nicholas Grimshaw.

Reyner Banham was essentially a radical theorist and his book The Architecture of the Well-Tempered Environment published in 1969 presented historical perspectives on the environmental function of modern buildings. To Banham the technology of environmental control held the key to an alternative understanding of the history of modern architecture. He openly challenged the thesis promulgated by Nikolaus Pevsner[8] that structure and construction were the primary agents in giving form to architecture, not environmental design. Until Banham voiced his concerns, the relationship between energy use and building design was a subject for specialists with their own ethics, values and professional bodies rather than architects. A typical student of architecture in the 1960s (like the author of this book) was encouraged to believe that heat, light, comfort and

Fig 182
This design by Foster and Partners is an expression of a well-tempered environment in difficult climatic conditions. Central Markets project in Abu Dhabi.
Source: Foster and Partners

257

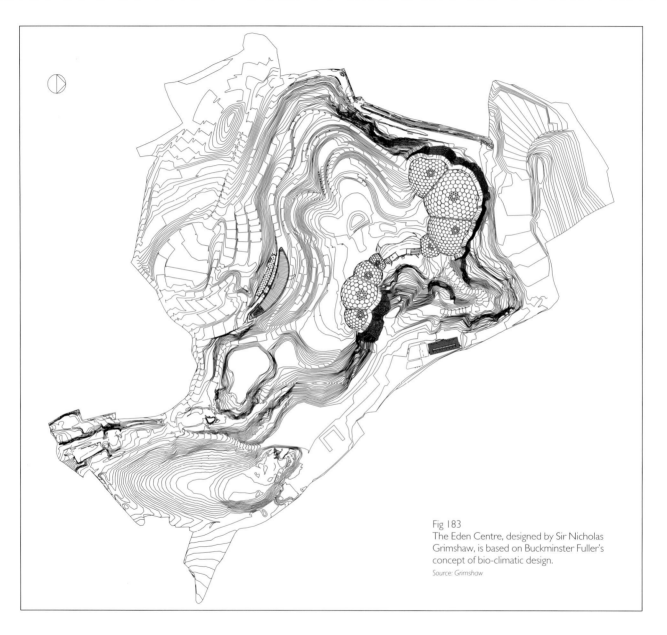

Fig 183
The Eden Centre, designed by Sir Nicholas
Grimshaw, is based on Buckminster Fuller's
concept of bio-climatic design.
Source: Grimshaw

sound were design problems to be handed 'over to the emerging profession of mechanical and electrical consultants'. Banham argued that environmental technologies were as important as the development of reinforced concrete or steel-framed construction in giving shape to 20th century architecture.[9]

Impact of the Oxford Conference, 1958

Banham's ideas gave expression to a movement whose origins lay in the Oxford Conference on Architectural Education sponsored by the Royal Institute of British Architects in 1958. The RIBA sought to ensure that architectural education was located in universities, and with that emphasis went a preoccupation with rational design methods underpinned by research. The former art college tradition and office-based system of pupillage was replaced by one where acquiring technical knowledge was as important as drawing and professional know-how. This encouraged a recognition that the environmental agenda was crucial to architectural design and the assessment of building performance. Building science emerged as a discipline almost as important as architecture itself. The aesthetics of design were absorbed within a wider lexicon of environmental concerns, a movement which gained momentum with the energy crisis of the 1970s.

Schools of architecture responded in different ways. Some, such as at Strathclyde and Liverpool Universities, became schools of 'architecture and building' or 'architecture and engineering science'; others adopted the title of 'centres for building engineering', where architecture existed alongside the portfolio of new disciplines. The ambiguity of nomenclature allowed research and teaching to embrace the concept of architects becoming scientists and scientists becoming architects. The outcome was a mushrooming of interest in the measurable world of climatic responsive design and ultimately of sustainability.

Modernist educators became the new heads of schools of architecture formed in the wake of the Oxford Conference. The change in the culture of architecture, into a scientific as opposed to an artistic discipline, benefited the teaching of environmental science. The former Beaux-Arts tradition had a coherent and consistent approach to design which largely denied the presence of the environmental agenda. Low-energy design existed only in the orientation of buildings to afford sun-traps or to cast powerful shadow patterns onto classical façades. What the post-Oxford Conference schools of architecture offered was a system of university education with an emphasis on scientific methods.

Another significant development was the election in 1970 of a president of the RIBA sympathetic to the environmental cause. Alex Gordon had earlier served on the RIBA council and, since 1960, had helped to steer the post-Oxford reforms. He had made his name in public service, mainly as chief architect for Birmingham City Council, and approached building design from the angle of social reform. Gordon combined his utopianism within a deep sense of environmental awareness. He is remembered today mainly for coining the mantra 'long life, loose fit, low energy' as the basis for architectural design. It is a legacy that combined elements of thinking from the Archigram Group, Buckminster Fuller and E.F. Schumacher, whose *Small is Beautiful* was published during Gordon's tenure in Portland Place.

Curricular reforms and the Layton Report

Although the 1958 Oxford Conference had little to say about the detailed content of the curriculum, this was addressed by the Layton Report of 1962.[10] This

Fig 184
Four student projects testing the understanding of technology and environment: (a) Leigh Brown; (b) Keith Dillon; (c) Michael Heath; and (d) Martin Bates.

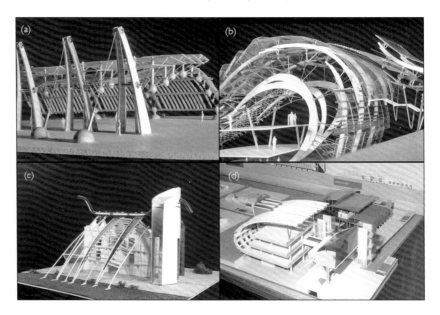

report introduced the notion that architectural education should be diversified by the introduction of technical specialisms such as building services design. The latter was one of eight 'scientific' specialisms which were intended to ensure that graduating architects had a good general knowledge of the integration of structure, services and construction. So, whereas the Oxford Conference introduced the quasi-scientific approach, the report of 1962 reinforced this by requiring the teaching of technology-based specialisms. As each was intended to be underpinned by research and tested through studio-based projects, the effect was to give further weight to the emergence of environmental design as an important element in the design of buildings.

Introducing 'environmental duty of care'

The RIBA and, more recently, the Architects Registration Board (ARB) have adopted standards of professional behaviour that place an environmental duty of care on practitioners. Inevitably, this has also been adopted into curriculum revisions since the late 1990s. Unlike the impetus for environmental understanding following the Oxford Conference and Layton Report, the origins of which were quasi-scientific, changes to the Code of Professional Conduct have an ethical basis at their core – environmental ethics has emerged now to stand alongside the wider professional responsibilities adopted by architects.

Ethics and the concept of environmental duty of care have a long taproot in professional perceptions. The ethical basis for architectural practice in the 20th century evolved from a duty of care to the client, through a responsibility to society as a whole, to one where the architect has to consider the environmental impact of the decisions taken. In 1962, Sir Robert Matthew in his presidential address to the RIBA declared that 'architecture today … is a service to the client and the community'.[11] Until then the interests of the client were uppermost, and this sometimes ran counter to wider social or environmental interests. Sir Robert Matthew was the first president to voice the legitimate interests of society as a whole. To Matthew, the ethical function of architecture was to help articulate a shared ethos – a compact between the client who commissions and pays for building work and the community at large which uses the building. It was a foundation of sufficient breadth to allow the absorption of subsequent environmental concerns. After all, 'a strict professional ethic, even if self-regarding in origin and imprecisely formulated, inevitably tends to generate an ideal of

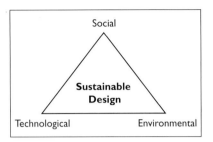

Fig 185
Three perspectives on sustainable design.

social service'.[12] This view, when applied to sustainability, allowed the UK government-sponsored Sustainable Development Education Panel (above) to suggest in 2000 that 'acting in accordance with sustainability principles is a defining characteristic of being a professional'.[13]

Today, the concept of environmental ethics has an impact on the choices architects have to make in the selection of building technologies and construction materials – it is no longer the purely physical, aesthetic or performance attributes which matter. Today's designers have to weigh up the impacts on the natural and social ecology and, because many construction materials are obtained from distant lands, ethical choices have to be made often with inadequate information. As sustainability becomes mainstream the ethics of construction choices emerges as an important design determinant.

THE EUROPEAN DIMENSION

As ethical codes evolved in the UK, a parallel impetus appeared in the mid-1980s, not from the RIBA but from the European Union. The Architects' Directive 85/384/EC required consistent standards of education, professional standards and codes of conduct to ensure the free movement of architects across Europe; and the Single European Act of 1986 introduced a number of minimum standards to ensure harmonisation of architectural services across the diverse professional landscape of the EU.

The impact was felt particularly acutely in terms of architectural education. A harmonised system of education for architects across Europe, implemented in 1987, required students to master 11 areas of study. Two specifically refer to environmental awareness: students are required to have an 'understanding of the relationship between people, comfort and buildings, and between buildings and the environment'.[14] This field of understanding suggests a tri-partite synthesis of people, buildings and environment with Vitruvian overtones.

Later the Directive says that students have to acquire an 'adequate knowledge of physical problems and technologies … so as to provide … internal conditions of comfort and protection against climate'. These clauses substantially increased the level of environmental teaching in schools of architecture and required the joint visiting boards of the RIBA and ARB (the latter body given specific responsibility to ensure that the Directive was implemented in the UK) to vet standards in architecture schools. The wording of the two environmental clauses had the effect of broadening the perception of the environment to embrace interests beyond low-energy design. Questions of climate-responsive design, comfort, global warming and the bigger agenda of sustainable development now crept into the curriculum.

The 'Professions Directive' 2005/36/EC

To strengthen the harmonisation of professional services across Europe, including architecture, the Professional Qualifications Directive (2005/36/EC) was introduced in 2005. It absorbed the earlier Architects Directive, but had the beneficial effect of strengthening the professional status of the architect and as a consequence of the mandatory green elements of training, ensuring that professionals across Europe had a sound grasp of sustainability. One practical consequence is the ease with which UK-trained architects can practise or set up office in EU Member States. Although in many parts of Europe green design was well established, in some of the newer member countries, sustainable design and green construction was a rarity. The Professional Qualifications Directive (sometimes known as the 'Professions Directive') not only ensured that non-UK-trained architects working in Britain had comparable 'green design' skills to those architects educated on RIBA/ARB validated courses, but it provided a stronger platform for taking UK skills into the new enlarged Europe.

The Directive also strengthened the use of the title 'architect'. In the UK the word 'architect' is protected under UK law and now the Professions Directive extended this provision to the whole of Europe. Such protection carries a responsibility to behave professionally – to be knowledgeable in the new science of sustainability as part of the privilege of being called an architect. Being a professional requires knowledge of the key issues and opportunities available but also an obligation to carry out services with regard to ethical understandings in the area of global warming, world poverty and energy scarcity.

UNESCO and Bologna

The standardisation of architectural education across Europe helped consolidate the central role of environmental understanding. Under the Bologna Agreement adopted in 2001, the education of architects was formally structured in to a three-year bachelors degree plus a two-year masters degree. The first programme provided the benchmark of general ecological appreciation, while the second postgraduate degree gave the student the chance to develop a specialism in energy or environmental design. Although there are some differences of nomenclature and structure to reflect different cultural traditions, the Bologna Declaration standardised the length of study and award of credits to the benefit of providing sufficient time to imbed sustainability into architecture courses across Europe.

In parallel, the Union of International Architects (UIA)/UNESCO Charter for Architectural Education adopted in 1996 and extended in 2000, reinforced the move towards reconciling human and ecological needs. The charter talks about the way architectural schools should include among their goals the cultivation of 'an ecologically balanced and sustainable built environment' (clause 8).

Under the extension of 2000 which lists 'Environmental Studies' as a core capability to be acquired during study, students are expected to have the ability to act with knowledge of 'natural systems', to understand 'conservation and waste management systems' and have an understanding of 'life-cycle of materials, issues of ecological sustainability, environmental impact, design for reduced energy use, as well as passive systems …' (see clause B2). The impact of European and international agreements not only altered the priorities and codes of professional bodies (such as the RIBA) but the curriculum and ethos of architectural schools.

THE GLOBAL DIMENSION – IMPACT OF WIDENING ENVIRONMENTAL CONCERNS

The UN Earth Summit in Rio de Janeiro in 1992 alerted world's governments (almost for the first time) to the looming environmental and ecological problems associated with urban development. Across the globe 182 governments signed up to a series of declarations, aimed not only at reducing adverse environmental impacts but also at adopting measures such as Agenda 21 initiatives to take positive action at a local level. The impetus from the declaration influenced the construction industry professions in the UK, some of which subsequently adopted new codes and standards. The RIBA took the lead, instituting a new committee to steer action. Known originally as the Energy Committee (from 1992), then the Energy and Environment Committee (from 1994), it became the Sustainable Futures Committee in 1998. The changing title reflected the altering perception of environmental problems. Traditionally, the construction industry had concerned itself with low-energy design, supported enthusiastically by quasi-governmental bodies such as the Building Research Establishment (BRE). However, after the Rio Earth Summit, the emphasis shifted towards wider ecological concerns such as rainforest destruction and biodiversity. Initially, the design professions were slow to reorient their environmental focus, but with government moves towards adopting the broad agenda of sustainable development, the professions and construction industry saw the benefit to their members.

One resource that gained the urgent attention of the profession was water. Although many understood that heating, lighting and ventilation of buildings was responsible for about half of UK fossil fuel energy use, few realised that about 50 per cent of all water consumption was building related. With growing stress on water reserves, a series of droughts in the late 1990s and increasing water utility bills following industry privatisation, architects and engineers began to design for water conservation. In parallel, the need to examine the source of hardwood timbers employed in building meant that the building industry woke up to its central position in helping to address sustainability.

The Rio Earth Summit provided a framework for development which has been adopted in many curriculum revisions, especially for those degree courses in sustainable design or sustainable architecture. Four main areas were addressed at the summit – energy conservation, rainforest conservation and associated ecological management, biodiversity, and action plans for environmental recovery. The latter, known as Agenda 21 ('Action for the 21st Century') led to initiatives from central and local government, the professions, grass roots organisations and universities.

Maastricht and the Architects Code of Conduct in Europe

The adoption of the Maastricht Treaty in 1992 added further weight to the environmental argument emerging from the Rio Earth Summit.

Various articles of the Treaty strengthened laws on the environment, such as article 130v, which introduced policies for 'preserving, improving and protecting the quality of the physical environment, protecting human health and encouraging the prudent use of natural resources'.[15] Architects and educators in the built environment became increasingly aware of their environmental responsibilities and the impact of buildings on the quality of life, health and resource consumption.

The Maastricht Treaty also introduced four important principles that span sectoral interests but which had serious implications for the way buildings are designed and architects educated. The first was an obligation to use best environmental knowledge – to incorporate the benefits of environmental innovation into building design. The second was to follow the 'precautionary principle' with the implication that risks should be assessed and caution exercised in the use of new materials and construction processes. The third was an obligation to rectify environmental damage at source rather than disperse pollutants into air or water. This meant that the polluter paid for the clean-up operation. Since many buildings pollute, the principle questioned the gas-guzzling technologies of modern air-conditioned development and, in theory at least, exposed the architect to potential litigation. The final principle was the need to consider all ecological impacts and to incorporate consistent environmental practice across Europe into local laws and codes of practice. This led to a revision of the Architect's Code of Conduct in 1997.

ARCHITECTURAL EDUCATION FOR THE 21ST CENTURY

The Toyne Report

Radical changes within UK higher education system, in the form of the Toyne Report of 1992, proved to be an important milestone for architectural education in particular.[16] This report, under the chairmanship of Peter Toyne, vice chancellor of Liverpool John Moores University, advocated a range of measures including the greening of courses which traditionally had ignored environmental issues. Cross-curricular greening, whereby undergraduates experience sustainability best practice from other courses, proved an important avenue for the broadening of environmental understanding in schools of architecture. Toyne also suggested the use of the university campus itself as the test bed for environmental innovation. As a consequence, a generation of green buildings was constructed, some for built environment faculties, which were used in teaching and research (a good example being the School of Engineering building at De Montfort University built in 1995).

By the end of the 1990s, therefore, there was pressure to incorporate sustainability into architectural education from three important quarters – changes to the code of conduct governing architectural services, European legislative reforms, and pressure from the university sector itself via the Toyne Report. The latter gained further impetus when the UN General Assembly adopted the World Summit on Sustainable Development's recommendation that 2005 should mark the beginning of a 'decade of education for sustainable development'. Ratified by the UK Prime Minister, higher education authorities are now drawing up plans to take the green agenda forward, in terms of action both on the campus and in the curriculum.

Fig 186
Eco-masterplanning needs to address a wider range of issues than in conventional building design, including water management, pollution and waste recycling. Masterplan for Queen Margaret University, Edinburgh.
Source: Queen Margaret University

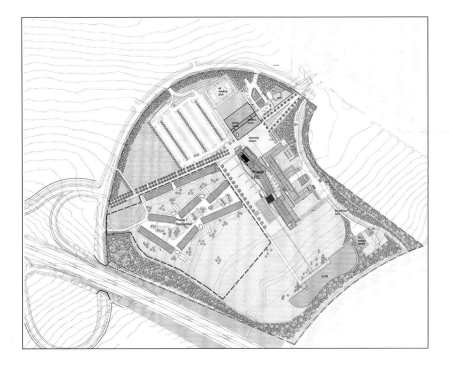

The Oxford Conference 2008

Fifty years after the original Oxford conference, a new one was held to 'reset the agenda for architectural education'. Addressed by Sunand Prasad, President of the RIBA and luminaries such as Christopher Alexander, Rab Bennetts and Susan Roaf, the conference reinforced the message of sustainability being part of the core curriculum for architects. In some ways the 2008 conference saw the maturing of the seeds planted at the 1958 conference. All but one of the keynote speakers centred on ecological and environmental themes, with Nina Maritz from Zambia arguing for the 'inclusion of environmental sustainability as a non-negotiable underlying ethos for all architectural endeavour'. David Gloster, RIBA Director of Education, reflected on the state of cities in which architects work with their conflicts between constructional innovation and the emergence of intermediate and low technologies. Tom Woolly, Professor at the Centre for Alternative Technology Wales and elected member of ARB, warned that for many students 'green' was a bolt-on rather than a means to create exciting architecture within a 'humanistic, socially responsible, ethical approach'. However, whatever their perspective, the speakers chose to highlight the importance of sustainability in all its complexity to architectural education. However, there was a subtle shift from that of environmental awareness residing in the building sciences in the 1958 Oxford Conference to a broader more cultural understanding in 2008. Sustainability is as Paul Oliver noted, part of the student's education on the relationship between architecture, society and culture.[17]

Professional practice

The Union of International Architects (UIA), the umbrella group which coordinates architectural institutes across the world, has adopted a set of principles intended to form the framework for action at national level. Principle 2 states that 'architects have obligations to the public ... and should thoughtfully consider the social and environmental impact of their professional activities'. Principle 3 goes further: architects, it states 'shall strive to improve the environment and the quality of the life and habitat within it in a sustainable manner'.

In 1999, the ARB of the UK amended its code with regard to the environment. The new Code of Conduct stated that while 'architects' primary responsibility

Architectural education and sustainability through the ages		
Date	Milestone publication	RIBA/ARB syllabus response and awakening professional consensus
58BC	Vitruvius (environmental triangulation of comfort, climate and design)	Architecture has climatic dimension
1860	John Ruskin (nature as guide)	Gothic revival adopts high ground
1880	William Morris (small, sustainable communities)	Arts and crafts based architectural education
1910	Patrick Geddes (ecology of cities)	Garden City Movement
1930	Frank Lloyd Wright (nature as inspiration)	Landscape design emerges as sub-discipline of architecture
1948	Lewis Mumford (environment of cities)	New Towns Movement
1965	Richard Buckminster Fuller (bioclimatic cities)	Building services incorporated into syllabus after Oxford Conference of 1958
1970	Ian McHarg (Design with Nature)	Layton Report on strengthening technology awareness on architecture courses
1970	Club of Rome report (limits to growth)	Conservation courses established in architecture schools in UK
1972	Concept of 'long life, loose fit, low energy' espoused by RIBA President Alex Gordon	Low-energy design in RIBA syllabus
1987	UN (Brundtland) Our Common Future	Emergence of term 'Sustainable Development'
1987	EU Architects' Directive	Environmental duty of care as principle
1992	Rio Earth Summit (integration of energy, ecology and environment)	Environmental understanding introduced to syllabus by ARB criteria changes (1995)
1992	Maastricht Treaty (EU environmental policy)	Sustainable Futures Committee established at RIBA
1997	Kyoto Protocol (global warming)	Increase in awareness of energy use
1999	Urban Task Force Report (Rogers)	Sustainability in syllabus as concept
2002	Johannesburg Conference (sustainable development)	Further revisions to RIBA and ARB criteria for Validation especially at Part I Full range of sustainability issues in syllabus via revisions of 2003 affecting Parts 1 and 2 'Environment' now a core theme of ARB Prescription
2006	Helsinki Conference (climate change)	RIBA introduces 'Sustainability Prize'
2007	Poznan Conference (carbon trading)	RIBA expands sustainability website with examples of best practice

is to their clients, they should nevertheless have due regard to their wider responsibility to conserve and enhance the quality of the environment and its natural resources'.

These revisions to the Code have wide implications for architectural education since, whereas ARB regulates through the prescription process 36 schools of architecture in the UK, the RIBA helps to validate these and a further 70 worldwide. As a consequence, the RIBA influences the ethos and curriculum of around a quarter of architectural training globally. One repercussion is that sustainability now assumes subject importance in its own right rather than being taught as an aspect of technology. Ecological design has almost moved to centre stage in design projects. The latter is important since about half of credits awarded in a typical school of architecture are design based, and unless sustainability engages with the studio culture, it fails to address the core of design education.

Although the legislation and Codes of Conduct described above are specific to the architectural profession, similar provisions exist for other professions such as the Institution of Civil Engineers, The Royal Institution of Chartered Surveyors and the Construction Industry Council.

Trends in the adoption of 'sustainability' in architectural education in the UK	
Positive trends	Negative trends
Growth in understanding of green issues required in RIBA/ARB criteria for prescription of courses	Student difficulty in dealing with the complexity of sustainability and the complexity of architecture
Growth in subject specialists in green area of design and technology on recognised courses	Green design becomes a specialist rather than a generalist topic, particularly at postgraduate level
Shift in emphasis from energy to other green issues	Architectural design and green technologies not always well integrated
Growth in green research and postgraduate courses on sustainability	

TAKING STOCK: SUSTAINABILITY TODAY

As this review has demonstrated, the history of architectural training in the 20th century is one of growing technological and environmental awareness – of a shift from art to science as the basis for design education. Although the early years of the 21st century saw the re-emergence of art architects (Frank Gehry, Zaha Hadid), the agenda of sustainability will in time embrace both camps. Then sustainable design will become a cultural movement which unites art, science and nature. However, there is one obstacle still to be overcome. The growing influence of theory in architectural education, not just in the UK but elsewhere particularly in the USA, means that building science and study of the making of buildings (what is generally called construction) is not always given enough attention.

Some architecture schools play down the centrality of technology and hence sustainability – not so much in time but in terms of the high ground of the design studio. Those professors who are most admired have an interest in conceptual or abstract design, not the practicalities of building technology. It is important that green issues are not seen as design afterthoughts but as one of the primary generators of architectural form.

The situation in much of Europe is similar but here there are different roots. In Germany and Denmark for instance, a distinction is made in architectural education between 'constructing architects' and 'design architects'. Only the latter are covered by the European Union Directive on the registration of architects. The irony is that it is in the construction schools that the knowledge of sustainable practices tends to reside. Although the design schools (many of which originated in the large art academies of Europe) teach sustainable construction, the students equipped with the best skills in green technologies are not allowed to call themselves architects. As a consequence, students who initially enrol on courses as constructing architects, move on graduation to mainstream architecture programmes. Their education may end up taking eight or more years (although some dispensation is given for their prior technical learning). This distinction, mirrored to a smaller degree in the UK in the division between architecture and architectural technology courses, does not help in embedding sustainable design into the core of professional understandings.

The Special Contribution of Richard Rogers

The contribution to the design culture of sustainability from the architect Richard Rogers (Lord Rogers of Riverside) should not be underestimated. His

Fig 187
At the Welsh Assembly Building by Richard Rogers Partnership, local materials such as Welsh slate and oak were selected to reduce the carbon footprint and ensure cultural continuity.
Source: Winnie Friis-Møller

Fig 188
Natural light and timber used in the eco-friendly Barajas Airport in Madrid, designed by Richard Rogers Partnership.

chairmanship of the UK's Urban Task Force (1999) was influential in redirecting government attention towards urban sites and the value of sustainable design. One valuable principle set out in the subsequent report is that 'social well-being and environmental responsibility' are fundamental to 'design excellence'.[18] His Reith lectures of 1998, his books such as Cities for a Small Planet (with Philip Gumuchdjian) published in 1997, and the example of his buildings such as the Welsh Assembly, had ensured that by the beginning of the 21st century sustainable development was having a significant impact on professional perceptions.

To a large extent the views of early pioneers of green design have become mainstream. Within a generation authors like Ian McHarg, whose book Design with Nature was almost underground reading in the early 1970s, find their principles now underpinning architectural education. The broadcaster and journalist Jonathan Dimbleby, giving the first RIBA Annual Lecture in May 2002, went even further. He suggested that architects should refuse to undertake unsustainable jobs, arguing that the ethical basis of the profession was undermined by commissions which did not place sustainable design to the fore.[19] Dimbleby called for a new awareness of the 'broad picture of sustainability' where 'ecological concerns, economic development and community identity' were brought together.

THE NEXT 50 YEARS

In the professional world beyond architecture schools, the construction industry as a whole has had to grapple with course changes to accommodate the rapidly evolving educational demands made by the adoption of the concept of sustainable development.

However, action across the industry as a whole has been hampered by a number of institutional and cultural impediments:

1. There is a wide interpretation of the term 'sustainability' across the various higher education built environment courses in the UK. Although the Brundtland definition is cited in much course material as a unifying definition and set of values, in reality the interpretation is distinctive to disciplines rather than universal. As a result, different priorities tend to be promoted, with

the risk that students lack either a common language of terms or a shared perception of solutions.

2. The professional bodies have a significant impact on the priority awarded to sustainability in the higher education curriculum. With various professional bodies involved (RIBA, ARB, CIAT, ICE, RICS, CIBSE, CIOB, RTPI) comes an inevitable diversity of approach within the courses that they validate. If the professional bodies were to agree a set of core values, environmental principles and body of knowledge (especially at undergraduate level), it would be easier to foster mutual understanding and interdisciplinary teaching across the industry as a whole. Recently a number of courses have grown up which give joint professional recognition for students who have completed the degree programme (e.g. at Sheffield, Bath, Strathclyde in the UK). Here, students have a more general undergraduate education, often focussed around sustainability issues, with the opportunity to move at postgraduate level into the profession of their choice. The jointly recognised undergraduate courses tend to have an architecture/engineering basis or an architecture/urban planning basis. However, upon the award of the degree students also obtain professional qualifications from more than one body.

3. Where sustainable design and construction is taught there appears to be little correspondence between knowledge acquisition via lectures, and knowledge application via practicals or design projects. Similarly, there is inadequate linkage between what is taught in the universities and the topics being researched under the umbrella of sustainability by research institutes.

4. Building development on university and college campuses is beginning to expose students (and staff) to the reality of sustainable design or good sustainable management. Thanks in part to the pioneering Toyne Report (HMSO, 1992) the UK compares favourably to the rest of Europe in terms of green demonstration projects built on university campuses (promoted, in part, by the Environmental Association for Universities & Colleges (EAUC) and its Green Gown awards[20]). As a result, there is a growing number of examples of the application of photovoltaic technology to new or refurbished buildings, passive solar student housing, water or waste recycling and car-free campuses. However, without a triangulation between teaching, research and physical

Fig 189
Informatics Building at Edinburgh University designed by Bennetts Associates sets an example on campus for architecture students to follow.

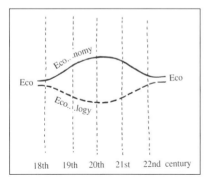

Fig 190
Future fusion of economy and ecology.

development on campus, the student can hardly be blamed for not taking sustainability seriously.

5. Too little interface seems to exist between further education (FE) and higher education (HE) institutions in the field of sustainable design, technology and construction. This is surprising given the extent of education available to building operatives (such as plumbers, electricians and bricklayers) in FE colleges. Although ladders exist between FE and HE in the area of admissions policy, no comparable exchange appears to exist in the pedagogy of sustainability or in the area of practical training of architects.

So, in spite of initiatives from individual professional bodies, such as the RIBA and ICE, and encouragement from government, the broad agenda set out by the Toyne Report has yet to fully influence the wider culture of education for the construction and design professional. This is all the more regrettable, given the interdisciplinary nature of sustainable development.

There is one final element in the education for sustainability debate, and that is the education of the public. Global education for sustainable development involves not just schools, universities and the professions but clients, governments and NGOs. There remains a considerable lack of awareness of the interrelated nature of human impacts on the environment. The involvement of users at the design stage in a project helps to ensure that green issues are addressed before economics takes a grip. Similarly, adjustments to the RIBA Plan of Work to include sustainable development principles in the early briefing stage of a project ensures that the environmental agenda is an integrated element.

A key is a well-informed public. Clients are increasingly knowledgeable about sustainability and some will only employ architects who are ISO14001 registered. However, users and the general public have an important role to play in influencing the brief for a project. Initiatives such as the Stirling Prize and the TV programme 'Grand Designs' act as a spur to the commissioning of green architecture.

Education strikes at core values; it is not sufficient to see a body such as the RIBA or ARB addressing educational standards alone. Changes in professional codes of conduct and in the ethics of practice are needed to ensure that environmental connections and commitments are made.[21]

NOTES

[1] Mats Lundstrom and Maria Nordstom, *The City at our Fingertips*, Malmo, 2001, pp. 58–9.

[2] Edgar Morris, *Seven Complex Lessons for the Future*, UNESCO, Paris, 1999, preface.

[3] For Eco Schools Handbook see www.ecoschools.co.uk

[4] UNESCO, *Action Plan for the Human Environment*, UN, Stockholm, 2003.

[5] Sustainable Development Education Panel, *First Annual Report*, 1999, p. 3.

[6] Reproduced (with amendments) from Brian Edwards, 'Sustainability and Education in the Built Environment', in John Blewett and Cedric Cullingford (eds), *The Sustainability Curriculum: The Challenge for Higher Education*, Earthscan, London, 2004.

[7] Dean Hawkes, *The Environmental Tradition: Studies in the Architecture of Environment*, Spon Press, London, 1996, pp. 10–11.

[8] Nikolaus Pevsner, *Pioneers of Modern Design*, Penguin, 1960.

[9] Reyner Banham, *The Architecture of the Well Tempered Environment*, Architectural Press, Oxford, 1969.

[10] Elizabeth Layton, *Report on the Practical Training of Architects*, RIBA, London, 1962, p. 2.

[11] Derek Senior, *Your Architect*, Hodder and Stoughton, London, 1964, p. 23.

[12] Ibid.

[13] *What Sustainable Development Education Means for the Professions*, HMSO, London, 2002.

[14] Architects' Directive 85/384/EEC, clause 11.2; see also 11.3.

[15] Brian Edwards, *Sustainable Architecture: European Directives and Building Design*, Architectural Press, Oxford, 1999, p. 9.

[16] *Environmental Responsibilities: An Agenda for Further and Higher Education* (The Toyne Report), HMSO, London, 1992.

[17] See www.oxfordconference2008.co.uk

[18] *Towards an Urban Renaissance: Report of the Urban Task Force*, E&FN Spon, London, 1999, Introduction.

[19] *RIBA Journal*, 2002, p. 96.

[20] See www.eauc.org.uk

[21] Brian Edwards, *Green Buildings Pay*, 2nd edn, Spon Press, London, 2003.

Epilogue – Sustainable Design at the Cutting Edge

Sustainability is rapidly evolving, while at the same time broadening and deepening its influence on architectural practice. It is changing design methods, design priorities, building types, urban patterns and design criticism. However, it is possible to single out some of the emerging green debates and areas of innovation which are likely to fashion architectural practice over the next decade:

- **Value** – Traditional measures have valued construction materials according to their usefulness and performance over time. Value resides in structural and mechanical properties, i.e. the ability of materials and products to hold a building up and to provide internal comfort. Today the value of construction materials lays in their scarcity and recyclability. True value lies in a balance of performance and ecological life-cycle impacts. That means it is unacceptable to specify a polluting material such as oil paint simply because it provides short-term protection. Better to find less damaging coatings, which may cost more but which damage personal and global health less and allows for the reuse of the material at the end of a building's life. Value is not just about cost, but is a matter of balancing performance with moral or ethical choices. As Chris McCarthy notes,[1] society values highly materials such as gold which have no use and simply burns materials such as timber which has a variety of uses, and treats plastics as if they have no value, irrespective of their indispensable role in construction and high level of recyclability.
- **Waste** – Waste has value and should be utilised more in construction. The UK construction industry is responsible for about 32 per cent by volume of landfill waste yet rarely employs reused materials or actively recycles its own waste. Over the next decade waste will enter the 'food chain' of typical construction either in the form of crushed and recycled materials used as aggregates, or in the form of reused structural members and building elements (bricks) or in the form of domestic or industrial waste refashioned into new construction products. Waste is a potential resource which will have a growing influence over the next decade. The drivers of change are the cost of landfill, the scarcity of many minerals, pollution controls, the use of 'cradle-to-cradle' approaches, and developments in material science.
- **Towers** – After a period of unpopularity in much of Europe, the tower block is emerging as a potential answer to urban sustainability. It offers many advantages over low- or medium-rise development, such as energy exchange between parts, density of land occupation, access to renewable energy, and distance from polluting streets. With diversified uses, tenure and wealth types, the

modern tower can become a mini-sustainable city. Heat loss from one part can readily become the gain for another, water can be recycled, air currents can be channelled to spiral through the core, nature can clad the outside and fill inner courts, making the tower a self-sustaining model of an ecological future. Of course, we have a long way to go, but towers work like the big trees of the forest – they sustain life in the canopy and their falling leaves (i.e. waste) supports a recycling economy in the under-storey. Sustainable high-rise is the future.

- **Shape** – Plan shapes such as circles and squares, which reduced the surface area relative to volume, were preferred for energy efficiency for many years. In housing this led to simple square plans with bedrooms in the roof space and to square offices with atria in their centre. The control of the perimeter was seen as a priority in terms of excluding external conditions. Today, the focus has shifted from heating, and hence thermal insulation, to electricity consumption. Electricity per unit of power is over twice as damaging in CO_2 as energy delivered by other means. Reducing electricity consumption means maximising access to natural resources – daylight, solar energy and wind. All of these challenge earlier assumptions. Buildings should not be fat but thin. Thinness gives access to renewable energy since there is potentially a long façade and a shallow plan depth in which to distribute the energy gained naturally.

- **Infrastructure** – Rather than focus on buildings, the green future will shift the emphasis onto public infrastructure. There is already a rebalancing between roads and rail, between road space for cars and that needed for buses, cyclists and pedestrians. However, all infrastructure projects whether schools, hospitals or libraries will be expected not just to display CO_2 emissions (as in the UK) but to set an example to others of greater energy efficiency. Public buildings provide the opportunity to test new green technologies, to educate the public about sustainable practices, and to teach our children how to survive in a resource stressed future. A key area of infrastructure is that of public transport. Here there has to be 'feet before wheels and narrow wheels before wide wheels'. That means putting the pedestrian first, giving priority to cycling, to rail (metro and heavy) with cars and lorries paying the full carbon cost of transport. Urban sustainability depends upon the development of new models for infrastructure provision – the integration of buildings, transport and energy.

- **Prefabrication** – In spite of the diversity in nature, human habitats are largely made of repeated elements. The challenge today is to use industrial production to produce a rich, varied and energy-efficient architecture – buildings whose

Fig 191
View of Green Lighthouse at University of Copenhagen, which incorporates many new technologies including photovoltaics, active climate screens, and phase-change materials to provide a carbon neutral science faculty building. Architect: Christensen & Co.
Source: Adam Mørk

'genetic code' is green but whose forms are largely industrialised. Prefabrication offers economy of means, reduced cost and higher quality control. It will allow the fruits of pioneer green design such as BedZed in London and Bo01 in Malmo to become mainstream. Mass production carries risks: in nature a small level of variety is built in across the generations allowing species to evolve on the basis of natural selection. In the construction industry natural selection should be under the control of consumers and their architects, not big business. A recent project by Danish architects BIG demonstrates how using the repetitive elements of Lego, a rich, varied and exciting architecture can emerge through prefabrication.

- **New materials and nanotechnology** – Great strides are underway to develop new materials based on lightweight composites, bio-plastics and nano-scale structures. Three are worthy of note because of their likely impact upon sustainable design and construction. New materials based upon crystal spun textiles, electro-spun textiles and carbon nanotubes offer potential to achieve more performance per unit of weight than traditional materials like concrete and steel.[2] The shift from macro- to micro-scale is similar to the innovations in the gene profiling of the natural world. In theory, advanced composites based on fibre- or textile-reinforced polymers offer greater economy, improved strength and enhanced plasticity over traditional materials, thereby achieving more with less means which is itself part of the ethos of sustainability. 'Aerogel', which uses molecular-scale structures to provide a new generation of lightweight materials with exceptional thermal properties and weight to strength ratios, is set to revolutionise construction. Replacing the sand in cement with expanded recycled glass pellets and the gravel with aerogel results in concrete with is both strong and offers high levels of insulation. Another innovation is in fabric-formed concrete, using flexible means of casting to model natural forms and exploit new aesthetic possibilities more akin to biology.[3]

FROM A CARBON TO SOLAR ECONOMY

We have now reached 'peak oil'– the stage at which production equalled or exceeded supply – and face a future of declining supplies, rising prices and global stress over available resources. As we do so, over the next decade or two, there will be a shift from a world economy based around fossil fuels to one where solar energy is the lifeblood of commerce. Although other renewable technologies will

Fig 192
New solar technologies used at Alexandria
Library, designed by Snohetta.

be important and there may be a contribution from nuclear power (until global uranium begins to run out in perhaps 2045) the major energy source will be sunlight.

Solar power will drive the electricity production of the future with super grid highways running on DC (instead of AC) current carrying electricity around the world. As solar takes over from fossil fuels, there will be a shift in political power from the cold grey north to the sunny south with Africa perhaps providing Europe with the bulk of its energy just as Russia does today. Buildings will reflect this trend and will become micro-generators of sun power. Sites with good solar access will be sought after and there may be battles to protect solar access.

Over the next few decades buildings are likely to produce their own energy, capture and recycle their own water, employ recycled materials, reuse their own waste, and balance carbon dioxide (CO_2) released during construction and building occupation against CO_2 converted back into oxygen by planting trees elsewhere. It is a difficult design challenge and will alter the look of buildings and change the way we measure performance. It will also require new skills of the architect and engineer, new outlooks and new professional standards of competency in the move towards the solar century.

The advantage of looking at individual buildings rather than whole urban areas is their relative simplicity. Buildings have predictable performance characteristics, with more readily measured inputs and outputs. If society accepts the idea of sustainable design in buildings, then the sustainable development of cities will follow. In fact, it is sustainable construction that informs sustainable design, which, in turn, influences sustainable development, not vice versa.

The complexity of the development of sustainable cities is a barrier to action, whereas in individual buildings, the interaction of resource impacts can be more easily understood and exploited to allow the new generation of green architecture to shine as a beacon for change. Increasingly, this is the agenda adopted by some of the world's most highly respected designers – Lord Foster, Renzo Piano, Sir Nicholas Grimshaw and Lord Rogers.

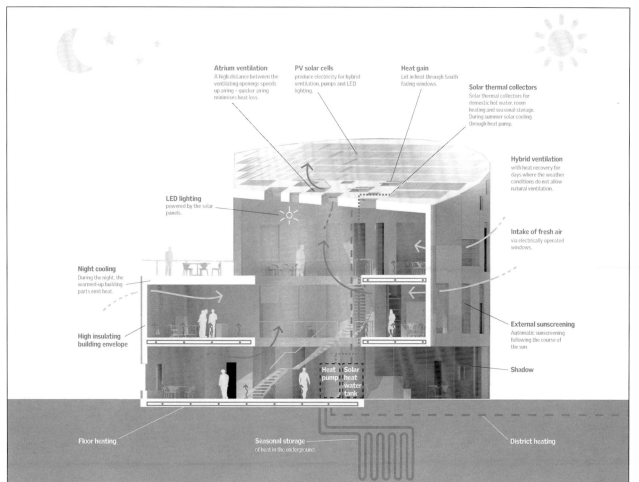

Atrium ventilation
A high distance between the ventilating openings speeds up airing – quicker airing minimises heat loss.

PV solar cells
produce electricity for hybrid ventilation, pumps and LED lighting.

Heat gain
Let in heat through South facing windows.

Solar thermal collectors
Solar thermal collectors for domestic hot water, room heating and seasonal storage. During summer solar cooling through heat pump.

Hybrid ventilation
with heat recovery for days where the weather conditions do not allow natural ventilation.

LED lighting
powered by the solar panels.

Intake of fresh air
via electrically operated windows.

Night cooling
During the night, the warmed-up building parts emit heat.

External sunscreening
Automatic sunscreening following the course of the sun.

High insulating building envelope

Shadow

Heat pump | Solar heat water tank

Floor heating

Seasonal storage
of heat in the underground.

District heating

Architecture is inevitably influenced by the socio-political context acted out in building regulations and planning law. The market-led ethos that supports individualism has tended to prevail at the expense of community values, although the European Union sets a good standard for intergovernmental environmental action.

Sustainability as a series of ideals is a concept grounded in the ethics of environmental responsibility. The techniques and technologies of green design are now generally understood – what is still lacking is an architecture profession which gives priority to ecological issues and a construction industry which puts sustainability at the heart of its operations. Recently, however, the UK's major architecture award, the Stirling Prize, has short-listed green projects such as BedZed housing in south London, Brighton Public Library and Accordia, a housing development in Cambridge which won the prize in 2008. The Royal Institute of British Architects (RIBA) also awards an annual sustainability prize which sends a message of environmental care to the public at large. The winning projects reveal is the growing ethical concern over ecological design.

In the RIBA brochure *Gateway to good architecture* published in 2008 there are two encouraging statements from what is arguably the world's most influential architectural professional body. The first states that through its control of education and membership, the RIBA makes sure that: 'every young architect has the ability to sell greener design to clients'.

The second argues that the greatest force for sustainable development is the audience for architecture, that is clients and users of buildings. The emphasis on the interests of users is encouraging, for they too have a vested interest in a green, healthy environment. The RIBA website *www.architecture. com* also has an online sustainability section with case studies which 'show you how you can improve the health of the planet' through better design of houses, schools, hospitals, shops and museums. By way of contrast the construction industry in the UK and most of Europe appears more concerned with on-site efficiency and profitability. Building standards, prefabrication and cost-effectiveness are themselves of little value unless what the construction industry creates are resourceful, environmentally robust and spiritually uplifting buildings.

The Olympic movement has also signalled a move towards more sustainable design practices over the past decade. Starting with the Barcelona Olympics, which deliberately sought a site that would help with wider social and economic regeneration, to Sydney with its energy-efficient athletes' village and new train line and Olympic station, to Beijing with its birds-nest stadium and experimental eco-technologies, the world of sport has been used to showcase green design. It is expected that London in 2012 will follow in these footsteps in spite of the recession in the British economy in the build up to the games. Movements such as the Olympics, which are free of dogma and have a pedigree of design excellence, can do much in presenting new eco-visions to the wider public.

NOTES

[1]   Chris McCarthy, 'New Construction Materials', in Lotte M., Bjerregaard Jensen and Jacob S. Møller (eds), B150 *Civil Engineering Futures*, p. 57.

[2]   Kasper Guldager Jørgensen, 'Next Generation Construction Materials', in Jensen and Møller, op. cit., pp. 60–3.

[3]   Anne-Mette Manelius, 'Liquid Stone', in Jensen and Møller, op. cit., pp. 70–4.

Selected Bibliography

– Blewitt, J. and Cullingford, C. (eds), *The Sustainability Curriculum: The Challenge of Higher Education*, Earthscan, 2004.
– Dahl, T., *Climate and Architecture*, Routledge, 2009.
– EAA report, *Impacts of Europe's changing climate-2008 indicator based assessment*, Joint EAA/JRC/WHO report, 2008.
– Edwards, B. (ed.), *Green Buildings Pay*, 2nd edition, E&FN Spon, 2003.
– Edwards, B. and Turrent, D., *Sustainable Housing: Principles and Practice*, E&FN Spon, 2000.
– Goulding, J. R. and Lewis, J. O. (eds), *European Directory of Sustainable and Energy-efficient Building*, James and James, 1999.
– Halliday, S., *Sustainable Construction*, Butterworth-Heinemann, 2008.
– Hawken, P., Lovins, A. B. and Lovins, L. H., *Natural Capitalism: the Next Industrial Revolution*, Earthscan, 1999.
– Hawkes, D., *The Environmental Tradition: Studies in the Architecture of Environment*, Spon Press, 1996.
– Hawkes, D., Jane McDonald and Koen Steemers, *The Selective Environment: An approach to environmentally responsive architecture*, Spon Press, 2002.
– Porteous, C., *The new eco-Architecture*, Spon Press, 2002.
– Roaf, S., *Closing the loop: benchmarks for sustainable buildings*, RIBA Enterprises, 2004.
– Rogers, R., *Cities for a Small Planet*, Faber and Faber, 1997.
– Sassi, P., *Strategies for Sustainable Architecture*, Taylor and Francis, 2006.
– Smith, P., *Architecture in a Climate of Change: A Guide to Sustainable Design*, Architectural Press, 2001.
– Thomas, R. (ed.), *Environmental Design*, E&FN Spon, 1996.
– Thomas, R. (ed.), *Photovoltaics and Architecture*, Spon Press, 2001.
– *Towards an Urban Renaissance, Urban Task Force Report*, E&FN Spon, 1999.
– Turrent, D., *Sustainable Architecture*, RIBA Publishing, 2008.
– Williams, D., *Sustainable Architecture: ecology, architecture and planning*, John Wiley and Sons, 2007.

USEFUL WEBSITES

www.bre.co.uk
www.breeam.co.uk
www.carbontrust.co.uk
www.cat.org.uk
www.dti.gov.uk
www.energysavingtrust.org.uk

www.eurec.be
www.rmi.org
www.ukgbc.org
www.usablebuildings.co.uk
www.usgbc.org
www.get-sust.com

Index